Our Roots Are Deep with Passion

Our Roots Are Deep with Passion

Creative Nonfiction Collects New
Essays by Italian American Writers

EDITED BY

Lee Gutkind
Joanna Clapps Herman

OTHER PRESS • NEW YORK

Copyright © 2006 by The Creative Nonfiction Foundation

Production Editor: Robert D. Hack

Book designed and set by Rachel Reiss

ISBN-13: 978-1-59051-242-5

10 9 8 7 6 5 4 3 2 1

LIBRARY OF CONGRESS CATALOGING-IN-PUBLICATION DATA

Our roots are deep with passion : Creative nonfiction collects new essays by Italian American writers / edited by Lee Gutkind.
    p. cm.
    ISBN 1-59051-242-1
    1. American essays—Italian American authors. 2. American essays—21st century.
3. Italian Americans—Social life and customs. I. Gutkind, Lee. II. Creative non-fiction.
    PS683.I83O97 2006
    814'.6080851—dc22

                                                                    2006000625

To all the Jews and Italians who have found their way to each other throughout history, in the Mediterranean, in America, and in this book.

Joanna Clapps Herman especially dedicates this book to her beloved Jewish husband, Billy Herman.

Contents

Acknowledgments IX

Foreword XI
Joe Mantegna

Introduction: The Evolution of an Anthology
    and the Living Tissue of Passion XV
Lee Gutkind

'Mbriago I
Louise DeSalvo

Words and Rags 15
Joanna Clapps Herman

These Innocent Lambs 28
Laura Valeri

The Walls of Gela 46
Edvige Giunta

I Denti Famiglia 68
Phyllis Capello

Sacrifice 71
Maria Laurino

My Father's Music 87
Ned Balbo

Washington Square 104
Carol Bonomo Albright

The Names of Horses 121
Annie Rachele Lanzillotto

Dagos in Mayberry 133
Peter Selgin

I Heard You the First Time, Daddy 148
Rita Ciresi

Bitter Herbs? 157
Sandra M. Gilbert

St. Sebastian in Boston 177
Randy-Michael Testa

Daughters of Mongrassano 190
Jeanna Lucci Canapari

Allium Longicuspis 199
Stephanie Susnjara

Jealousy, or The Autobiography
    of an Italian Woman 211
Gina Barreca

Il Pasto Che Parla 223
Valerie K. Waldrop

Selling the House 234
Marianna De Marco Torgovnick

Italian American: The Next Generation 244
Christine Palamidessi Moore

Mama, Che Cosa Vuoi Che Faccio? 255
James Vescovi

Italian Bride 271
Mary Beth Caschetta

About *Creative Nonfiction* 287

Acknowledgments

Special thanks to an anonymous donor for endowing the $1000 Laura Pizer Prize in Creative Nonfiction and generously supporting this volume of Creative Nonfiction.

The Creative Nonfiction Foundation gratefully acknowledges the Juliet Lea Hillman Simonds Foundation, Inc. and the Pennsylvania Council on the Arts for their ongoing support.

Special thanks to the editorial board of *Creative Nonfiction:* Laurie Graham, Dinty W. Moore, Patricia Park, and Lea Simonds. Thanks also to managing editor Hattie Fletcher, assistant editor Maria Wrzosek, and our literary agent Andrew Blauner.

Foreword
· · · · · · · · ·
Joe Mantegna

On occasion I've been asked, "What's it like being an Italian American?" I've come to realize one might as well ask, "What's it like to have brown eyes and black hair?" the answer being, "I don't know what it's like NOT to." Perhaps other ethnic groups strive to permeate every molecule and fiber of their being as Italians do, but that question must be asked of those to whom it applies. For me, it just is.

You get your first glimpses of it when you become a young adult and find yourself gravitating toward sounds, sights, and smells that, at best, you thought were barely tolerable as a child. It's not that you didn't like eggplant sandwiches in your lunch bag for school—it's just that the kid next to you who wanted to trade his bologna or peanut butter and jelly for something different hadn't bargained for anything THAT exotic.

Did everyone's grandfather tear up a perfectly beautiful grass lawn to plant tomatoes and peppers, or walk along highways looking for dandelions and maybe even a wayward rabbit? If other kids came home during the holidays and found a goose or a lamb in the backyard, they'd be thrilled with the anticipation of the coming year with new and beloved pets. Didn't they know not to get too attached? By early January, these new additions would mysteriously disappear during weeks of culinary extravaganzas.

As a child, I'd marvel at my father's passion for bitter, wrinkled black olives and orange slices with pepper and garlic. I never saw items like that on the Andersons' table on *Father Knows Best,* the black-and-white TV role-model family we all worshiped in the 50s. Why do we eat peppers and eggs on Friday, clams on Christmas Eve, and how did that fish that started out like a plank of wood end up in our bathtub? And does everyone else alternate Sinatra, Dean Martin, and Louis Prima with Mantovani and Mario Lanza as the background music of choice for our daily lives? All of this mystified me as a boy and all of it I embrace and cherish as a man. I have more than once strolled the aisles of an Italian deli to do nothing more than reminisce about my life using only my sense of smell as my guide.

I know it's not uncommon to become our parents. I just somehow feel that Italian Americans often take it to an extreme. Our roots are deep with passion; I shouldn't be surprised.

Of course, there's a lot more to our heritage than just those delights of the palate and the ear; we are the ancestors of arguably the greatest civilization this earth has yet spawned. The lineage of literature, arts and science, philosophy, and the like is long and strong within the Italian culture. From fennel to fusion, from da Vinci to DiCaprio, the footprints we've left on the path of man's history are numerous and indelible. With these thoughts in mind, I've had the pleasure of exploring that deep passion with this collection of essays.

What awaits you is a marvelous combination of thoughts and ideas, dreams and dreads, laughter, tears, love, anger, and every other form of emotion and feeling that one would expect from a group of writers who also share that commonality of being the sons and daughters, however removed, of Bella Italia. There are stories here that explore the depths of home, food, music, family, friendship, regionality, and religion. What other culture will give you a potpourri of riches that mix garlic, wine, *nonna,* Catholic school, ghosts, the Mafia, jealousy, gay pride, an uncle named Zio Augie Doggie, and an ode to a dishrag in one collection of writings? For me, reading these essays was like walking into Grandma's house on bread day. You've arrived someplace safe, warm, and inviting, and at this moment, there's no better place on earth.

In many ways it's like taking a trip to the "old country" itself. It's a trip laced with beauty and ugliness, laughter and pain, tranquil vistas and craggy coasts, but at the end of the journey you feel you've visited someplace that transcends unforgettable; it feels like someplace you want to return to. It feels like home. And whether you experience it as someone who can relate to almost every word, or as someone to whom this insight is new and fascinating, I know at the end you'll feel glad you took the trip.

Buon viaggio. May your journey be as rewarding as it was for me.

Joe Mantegna
NOVEMBER 19, 2005
TOLUCA LAKE, CALIFORNIA

Introduction:
The Evolution of an Anthology and the Living Tissue of Passion
· · · · · · ·

Lee Gutkind

So far, I have edited nearly thirty issues of *Creative Nonfiction,* a half dozen of which have been turned into books like this one, along with another three collections published exclusively as books. Some of these projects—books and issues—have come together smoothly and sweetly, without a hitch, while others exploded in a rush of inspiration or a confused clamor to make a deadline. This collection has been simultaneously sweet and explosive and, perhaps because of that, irrepressibly inspiring.

It began in 2001 at dinner at the writer Gay Talese's house in Ocean City, New Jersey. At least a dozen people, mostly from the Italian American community, were sitting around Gay's long rectangular table on his screened-in side porch. The Italian consul had come up from Washington, and a surgeon who was president of a prominent international Italian American organization was in attendance, along with the dean of a large college. The details have faded, but the intensity of the dialogue that night, capturing and confronting Italian heritage and identity, was unforgettable—a palpable force that I had never experienced in my own home.

I grew up in a Jewish family, and although we Jews had a religion and a culture in common, I had always felt that we were all freelancers— religious and cultural independents. The glue that might have kept us together—the connection I sensed among these Italians sitting at the Talese table, revolving around roots and heritage—was missing for us. We were Jews, for sure—we felt the bond—but it was never a subject to dwell upon or trumpet. Most American Jews from my parents' generation did not consider Israel a homeland in the way that Italians do Italy. Israel was more of a beacon of belonging—a place to visit, to plant trees, to give money, and to flee to if, God forbid, the dreaded persecution returned. But here, with all of this Italian pride and angst surging like testosterone, I was intrigued and a bit jealous.

The following year I was asked to speak at a conference entitled "Italian Roots/American Soil." I talked about the evolution of the creative nonfiction movement and how the memoir explosion has invigorated the literary landscape and encouraged nonwriters to look back and preserve what they remember of their past for future generations. After my talk, I took some questions—and again I was flummoxed by the amount of energy and emotion exerted in relation to the Italian American experience. There were many eloquent statements filled with anger, resentment, and love toward the homeland and its magnetism. I decided then that I would one day devote an issue of *Creative Nonfiction* to this Italian American spirit and experience, featuring writers who dramatically articulate the complicated, powerful, and often unresolved feelings of being American and Italian simultaneously, if such a combination is even possible.

But first, I needed financing for this project. In order to do a special issue, we often raise money for marketing to solicit original manuscripts and to offer a cash award for the best original essay submitted to us for publication. In this case, Louise DeSalvo's essay, "'Mbriago," was eventually selected from approximately 300 submissions as the winner of the $1000 Laura Pizer Prize in Creative Nonfiction, given anonymously in the name of a Neapolitan Jewish woman whose love of the Italian language led her to a life as a scholar of Italian language and literature.

But long before this issue was a certainty and the prize was a reality, I had directed one of the graduate student interns in our office to e-mail people who had submitted manuscripts to us but were not subscribers, to ask if they would like to take advantage of our special rates to subscribe. If they think we're good enough to publish their work, perhaps we're good enough to read and put by their bedsides, I reasoned. During this process, this intern, whose married name is Italian, received a return e-mail asking, from one Italian woman to another, why *Creative Nonfiction* didn't publish more essays by Italian women writers. The intern asked me how to respond, and I told her to say nationality had little to do with why we accept or reject essays, but that I had, in fact, a special Italian American issue in mind, and we needed funding to get it going.

Eventually the answer came back from Joanna Clapps Herman, a writer of fiction and nonfiction and a professor of creative writing at The Center for Worker Education at City College of New York and at the Graduate Writing Program at Manhattanville College, who suggested that she might be able to help. I met Joanna in New York a few months later, and we forged a friendship that began with a lavish dinner at her spacious Riverside Drive apartment with a cast of at least half a dozen Italian American writers, almost exclusively women, who wanted to hear about my idea for a special issue and tell me about the essays they intended to write for it. Four hours of inspired and revealing conversation and what seemed like dozens of courses of food and unlimited bottles of wine later, we had all forged a bond. Essays by three of the writers I met that night, including Joanna, who is the co-editor of this collection, Edvige Giunta, and Annie Rachele Lanzillotto, are in this book. Joanna eventually reached out to an anonymous donor, an Italian American woman, to help fund the original essay prize and the marketing that went with it.

All of this took place a couple of years ago, as I said; anthologies can be slow in coming together. And we at *Creative Nonfiction,* like many other literary journals, seem to suffer from a slowness syndrome ourselves—until our anonymous donor, represented by my impatient co-editor, Joanna, began to scream and yell. Facing the wrath of an angry Italian New Yorker, we got moving—fast. Joanna was and is a rarity—a force of energy and commitment. Although we advertised and solicited manuscripts in many venues for more than a year, Joanna's personal connections brought the bulk of the best pieces in this book, including her own, "Words and Rags."

I make a point now to say I have never been involved in an issue or an anthology in which the entire ensemble—writers, editors, and benefactors—invested so much emotion and energy in nearly every phase of the project, from the selection of the essays down to the barest and most minute details of copyediting. I even had the husband of one of the writers we initially rejected telephone me at home one evening to beseech me to change my mind and accept his wife's essay, for she was distraught; she needed to be part of this select group of Italian American voices. There was no alternative; I acquiesced. The writer revised her work repeatedly and is now included in the collection.

Many of the editorial suggestions made by my staff at *Creative Nonfiction* and the editors at Other Press, which is copublisher of this collection, were rejected outright by some of our contributors—with shock, resentment, and threats of withdrawal, as if we were all clueless as to how to edit. (We did not, a few of the writers said, have a sense of history.) One thing I know: for good or bad, the writers in this book believe in themselves and their words and ideas, down to the barest minutiae of punctuation. Under other circumstances, I might have wielded my limited editorial power and insisted, as I have done in the past, once or twice, that it has be my way or no way. The editors at Other Press could have acted similarly.

But faced with the writers' fierce passion for their ideas and commitment to their prose, it is accurate to say that we—editors at *Creative Nonfiction* and Other Press—acceded almost every time. And, in fact, we have been delighted to do so. I have been writing, editing, and teaching writers, young and old, for many years, and if there is one thing missing in much of the nonfiction work I read today from students and highly experienced professionals alike, it is what the writers in this book vividly and universally exhibit: the passion of conviction—that cacophony of emotion with which I was first enamored at Gay Talese's dinner.

For a long time—more than a year—the working title of this collection was to be *Old Ways in a New Land.* No one, Joanna especially, was completely satisfied with this title, but I always assumed that something better would come along when least expected. But as time passed and the deadline to go into production crept closer, we couldn't collectively find the appropriate words to capture the deep and magical essence of the Italian American experience as reflected in the essays we were about to publish, until the Tony- and Emmy-award winning actor Joe Mantegna provided the answer.

A friend, the writer Paul Paolicelli, had participated in a panel about Italian American literature moderated by Mantegna, and I asked Paul to connect me with the actor so I could ask him to read our anthology and perhaps write a foreword to the book. Obviously, Joe agreed. I knew him as a great actor whose extensive career has spanned television, theater, and film roles, but I didn't quite understand, until I received his foreword, what a brilliant and incisive writer he is.

Joe Mantegna perfectly captures the mood and the deep power of reflection, observation, and confession inherent in this collection. I knew this the moment I began reading his contribution. Each sentence struck home with raw warmth. But when I read that special phrase, buried in the middle of his text, I understood that Mantegna belonged in this book and that he had expressed with clarity and empathy the very essence of all of the words published in these pages: *Our Roots Are Deep with Passion.*

Joe Mantegna nailed it in a powerful and definitive phrase. There is nothing more to add, except my appreciation to Joanna Clapps Herman, to all of the writers in this beautiful and passionate collection, to Other Press for seeing the strength in this work, and to Mantegna himself, who recognized the living tissue of passion that united all of our voices.

Our Roots Are Deep with Passion

'Mbriago

. . . .

LOUISE DESALVO

A Knock at the Door

It would happen like this. A knock on the crackled glass of the door
to our tenement apartment in Hoboken, New Jersey. My mother, not
expecting a visitor, opening it as she would for anyone who troubled to
climb the four steep flights of stairs. She had nothing to fear. She knew
that if the visitor was a stranger, by the time he got to our door, he
would have been stopped, thoroughly checked out, and granted passage up to our apartment by one of the young men hanging out on the
corner of Fourth and Adams in front of Albini's Drugstore, by the old
woman leaning out the window on the first floor of our building, or by
the old man sitting in the sun on our front stoop.

So because there was nothing to fear from a knock on the door
(World War II was over, my father back home unharmed, at work a few
blocks away), my mother would put down her mending, or turn away

. . . . .

LOUISE DESALVO, winner of the Laura Pizer Prize in Creative Nonfiction, is Professor of English and Jenny Hunter Endowed Scholar for Literature and Creative Writing
at Hunter College. She has published four memoirs, among them *Vertigo*, winner of
the Gay Talese Award, and, most recently, *Crazy in the Kitchen*, and is at work on another memoir.

from her ironing board, or pull a pot off the coal stove and open the door, hoping, perhaps, that it was my father home from work early or Argie from down the block—the only friend who could lure her away from the punishing rounds of her daily household chores.

Outside the door, not my father, nor Argie, but an old Italian man. Short, stooped, ruddy-faced from years of work in the sun, wearing a cap like my grandfather's. Surprise on his face. Then, shame. A slight bow, as he took off his cap. *"Mi dispiace proprio,"* he'd say. "I'm very sorry." He hadn't known a woman would open the door. *"Mbriago?"* he'd ask. *'Mbriago,* the drunk. My grandfather's nickname. The man had come to see him. He would be a distant relative from Vieste, my grandfather's village in Puglia, or a crony from his railroad days in up-state New York, or a pal from his years of working on the docks in New York City. And he would be needing a loan.

Ours was a neighborhood of nasty nicknames—"Joey the Fat," "Jimmy Goose Face," "Bobby Snot Eater." Even mine—"Miss Prim," "Miss-too-big-for-your-britches," or "Miss Smarty Pants"—given me by my father, were far from endearing, revealing my father's disgust at what he called my holier-than-thou attitude. So my mother never re-coiled at her father's being called *Umbriago.* There were many old Ital-ian men like my grandfather who worked all day, drank wine all day to fortify themselves for work, staggered home drunk, washed themselves at the sink, changed their clothes, poured themselves a little glass of wine to restore their spirits while they waited for their suppers, poured themselves a large tumbler of wine to accompany their meals, poured themselves a little glass of *digestif* so they would sleep all night. They, too, were called *'Mbriago.* And even the ones who weren't called *'Mbriago* were drunk much of the time.

"Next door," my mother tells the visitor, pointing. She knows that anyone who comes to see her father comes for a loan, the bargain sealed by a few glasses of my grandfather's homemade wine. My mother, wor-rying about how my grandfather will support himself when he retires if he gives money to everyone who comes to his door, and because she embraces the American doctrine of self-reliance, slams the door on the old man, shakes her head, and grumbles her way back to her work.

The Table

In all the photographs, in all the moving pictures of my grandparents' table, there is always bread, just enough food for satiety, and always a flask of wine. But there is never water. Not a pitcher of water, nor a glass of water. My grandfather, so far as I know, never drank water. Nor did my grandmother, much. A little glass of water for her on the hottest of days is all I can remember.

When I am young, I never notice that my grandfather does not drink water, that he drinks only wine. And his nickname, *'Mbriago,* tells me nothing more about him than if he were called something else. For his drinking wine instead of water when he was thirsty was not something I questioned or remarked upon. It was as natural to me as the green of the trees in the park around the corner in springtime, the sweat of summer, the melancholy falling leaves of autumn, or the death of the soul in wintertime.

Home Movie

In one moving picture, taken by my father, my grandfather is standing behind his kitchen table, miming drinking down an entire flask of wine. My grandmother looks annoyed, tries to take the flask from him. He pulls it away from her, mimes drinking the entire flask of wine again. She becomes annoyed again, grabs his arm, tries to take the flask away again. But he turns away from her. He is the hero in his son-in-law's home movie; he is enjoying playing the drunk that he is.

My mother sits at the table, looks away, cups her face in her hand, a gesture that I have come to understand indicates her displeasure at what is going on. There is an antipasto on the table. Another flask of wine. A cup of milk for me. But no water.

Water, Water

My grandfather began to work in the fields of Puglia when he was seven years old. When he worked in the fields, he was not given water to drink by the landowners or their overseers. Water was scarce; water was needed for the crops and for animals, who were viewed as more valuable than farmworkers who could more easily be replaced if they sickened and died.

In the fields of Puglia, as in fields all across the South of Italy, people working in the fields drank wine to quench their thirst, not water. Wine was abundant; wine was cheaper; wine was safer to drink—at least that's what the farmworkers believed. Even now, if you travel to the South, if you see a group of farmworkers stopping their work for a few moments to rest, you will see them passing a flask of wine among themselves, you will see each man or woman wiping the mouth of the flask before passing it on to a comrade. "Passing the saint," they call it.

And so, my grandfather began "passing the saint" when he was seven years old as he worked in the fields; he "passed the saint" each day of his farm work in Puglia until he left for America. And one of the reasons he left for America—one of the reasons many people of the South left for America—is because the South was arid, the South was drought-stricken, and because of this lack of water, farmworkers did not earn what they needed to support themselves during bad years. So, at the beginning of the twentieth century, when there were a series of droughts that left many unemployed, America beckoned. And by the time my grandfather left Puglia, the habit of drinking wine, not water, to quench your thirst was ingrained. Water was dangerous, he believed (and it often was); wine was safe (even though drinking wine long term would kill you, but this he did not know).

If my grandfather had lived in Puglia until 1939, if he had not emigrated to America very early in the twentieth century, he would have witnessed the completion of the great aqueduct that now delivers water to Puglia, albeit inadequately. It was begun in 1906 and encompasses 213 kilometers of subterranean tunnels built by 11,000 workmen. During the Roman Empire, eleven aqueducts served the imperial city. But the Pugliese people had to wait until almost the middle of the twentieth century for water to be brought to their arid land.

Perhaps my grandfather would have been one of the men building that aqueduct. But he was not. He lived in Puglia when water was scarce; when whatever potable water was available was sold to the poor at exorbitant prices; when much of the water of Puglia was tainted and undrinkable; when much of the water of Puglia was standing water, which bred mosquitoes, which gave the people of Puglia malaria, which killed the people of Puglia in astonishing numbers, especially the children and the old and the weak.

But the South of Italy was not always an arid land. The aridness and the lack of safe drinking water in the South when my grandfather lived there was caused by human beings and rooted in history and racism— the history of conquest, exploitation of the land and its people, and the refusal of the governments of the North to provide the South with the water it needed to sustain life.

The Englishman Norman Douglas traveled through Puglia and Calabria in 1922 to see how the modern South compared to descriptions of the region in ancient texts, such as those in the odes of the Roman poet Horace (65–8 BCE), who was born in Puglia, and the *Iter Venusinum* of Lupoli, and the texts of Virgil, Martial, Statius, Propertius, Strabo, Pliny, Varro, and Columella. He wrote about what he discovered in *Old Calabria,* originally published in 1915. Everywhere he went Douglas looked for rivers, or streams, or springs mentioned in these ancient texts, and he discovered that virtually all of them had disappeared. He remarked upon how waterless the modern South is. How in the South, unlike the North, rains come during the winter when nothing is growing—in spring and summer, instead of rain, there is hot dry air, which makes it essential for the government to provide a system whereby water is captured when it's plentiful and distributed when it's not, only this isn't done. How the only water to be had is bottled from mineral springs and sold by vendors. How peasants and farmworkers drink wine, not water; how they're often drunk by midday.

But in Horace's time, the South was "covered with forests," and the forests were full of "hares, rabbits, foxes, roe deer, wild boars, martens, porcupines, hedgehogs, tortoises, and wolves," virtually none of which survive now because the forests have been cut down or burned by invading armies. For Douglas, the South's poverty was linked to how despoiled the land had become; he attributes the lack of water to deforestation; he attributes the diseases that have plagued the South—cholera and malaria—to what has happened to the water in the South because of deforestation.

He tells of the "noisome" waters that exist in this generally "waterless land" of the South, of how little the government has done to drain the swamplands that breed mosquitoes. He writes about how prevalent malaria is in the South, how taking doses of quinine is necessary to prevent malaria, but how the poor can't afford quinine.

"I dare say," writes Douglas, "the deforestation of the country, which prevented the downflow of the rivers—choking up their beds with detritus and producing stagnant pools favourable to the breeding of the mosquito—has helped to spread the plague [of malaria]." He writes how cholera is increasing, and how the government's not providing adequate sanitation in the South has made its spread inevitable. He tells how, because of deforestation, there are more frequent landslides, and of how, after landslides, the threat of cholera becomes greater.

Centuries of invasion left their mark as well. Invading Turks burned down everything they encountered—towns, cities, forests—as they rampaged through the South. Spanish viceroys and Bourbons and Arab invaders destroyed the land. The Adriatic seacoast was depopulated during the Arab invasion, and villages and towns were destroyed: everything in the path of the invading army was burnt to the ground, and "the richly cultivated land became a desert."

And what the foreign invaders began, the government in the North completed. Northern and German industrialists acquired rights to the timber of the South, and Douglas saw the slopes of existing forests felled during his journey. To denude hillsides of trees in countries with abundant rainfall was one thing. But to do so in a country with insufficient rainfall was "the beginning of the end."

Douglas believed that politicians and industrialists were greedy and did not care that their practices would lead to disaster for the economy of the South in the future. Once hillsides were denuded, rainfall washed the soil away, exposing the rocks beneath, making reforestation impossible. But why should they care? They did not live there. The immense profits gained from these destructive practices went north, went out of the country, and often the workers who cut down trees were imported. So the people of the South did not profit from their country's abuse.

Centuries of conquest coupled with the ravages of exploitative capitalism left the South devoid of two important natural resources, forests and water, and turned the South into the arid land my grandfather left. These acts changed the character of the people of the South. It led to the kind of "bestialization" and "anguished poverty" that Douglas observed—until the 1880s, the poor sold their children by officially sanctioned contracts.

Douglas tells how haggard the people are, and how "distraught" from hunger and thirst. He believed that it was because the land could not feed its people, could not provide employment for its people, could not quench the thirst of its people, that the great emigration of the people of the South to America occurred.

Later in the twentieth century, Carlo Levi's observations were essentially the same as Douglas's. Levi spent time in Lucania, the desolate region between Puglia and Calabria, as a political prisoner. In *Christ Stopped at Eboli*, Levi describes the state of this region when he lived there.

Hills of clay had become its most prevalent geographic feature. Wondering how they have been formed, Levi asks a local and is told that the trees have long since disappeared and the once fertile topsoil has eroded, leaving clay. Now, because there are no trees to hold the clay during the rainfalls of winter, there are frequent landslides. "The clay," he is told, "simply melts and pours down like a rushing stream, carrying everything with it. . . . When it rains, the ground gives way and starts to slide, and the houses fall down . . . the clay simply melts and pours down like a rushing stream, carrying everything with it."

Because the earth can't support agriculture, many of the men of the region emigrated to America, destroying the family structure of the region. "For a year, or even two, he writes to her, then he drops out of her ken . . . ; in any case he disappears and never comes back." The women form new attachments, but they cannot divorce, so that many of the children are illegitimate. But the children die young, or "turn yellow and melancholy with malaria."

Levi believed that the South became poor because "the land has been gradually impoverished: the forests have been cut down, the rivers have been reduced to mountain streams that often run dry, and livestock has become scarce. Instead of cultivating trees and pasture lands there has been an unfortunate attempt to raise wheat in soil that does not favor it. . . . [M]alaria is everywhere."

For Levi, the effect of chronic malaria has been inscribed into the character of the people of the region. Malaria has robbed the people of the South of their ability to work and to find pleasure in the world.

Luxury Travel

When I take my husband to Sicily for his sixtieth birthday, we stay in a fancy hotel in Agrigento, overlooking the famous Greek temples.

At the end of the day, I take a long, hot bath. It is the time of the winds that blow up from the Sahara. There is grit on my body, in my hair, on my clothes.

Later, in early evening, I take a solitary walk into a village. I hear old women complaining to each other about how, for yet another day, there has been no water. A thousand yards down the road, in our hotel, there is an ocean of water. Here, none. Why?

When I return home, I ask a Sicilian friend. He laughs at my ignorance. "The Mafia," he says. "They control the water." He tells me to read Mary Taylor Simeti's *On Persephone's Island.* There I learn that in Sicily's interior, very often there is water only once every five or ten days. This is not the fault of nature, says Simeti. For Sicily is "rich in water that flows to the sea unexploited" because of government neglect, and because the Mafia "controls the major wells and springs that tap subterranean water layers, and...sells its water at high prices" and interferes with any attempts to ensure a cheap, safe water supply for the people.

Working on the Railroad

My grandfather came to America when he was a young man. He came for a better life, yes. But he came, too, because he was afraid that if he stayed in Puglia he would die. Die from a bullet to the chest during the workers' rebellions. Die from thirst. Die from starvation. Die from malaria. Die from cholera. Or die for no reason at all.

And regardless of the stories we have been told of the people of the South leaving because they wanted a better life in America, it was terror, more than anything else, that propelled him and the scores of others like him up the gangplank to the ship that would take him to America. Terror, and, yes, a job promised him by a boss recruiting men from his village to build a railroad line in upper New York State. The deal was simple. If you put your mark on a piece of paper, you'd get free passage to America. When you got there, you worked until you paid off your passage. Until then, the railroad would take care of you. There would be nothing for you to worry about.

And so my grandfather came to America, and worked on the rail-road, and slept in his filthy work clothes—there was no place to wash, no water to wash with—on vermin-infested bags of straw, covering himself with a discarded horse blanket, eight men to a roach-infested, windowless boxcar. He awakened at three in the morning, just like in Italy, and walked the line to the day's worksite, and worked from five to twelve without stopping. For lunch, there was bread, and sometimes there was water, but not always, because fresh water was in short sup-ply. In a 1916 essay called "The 'Wop' in the Track Gang," Dominic T. Ciolli reported how the *padrone* of a gang like my grandfather's com-plained to him because the laborers complained that they had no fresh water, had had no fresh water to drink or to wash with for weeks, and how the *padrone* said, "These dagoes are never satisfied.... They should be starved to death.... They don't belong here."

But, like in Italy, my grandfather said, there was wine, there was al-ways wine for the workers to drink. Wine: antidote to rebellion. Wine: pacifier of those plagued by injustice. Wine: quencher of the rage. By the time my grandfather paid off his passage and moved to Hoboken to work on the docks, he was an alcoholic. But that word does not de-scribe who my grandfather had become: a wounded man who had lost whatever hope he'd managed to salvage from the rubble of his life.

When my grandfather talked about his days on the railroad, there was a rage in his eyes, a rage that could pummel a wife, that could start a riot, that could burn down a building, that could kill a *padrone,* but that did not. And so. He'd take a glass, pour himself some wine, and then some more wine. After his third glass, he looked for the rage, but it was no longer there. After his third glass, he'd miss his mother, his father, his *paisani*.

Last Supper

"The day your grandfather dies," my father says, "he's digging out the basement in the house of one of your grandmother's relatives. And it's hot down there, and it's hard work because he's got to put all the dirt he digs into a sack and carry it up the stairs and out to the back yard, and your grandfather is doing this to make a few extra bucks because his pension isn't enough to live on and because he's always giving his money away to anyone who comes to his door, and this pisses off your mother and your grandmother, but they can't do anything to stop it.

"And this day, he isn't feeling so good. He's tired and dizzy even before he starts working, and after a couple of hours, he wants to stop working, but they tell him a deal's a deal, and that he has to keep working. And to keep him working, those bastards gave your grandfather wine to drink. And, you know your grandfather, there wasn't a glass of wine he would ever refuse. So he takes the wine, quenches his thirst, forgets he's tired, and keeps right on working until mid-afternoon when the job is done. Keeps working through the heat of the day. Keeps working even though he's hot and tired and dizzy and feels like he can't breathe."

The rest of the day goes like this.

My grandfather comes home, washes himself at the sink, changes into a clean set of clothes, has a glass of wine and a bite to eat with my grandmother. After he finishes his meal, he pours himself another glass of wine, gets the spiral notebook that lists the money people owe him, sits down at the kitchen table, starts tallying his accounts using a system of his own devising—he's never gone to school, never learned arithmetic. He's scribbling away, getting angry, because it's a year later, and his wife's relatives in Long Island still haven't paid their debt, and he's tallying how much they owe him when he falls to the floor. He's had a massive heart attack.

A few hours later, my mother, my sister, and I come back home. My mother knocks on her father's door to ask for help. We've been shopping; she's tired of being with us; she wants him to take care of us while she puts her groceries away.

He doesn't answer. She panics: He's supposed to be home. She struggles my sister and me into our apartment. Tells me to climb through the open window out onto our fire escape. Tells me to climb through my grandparents' open window, tells me to unlock their door.

I do as I'm told. I've done this before when my grandfather's forgotten his keys. So this is why I'm the one who finds my grandfather dead.

Last Rites

At the wake, I go up to the casket to see my grandfather's body. He is wearing his one good suit, the one he wears to my First Communion. There is the smell of flowers from a few commemorative wreaths surrounding him, the smell of mothballs emanating from his suit, the smell of death.

"That doesn't look like Grandpa," I say. "And it doesn't smell like him, either." A neighbor stands behind me. She is watching me, listening to me, awaiting her turn to view my grandfather's body.

I am kneeling down, as I have been told to kneel by my father. I am supposed to be paying my last respects to my grandfather, as he has told me I must do. I don't know what last respects are, just like I don't know what first respects are, so I don't know what I'm supposed to do. But I have watched the stream of visitors go up to the coffin, kneel down, touch my grandfather's hands frozen in prayer, make a hasty Sign of the Cross, kiss their fingers, and move on. My mother kneels in silence next to me. She hasn't said much since the day her father died; she will say even less in the years to come. Sometimes it will seem that she has followed him to wherever he has gone.

Everyone in the funeral parlor cares about how she is "taking it." No one is concerned about how I am "taking it." My grandfather, the man who took care of me whenever he could, who sang me songs, who told me stories I couldn't comprehend of a land where wild seas drowned fishermen, where rainfalls were so powerful they made the land slide away, rainfalls so relentless that they washed away all the good earth and made it impossible to grow anything to eat; of a land where wolves ruled the night and men and women walked to the fields in the dark and worked in the blaze of day without a tree to shade them during their precious few moments of rest.

"And what did your grandpa smell like?" my neighbor asks.

I remember my grandfather, at his table, drinking wine. I remember my grandfather at *our* table, drinking wine. I remember my grandfather crushing grapes in the basement, stomping on them with feet that would stay purple until late summer. I remember my grandfather drinking wine when he took care of me, drinking it, sometimes, right out of the bottle. I remember my grandfather giving me watered wine to drink when he took care of me when I told him I was thirsty. I remember my mother being angry at my grandfather when she came back home and found me drunk, asleep on my grandparents' bed, under the giant cross on the wall with Jesus Christ bleeding.

(In high school, I am the girl who drinks too much at parties. The girl who is always thirsty but who never drinks water when she is thirsty, only booze. The girl who drinks so much she can't remember how she gets home. The girl who drinks so much that she passes out on the way home, once, in the middle of a four-lane highway.)

"And what did your grandfather smell like?" the woman asks again, for I have not answered her.

"Like wine," I say.

The woman laughs. *"'Mbriago,"* she says. "That's who your grandfather was: *'Mbriago."*

"No," I say. "That isn't who he was. He was my grandfather. Salvatore Calabrese."

Transubstantiation

In Pier Paolo Pasolini's 1966 film *Uccellacci e Uccellini (The Hawks and the Sparrows),* a contemporary Italian father and his son travel into the past, to the time of Saint Francis of Assisi, and become monks. The father, Brother Ciccillo, prays for a miracle. He prays that all the wine in the world be turned into water. He prays that there be no more wine in Italy. He prays that there be enough water in Italy so that those who have become drunks because they have had no water to drink will drink water, for they will no longer need to drink wine.

I read about Pasolini. Learn of his belief that the workers of the world, like my grandfather, will save the world. Learn that his father, like my grandfather, was alcoholic. Learn that his father, like my grandfather, died because he drank.

Brother Ciccillo's hoped-for miracle: wine into water, not water into wine.

Words and Rags
· · · · · · · · · · · ·
JOANNA CLAPPS HERMAN

There is a hierarchy of rags in my house on North Main Street: the very good dust rags, the regular rags, the polishing rags, and finally the under-the-sink rags. Our old clothes, old sheets, and *mappine*s are ripped into squares, and each is designated to its rag station. The rags descend from high to low as they rip and wear further, until they wind up under the sink to clean our filthiest messes. There, dried into dirty gray twists, these rags hang over the pipe. As said above to clean up our filthiest messes.

"Good dust rags" have the highest place and rank. After they're ironed and folded they are carefully tucked behind my mother's underwear in her bureau.

But the *mappin'* is the flag of our everyday life. Though not of the same high rank and station as the good dust rags, the *mappin'* is ever present, always ready to mop, wipe, dab every ordinary bit of mess and

· · · · ·

JOANNA CLAPPS HERMAN has published in *Massachusetts Review, Kalliope, Crescent Review, Critic, Paterson Literary Review, Inkwell, Earth's Daughters, Voices in Italian Americana, Italian Americana, Woman's Day, Sing Heavenly Muse,* and many other periodicals. Her fiction has been awarded The Bruno Arcudi Fiction Prize and second place for the Anne and Henry Paolucci Prize. Her essays have appeared in the collections *Don't Tell Mama* and *The Milk of Almonds.*

dirt. Slung over our shoulders, it is a mantle conferring affiliation in our female world. It's our job to keep nature and civilization perfectly balanced: nature with all its incumbent mess outside, us neatly inside. All dirt, grass, leaves, insects are to be swept, dusted, pushed back out through windows and doors. If they can't be pushed out, these bits of fluid nature always wanting back in are to be vacuumed, scoured, dumped, made to disappear. All wood must be scrubbed, waxed, and polished until it resembles a material as far from the wildness of nature as possible. All stone, clay, glass must gleam, glimmer, and shine— vested of every rough uneven bit of soil or tree or mountain it may have emerged from. Our rags are our implements—the female equivalent of hammers, chisels, and saws—but the *mappin'* is first among these, the most important tool in our polished female world.

"What a mess!"

"Quick. Where's the *mappin'*?"

"Wipe that up!"

Things are often *sciangiat', strisciliat', stambl', sporc'* in Waterbury. Respectively these mean broken down, tangled up, a mess, confused or dirty. There are a lot of dirty, mixed-up messes in Waterbury. What if you are *'broglon'*, someone who makes a big mess? *No' buon'* or *non* good. What if you're *stunad'*, out of it, stupefied, *citrull'*, a cucumber (that dumb), and brazen about it? This could mean that you're *scustomad', mal educa't, senza educazion'*, without custom, badly educated, without education, in short, ill-mannered, ill-mannered, ill-mannered. Bad, bad, bad.

If you know what's good for you, you'd better *stata citt'* and *fate fatti tui'*, shut up and mind your own business. Because if it turns out you're *fracomoda'*, too damn comfortable, so comfortable as to be unable to move, lazy—which definitely makes us the kind of girls who will *mai ess femini' della cas'*, never be good housewives—we're going to get straightened out but good, with such a *palliad'*, such a beating, because you're making your mother *sciatt'*, burst.

So it's essential to get these messes cleaned up, straightened up. *Subit' mo'!* Immediately! Now! If we're up the farm with Gramma and we answer back, "I didn't make that mess, Gramma. She did," then she'll say, *"Citt' na nonna."* Be quiet, Gramma, meaning, you be quiet, so you might as well just be quick about it and get that *mappin'*. Gramma, like all the old-timers, addresses the children with her own appellation. "Gramma, give Gramma kiss," Gramma says, extending her permanently wrinkled, permanently garlicky cheek toward you.

My mother, my sister Lucia, and I have a *mappin'* slung over our shoulders as we go about our work in the kitchen, to sweep past our mouths after we sample some steak *pizzaiol'* from the pan on the stove, tasting the combination of steak with peppers, tomatoes, onions, garlic potatoes, all simmering in olive oil. Does it need salt? A little more hot? Or if we grab a bit of salad from someone's plate when we're clearing the table, we hold the *mappin'* just under our chins as we lift the tomato dripping with dressing to our lips. Then we whip the *mappin'*, ready for us to wipe down the olive oil that dribbled onto the floor. A quick shake of the *mappin'* into the sink and it's clean again. Like kissing something up to God, shaking it out makes the *mappin'* immediately clean. Unless it's just come out of the *mappin'* drawer, it's always a little damp and makes the perfect rag to swipe every ordinary spill and mess.

The *mappin'* is as basic to our lives as food. We're out to clean the dirt off our hands and the manure off our peasant feet.

There are only two or three "good" *mappines* to use when company comes. The linen ones, always clean, ironed with perfect creases, are taken out of the linen closet a couple of times a year to dry the gold-trimmed etched glass water goblets that my parents still have left from their wedding presents. When company's coming we take the glasses down from over the fridge and wash them in very hot, hot water. Then we dry them with the linen towels—the good *mappines*—until the glasses squeak. But those are very rare occasions. Maybe it's because the New York relatives are visiting.

The everyday *mappine*s have been recently laundered (at least one laundry a day), ironed, and folded in the precise and prescribed way—first lengthwise in three, then folded in half, and laid in piles in the *mappin'* drawer exactly to the left of the equally ripped and ironed and folded cloth napkins. None of these are very far from their rag incarnation.

Mappin' is our dialect word for dishtowel, but how *'Merican* (pronounced Mer-i-KAHN) that sounds. But the word "dishtowel" connotes a neat cloth folded over a towel bar near the stove: clean, intact, more for show than use. It has nothing to do with the *mappin'* as we know it. If the idea is to convert this word back to what might be, what no doubt is, the original Italian word, in the singular it would be *mappina,* plural would be *mappine.*

The daily use of dialect words in the course of the day is one of the ways we knew we were Italian and not Italian American. Although my generation doesn't speak my mother's family's Tolvese dialect, we are definitely *Tolvese,* and Italian. We use the English nominative plural, the "s" to make the *mappine* into *mappine*s. To us "dishtowel" sounds stilted, pretentious. Dishtowel, dishrag, wash rag. These *'Merican* words sound awkward, unnatural. Don't *'Mericans* feel stupid when they use those words? A word like *mappin'* should have a kissing closeness to onomatopoeia.

"Colander," too, sounds so Anglo as to be Saxon. *Scola maccarun'* sounds real; it rolls off the tongue like it's supposed to.

"What does *scola maccarun'* actually mean, Mom?" This occurs to me in a burst of linguistic awareness as I'm reaching for it from under the sink. It's a Friday so we're making *aglia olio,* no meat.

The three of us are in the kitchen. Lucia's setting the table. My mother is frying the garlic in oil. I'm washing the parsley when my mother tells me, "Get the *scola maccarun,* Jojo." Until that Friday, it has simply been the word for the object we use to strain the water once the linguine is cooked. (NB: You only use linguine for *aglia olio.*)

She pauses, puzzled and amused by what she finds herself saying, after she stops near the sink with the aluminum pot full of linguine. She's ready to pour. "Well, actually it means 'strain the macaroni.'" We don't consider these words. We say them. They are our words. "Here, put it in the sink," she keeps our preparations going.

"You mean you're saying to us, 'Get the strain the macaroni?'"

"I know, but that's what it's called. What can I tell you?" She throws back her curls, just released from the bobby pins but not yet brushed through, and laughs. Dad isn't home yet and we're hurrying to get dinner on the table. She hasn't had a chance to run a brush through her hair and put her lipstick on, which she'll do when she hears the truck crunch over the gravel in our driveway.

I'm asking about the *scola maccarun'* because Miss Collins, our smartly dressed seventh-grade teacher, who's just returned from a trip to Italy over the summer, said something today in an uncharacteristically peremptory manner. Just before we lined up in the pink girls' side of the school basement to go back to our classroom, when we were talking about making *'a pizz'* in cooking class that day. "*'A pizz'* isn't a real Italian word. The real Italian word is *La Pizza* and it means 'a pie.'" Miss Collins stood there, head high, certain in her pronouncement. *La Pizza?* Not *'a pizz'!* How could that be? How could she knew more than us about our language? Where did she get this? Who does she think she is?

Miss Collins is one of the young women who went to normal school right after high school for two years to train to be a teacher. Teachers in that era were trained at two-year teacher training schools called normal schools. When these women accepted their teaching positions they signed an agreement not to marry. If they married they had to give up their jobs. Not so for men. Occasionally we'd hear a whisper about a female teacher who was secretly married until "they" found out. Then she was fired.

We are shocked that women would give up being married for a job, just as horrified as we are about their being punished, fired, for being married. We are shocked.

We know our family speaks dialect. *Tolvese* is our dialect and therefore *buon'*. "*Meh,*" Gramma laughs and covers the gaps in her teeth with one cupped hand when I ask her one day when she's making distinctions between people who are *Napolitano, Siciliana,* and *Barese,* "What about the *Tolvese?*"

"*Su bas,*" she says. Real low. Even so, being *Tolvese* is what we are and it seems inherently to be a good thing. Even if my generation doesn't speak *Tolvese* it's still ours. The dialect words lace our everyday cadences as naturally as English. They aren't part of another language for us.

The words we use often have to do with the house, *a cas'*, or food, *i' robb' 'i mangiar'*, and to do with insults, mess, confusion, vulgarities. It's a language of the home and street, at the margins of any lexical canon but at the center of our lives. So for example, "I have such a *vuli'*" means, "I have such a yen or desire for a particular food," but "yen really doesn't capture the same feeling," my father says every time he translates it for someone outside our family. *Bugiard'*, liar, *stravers'*, perverse or pigheaded, determined to do things your own way, and therefore the wrong way, *capa dost'*, thick-headed, *capa dur'*, thick-headed, *faccia dost'*, thick-faced, or thick-headed. Do you see a pattern here?

Manaccia diavol', damn the devil, *va'Napl'*, go to hell, or go to Naples, going to Naples being the equivalent of going to hell (I have no idea until I am a teenager that what we were saying had anything to do with Naples: the word meant how annoying), *manag' 'a 'Merican'*, damn the Americans, *malandren'*, bad boy, *mammon'*, mama's boy, but really anyone dumb or annoying, *u pazz'*, crazy, you make me *schiatt'*, you make me burst, said with fury, indignation, *che bellezz'*, what a beauty, really, you're unbelievably annoying, *canta tu*, sing you, or go ahead and talk, tell them everything you, ma sona ma beech bastid. These words can't be wrong. They are what we use to signify meaning and that meaning is communicated. That's called language.

I don't remember knowing there was another, "real" Italian until I am ten or eleven, though my mother always says about Grandpa

Clapps's second wife, Nanny Clapps, who was from Lucca, "Oh, she speaks such beautiful Italian. Her pronunciation is so beautiful." She takes the time to pronounce each vowel fully, even the final ones. Our dialect is hurried; our family has to get out to the *masseri'*, the fields. Is that why so many vowels are elided or clipped?

When I visited Lisbon, the old Portuguese women looked and sounded like my grandmother to me, something about the swing and clip of their words. We all know about the influence of the Arab "u" in the southern Italian dialects, but what about the influence of the Albanese, Francese, Tedeschi? What about the influence of all those eastern Mediterranean cultures? Like Comma' Luci's family who were *Grigiott'*, the Greeks, who lived in a certain neighborhood of Tolve. What does it mean that they were "Greek"? Does our dialect include residual Greek words and phrases? Whatever the elements are that make it up, our dialect has the sounds of intimacy, the sounds of an enclosed, hermetically sealed world.

The words Miss Collins used that day were the strange ones. If she was correct, she was not right. What did she know? She wasn't the one who made the weekly bread supply along with *'a pizz'*—to be eaten on Saturdays—in the woodoven Grampa built for his *'a Figliol'* (young girl) Gramma, down by the road once a week. She didn't help to slaughter a pig and then pour boiling water on the pig's skin to get the hair off, then gut its innards so that we could roast the pig carcass on a spit, or butcher it in order to make *salscici'* for the *ragu*, or *'a salscici'* that was then dried and preserved in *olio di'oliv'*. She didn't cure the *prosciutt'*, can the peaches. She hadn't gotten up before dawn to feed the chickens, collect the eggs, milk the cows before she went to school as my mother and her sisters did. She didn't shovel pig shit into barrels to fertilize the garden.

Miss Collins doesn't know the smell of pig shit on a hot summer day that filled the nostrils of my mother and her sisters one summer as they picked bones out of the pig manure to sell because it was a hard time for her family. She doesn't know the intense, salty, cheese and prosciutto smell from the wine cellar where all the drying cheeses, *prosciutt'*, and *salscici'* hang, the smell from the wine barrels soaked with intense red wine, the damp smell from the damp stone walls, and the smell of the fat crisping from the pig roasting on a spit in summer. She doesn't know the smell of tomatoes that have been picked in the summer heat, blanched in boiling water, peeled, then packed along with *basilicol'* into large glass jars that have been boiled on long hot summer afternoons in gigantic pots to sterilize them. This project alone took weeks every summer, as the tomatoes were jarred, then carried down the rickety stairs in bushel baskets to line the long *sciangiatt'*, creaky, wooden shelves in the side canning cellar, not in the root and wine cellar where the *prosciutt'*, *scamozz'*, and dry *salscici'* and other preserved foods that Gramma makes hang, not the main cellar where the *salscici'* is made. She hasn't laid the rest of the tomatoes out on large sheets in the sun to dry to make *'i conserv'*, which will thicken and sweeten the *ragu* all year long.

Still, Miss Collins has ripped a tear in the fabric of our mapped world. Our language wasn't "real."

Miss Collins went to grammar school with the movie star Rosalind Russell. "Even then she was a devil. She'd try anything. Oh, she was a wild one," Miss Collins said, proud to have had such a friend as a child. "She was always climbing over fences. One day she ripped her underpants and she took them right off and threw them on the ground."

She was short and elegant, sharp, and a snappy dresser. She traveled in the summer with Miss Burney, who taught second grade, who was quiet, sober, not sharp or a snappy dresser, but she wasn't sad and alone like Miss Martino, whose sadness made her mean. Miss Collins, the snappy dresser, liked us. There was always a light in her eyes that spoke of humor, pleasure at being alive, a lack of resentment at teaching us, the sons and daughters of the flotsam and jetsam that had floated ashore in America.

We girls, who sat on the stairs near the baseball field brushing our long flowing hair so the boys would notice us, couldn't reconcile our sense of our teachers as women who held great authority over us with the fact that they had agreed not to be married. Miss Collins alluded to romance. Men she met when she traveled in the summer? Did I make that up? Was she independent and didn't want the must and should that all the women in my family lived with?

Now I wonder if she and Miss Burney were more to each other than we could have understood. Was teaching a haven for gay women? Was the convent a sanctuary of professional life and respectability for our nuns who taught us catechism on Monday afternoons in the convent on Hillview Avenue?

In the fifties we felt so sorry for the nuns who were "married to Jesus," we said with our eyes round and shocked, heads shaking in a studied admiration that barely hid our disbelief, our condescension. Most of us would have signed right up to be nuns if it hadn't been for the prohibition against marriage and having babies. For our teachers it made even less sense. They weren't married to Jesus. "They couldn't get married back then. That's terrible. Then it was probably too late." Whose words are these, stored so carefully in my head? Our mother's, then ours?

Miss Collins, the snappy dresser, the very pretty, the teacher who traveled with Miss Burney, who had had Rosalind Russell for a childhood friend, who had the good sense of humor and real affection for us, said, "I went to Roma, this summer," with an unmistakable American pronunciation. "It's called *la pizza* and it means pie. It's not *'a pizz'*." I guess you could call it mutual condescension made of whole continents of misunderstanding.

Miss Collins didn't know that our dialect preserved the ancient first-person form of *sapere*, which is *saccio*, the word that Dante uses for "I know" in *L'Inferno*. In modern Italian it's been changed to *so*, even though the cognate structure for *fare* still uses *faccio* for "I made." *Fare* and all the "made" constructions are practically copulatives in Italian, used the way the infinitive "to be" is in English. At Boston University, years later, I sat through years of Italian taught by our old Pirandellesque professor who refused to do anything but read each book to us droning for an hour and a half on Tuesdays and Thursdays, reading the Italian, then translating it, looking up in disgust every half hour or so to ask, "Are there any questions?" daring us to even consider engaging him.

I learned nothing about Dante, but two things about our dialect. I noticed that Dante used *saccio,* just like we did. *Ma chi sacci', i sacci', no sacci' i.* Who knows, I know, I don't know, were all a part of our everyday parlance in Waterbury. Once in my Dante class, the word *sciagurato* came up in the middle of Book XX. When I heard from the periphery of my miasmic fog the professor ask if anyone knew what the word *sciagurato* meant I swam up out of my stupor and raised my hand for that one and only time and said, "I do. My grandmother used to say *'chiest' femmine si chiamano sciaguratu', remaniesc' senz u' marit' e senz' innamurat'."* These bad women who are called *sciagurat'* wind up without a husband or a lover.

He snorted in bitter recognition, then caught himself and stopped. "Yes, it means something like that, a person of a slovenly nature." That was the only spark of life I ever saw in that class. I learned that my dialect had some deep connection to an older world that I barely glimpsed that day.

Miss Collins and Miss Burney who sometimes traveled together in the summers didn't know that my grandmother sang to all her *creatur',* rocking them in their baby carriages, one foot rocking the front axle of the carriage, like the treadle of a sewing machine, the wheels of the carriage creaking in rhythm, her hands free to crochet in rhythm, while she chanted, *Ninna nonna, ninna nonna,* which means sleep grandma, implying sleep for Gramma's sake. It was common for a mother or grandmother to address her child by her own appellation, a commonplace of affection and connection. Individuation was not on our map, only connection, union and merging. It's not until I live in New York and I hear Spanish mothers and grandmothers saying this to their little ones,

"*Mami,* don't do that." Meaning "my child, child who belongs to me or even child with whom I am one, don't do that." We're one culture.

The summer my husband, Bill, and I went to Portugal, we spent days along the Tagus. The next summer we went to Turkey and spent the same overheated listless summer afternoons along the Aegean coast. Each end of this Mediterranean felt the same. At times I would look up and think, "Italy? No, Turkey, no, wait..."

Then the following year we had no money and we spent our long summer afternoons bleeding into evenings, bleeding from cerulean blue into indigo, along the estuary of the Hudson rushing out toward the western shore of the Atlantic, on the promenade in Battery Park City, in New York City. Here again, the same watery edge on the lip of a large expanse of sea or headway rushing into the larger body was the same. Always the golden glow, always the sense of being held just at the edge of the larger other that an immense highway of water brings to its shores. All my connections were here: the eastern antecedents of the Greek, Semitic, Turkish cultures that flooded over into Sicily and southern Italy, then the trip our Mediterranean ancestors made in distress via Portugal, Spain, France to the shores of America. These connections, the eastern Mediterranean, the western Med, rushing out into the Atlantic, which rushes across to American shores, they all hold the same hope, the same imprisonment, the same possibility.

Gramma said, rubbing our bruises in a gentle circling motion, *"San' e san', ogg' ruot, e crai è san'."* Heal, heal, today broken, tomorrow healed. Years later, when I was teaching a women's poetry class we began to discuss the ancient oral tradition of love poetry, or ritual songs and chants that women were often responsible for, marriage songs, funeral chants, birth songs. We began to discuss our own female oral traditions and I asked my students to bring in their mothers' and grandmothers' chants, blessings, sayings, and songs. When I sang my grandmother's healing chant of *san' e san'* to show them what I meant, Inez, a Puerto Rican student of mine, said, "My grandmother sang the same thing all the time, exactly the same way." Did that healing song travel the Mediterranean from southern Italy to North Africa to Spain, then to the New World? Did the Spanish bring it home with them after they conquered southern Italy? Did they bring it to us when they came and lived among us? This map of oral language was preserved in invisible ink and connected me to this woman's family. I felt a wave of connection between this Latina woman and the women in my family. Our grandmothers healed us with the same chant.

Miss Collins couldn't know that. She couldn't know that in places like Waterbury we've preserved these ancient words and songs and sayings long after Italians on the rest of the peninsula gave them up. When my mother and her sisters went to Tolve in 1986, our people laughed when they spoke the dialect language they had always used, the one my grandparents had brought with them when they arrived in the first decade of the twentieth century. Our relatives in Tolve had given up the dialect after radio and television took over their language. They didn't say, *"Si volema schi schiama nin se no, non schima scen,"* if we're going to leave, let's go, if we're not, let's not go. (Let's stay.)

What could Miss Collins know about a *mappin'*? I'm sure she didn't know that the word "map" comes from the same root word that *mappine* comes from. The Latin root word *mappa* means cloth or towel. In Medieval Latin, *Mappa Mundi* means sheet of the world because maps were originally drawn on pieces of linen. The word "mop" come from the same root. She didn't. And we didn't. But deep in the south of Italy, in the hill towns, this word root, this idea of the small piece of precious cloth that holds your world together, connecting worlds that you hardly know exist, held that meaning.

If a dialect is a language without an army behind it, the *mappin'* is our flag, our banner, holding aloft everything that has kept us at the edge. It's the flag that hails our marginality. We were the backwater to all the great Mediterranean empires that conquered southern Italy. So the words that come down to us are words without formality, without hegemony, entirely noncanonical words. Is that why the words of confusion, mess, disorder, the curse words, the words of ruin, crippledness, dirt are the ones that have passed down to my generation? We had *mappines* on our shoulders, shovels in our hands, dough under our fingernails, bits of sausage caught between our teeth. The church damned us on the one hand for being the pagans we were, and all the Italians north of us, which means most Italians, damned us on the other hand as "those Arabs down there, those Africans." They still say this even now, as they dismiss our people with a laugh and heads tossed in contempt, so afraid that they might be connected to us. They shouldn't worry so much. They're not. We're not. Connected.

Em beh', what are you going to do? If anything we're an ancient Semitic, Phoenician, Greek, Byzantine, Anatolian, maybe even Roman *misconbrulia,* mixed-up mess or confusion, an island of people that came loose from the eastern shores of the Mediterranean, more Near Eastern than Western, but from which in desperation, at the end of the nineteenth century, we floated ourselves across the Mediterranean in bits and pieces, in such tiny pieces we floated one or two people at a time through the Straits of Gibraltar and washed up on the shores of America. We collected in threes and fours along the edges of America. We made communities where the ancient mores of our culture preserve something so old it doesn't have a written record, only a song here and a rag there.

These Innocent Lambs

· · · · · · · ·

LAURA VALERI

An old Sardinian legend tells of a devil who came to live on this island, finding the rough seas, the rocky shores, the dust, and the desolate crags an abode more suitable than hell. The locals say they've seen tracks of fire where the devil's hooves pass, and that he pesters goat-herders by turning cattle into red ants. If you ask enough people, some even claim to have seen his winged shadow. This devil has company, Sardinians say: blood-sucking women who attack babies in their cribs, and murderers who turn into goats by night because of unpunished misdeeds and scratch their horns on the window-shutters of their victims.

Fortunately, in the early seventies, when our family spent its summers in the southern tip of this Italian island, my brother, my sister, and I were still unfamiliar with this particular stock of boogiemen tales. We were six, nine, and twelve respectively when my parents first bought a tight little cottage improperly called "little villa" *(villino)* on a shrubby, dry beach-cove called Costa Rei. There were only a dozen other cottages in the community, each one looking exactly like ours, and unless someone wanted to count the pizza joint seven miles north, the nearest

· · · · ·

LAURA VALERI is the author of *The Kind of Things Saints Do,* winner of the John Simmons and John Gardner Awards. She lives in Savannah, Georgia, where she teaches writing and is at work on a novel.

sources of groceries or entertainment were the cattle farms far up on the hills. We could have pigs, ducks, and goats slaughtered for a modest price; we could have fresh milk, and even homemade jelly, but we could not have television, or toys for that matter, except for the few we managed to sneak in the trunk of the Renault 16 that every summer shuttled us from Milan to Rome and onto the rickety ship that ferried us into the Sardinian port.

For entertainment we kids had ourselves—and the other twenty or so children whose parents vacationed there, decades before the Sardinian coast became the choice vacation spot of Saudi royals and European elites. We were a twenty-faced brat pack with three or four alternating leaders, middle-class urchins from cities of industry and crowd, eager to shed urban propriety. In the daytime, when we dared each other to tiptoe barefooted ever so slowly over a thirty foot stretch of pebbled road, then through the dune grass, and finally over the hot fine sand, all we knew was that the semi-precious St Lucy's eyes could be found on the shores along with starfish, and that underwater, if you dove deeply enough, you could see moray eels twisting through cracked terracotta jars abandoned by who knows what past century's galleon. But without movie theaters, restaurants, or even a fairly stocked supermarket, it took some ingenuity to fill the long evening hours. Even TV antennae were a luxury.

Parents organized nightly card tournaments and elaborate potluck dinners (kilos of ash-roasted pig, liters of cioppino, mountains of crème brûlée), to celebrate island scarcity with wine, fresh seafood, and chatter, and singing to Mina and Gianni Morandi, and calling out each other's pinochle trumps. But we, the kids, clustered noiselessly out on the porch, measuring boredom with tales: *Well, everyone's done the Ouija, with the little glass, but that's kid's stuff,* the kind forbidden by Catholic nuns, *I'm talking about possession here,* as if our lives were not uncertain enough, *You've got to be big like me, at least in the tenth grade,* that we needed ghosts to validate us, *It's not for little kids with milk on the lips,* to test our prepubescent courage, *You'd start crying and you'd chase away the ghost. Or worse,* to swap a yawn for a shiver: *You'd bring the devil. Yeah, I said the devil. You think it's funny, do you?*

The older kids could tease us, saying we were too small for a séance, but that would only get us begging for Lucia to help, the long-haired girl with the freckles and the pretty faraway eyes, the girl who looked at you without looking at you, whose voice was always a breath or two after her words; Lucia, who already spoke like she belonged to the ghosts, her long hair sweeping over the table top as she shook her head this way and that. She didn't mind telling us about the drowned girl, the ghosts that slipped inside her nostrils once, tying up her tongue and flouncing her about like a Neapolitan puppet. Dangerous, she said. So dangerous that after, she slept for a whole week.

But the next day, when the talk was sharpened by the heat and the salt, the older kids would remind us how Lucia smoked, how she was one of the "absent ones," this girl who dressed in men's suits three times her size, this girl who was caught at night drinking and sucking up joints. Everyone knew that Lucia was headed for "the bad finish." Not even her mother, Marta the drunk, could stop her, and her father, the Alitalia pilot, was too busy flying and womanizing to bother. Who was there to stop Lucia, who ran away at night sneaking through the window, such a pretty red-haired girl with wide green eyes, headed for a bad finish? We, the girls, we wanted Lucia's long eyelashes and the happy red strands of her hair, but we didn't want her life, and we certainly didn't want that gossip, rising after each of her footsteps like a black puff of dust.

"Ghosts?" The boys laughed. "You say ghosts? She sleeps all day because she's too tired from poking herself."

The older kids pushed on their veins and wiggled their eyebrows. And you were supposed to know, even if you were a little one, that it meant Lucia was a heroin addict. She was a lost one, they said. It had started like a joke, one or two joints once in a while, but it ended up like that, she and her ghost stories and her tragic family: her mother who drank, her father who cheated, her brother, Fabrizio, who was a delinquent and failed all his classes (at 15 he was still in the eighth grade), and little Marzio, the youngest, who had turned stupid from taking so many slaps on the head from his drunk mother, and from those nasty, nasty boyfriends of Lucia's who liked to use their hands, so much that Lucia sometimes sported a shiny pulpy cheek just under her eye and blamed it on the ghosts.

We local children went to Lucia's house every afternoon, that little stucco cottage complete with solarium and draping bougainvillea, its coarse, shepherd-style, chestnut furniture a mirror reflection of ours, and we watched, through her living room's windows, the preening Lucia with the long red hair looking at herself, her mother already too drunk to notice her. We'd shake our head at Lucia the beautiful for wearing these foolish-looking clothes, and she'd throw us a smile through the window and sometimes even asked us, "How do I look?" not realizing we were too shy to tell her that girls weren't supposed to wear boys' clothes, that pants and jackets on a girl didn't look so good, and she was *pazza!*, crazy-crazy, for asking us. But we always nodded, because in somebody else's house you had to be polite, and we said that she looked all right. So she glanced at herself once more, smoothing her lips with a wet finger, mussing a curl around her sweet oval face.

"Lucia, won't you tell us about ghosts? Won't you come and play the medium for us, for a *seduta spiritica,* a spiritual sitting?"

"But you kids are too young! You think it's a joke. You have to take things with respect, otherwise you can call on the devil. And once the devil is in your house, you can never get rid of him."

"We'll be careful, we promise."

"Oh, you promise, do you?"

"Oh, yes, please, Lucia. We want to see about ghosts."

"But who will be there to call on the ghosts?"

"You, Lucia, you're the medium, the psychic. Everyone knows you're the best."

Lucia looked scared sometimes, shaking her pretty red hair, her green eyes wide.

"No, no. Because...if you laugh? If you laugh, you attract negative spirits, even the devil. And who will pay for it, huh? I will! Because I will be in a trance. And do you think it's fun to be in a trance when the devil is about? This is serious stuff. I can't do serious stuff with foolish kids. Forget it."

But if we were patient, and if we insisted, sometimes, if her boyfriend had stopped coming around—if she didn't have a red Fiat or a metal-blue Alfa waiting out near her window — then she'd come and sit with us on the front porch under the flowering bougainvillea to drink fizzy sugar water, and listen to us talk about who was the cutest boy on the beach, who was the best body surfer, who had been the smartest and the funniest when old, crusty Mr. Duri came back to find his palm trees de-fronded.

So it went that the lights went out for a flicker, and someone foolish said, "Ooooh. Here comes Spirit to warn us."

"Shut up, stupid. Don't make fun of Spirit like that." It was that easy to rile up Lucia, a rebellious red lock already falling on her freckled cheek.

"Spirit is bullshit." Pietro Testa had a reputation for being good at making people "dick-off like a bull," pushing on buttons until those buttons popped off and hit you in the teeth. The mothers said it was because he was fat and had an insecurity complex. (They said that only when Pietro's mother wasn't around.) He did it just to show that he was somebody, the mothers said. And he always got the other kids—the good children, the innocent lambs—he always got them "in an ugly situation." But try to remind a mother of that explanation when her sandal is in mid-flight aiming for your head. She'd say, "Me? I would never say that about a child!" And for that, you'd get the other sandal, too.

"So the light went out," Pietro said, his voice like an out-of-tune mandolin. "It's all a bunch of shit. I don't believe in Spirit."

Except the lights went out again. Lucia spoke to the darkness. "Spirit, we apologize for foolish Pietro. He doesn't know better. Spirit, we humbly ask your permission that you restore the electricity in this house."

And just like that the lights came on again!

We held our breaths and looked at Lucia, who was trying to freeze Pietro with her eyebrows bunched up and low. But Pietro was unflinching, a smug smile stamped on his lips, his fatty cheeks pushing over his cheekbones, making his giblet eyes look even smaller.

"Yeah, Spirit, suck my cock!"

Lucia gasped, and we saw her reach over the table for Pietro, and just then the lights went out again.

"Pietro!" we all screamed.

"Come on! This is a fucking island. It's just a blackout."

The light bulb flickered a bit as Lucia muttered prayers, an apology to Spirit for the unbelieving boy who had dared call into question Its power.

When the light finally came back, Pietro was laughing.

Lucia pushed away from the table, all choked up and ruffled.

"I pay for this," she said, pointing at Pietro. "That's why I don't like to talk about this stuff with kids. Then Spirit takes it out on me."

She could not be persuaded to stay, but had we been any older we might have realized she relished somewhat the attention she had garnered in that one session of light flickering on the front porch of our house. What we noticed was only our thirst for this ghost business. Now that we had witnessed the Almighty Light Withdrawal, there was no mission nobler than persuading Lucia to lead a *seduta spiritica,* a séance.

During those evenings in Sardinia, the only thing we talked about was the night that the lights went out because stupid Pietro made fun of Spirit in front of Lucia. All we needed was little Marzio's official report that Lucia had been found the next morning on the floor of her bedroom, naked and beaded in sweat, her eyes rolling back in their sockets, her mouth coated in saliva, a gasping not unlike that of love-making heaving through her chest and neck. It convinced us without a breath of doubt that she had been punished by Spirit on Pietro's account, even if the adults dismissed this tale as yet more evidence that the Della Rosa girl was a junkie, a *drogata* headed for "a bad finale." She was sent to Rome, but came back three weeks later when her Alitalia pilot father got tired of taking care of her. We hailed her arrival with renewed insistence that she lead a séance. But it wasn't until Giovanna returned from Cagliari that we finally had our wish.

Giovanna was among the spottiest of the regulars at our little beach enclave. She was a Sardinian, a native of Cagliari, and thus had the freedom to come and go without the restrictions of plane fares and ferry schedules that those of us who resided on the Italian peninsula had to respect. We'd known her from early on, when Costa Rei was just a spatter of rocks and shrubs near the beach. There were only twelve cottages then, and it was us, the Della Rosas, the Testas, the Fornarinis, the Duris, and the Sobreos, Giovanna's family. We knew Giovanna as one of *the settlers,* and it didn't matter that she came and went, that some summers she was with us on every game and stunt, and some others she puffed up her cheeks and looked to the side with her mouth all puckered up and said with breath and boredom, "Pietro is an idiot and Fabrizio is a fool. I can't believe you're so hung up on their juvenile bullshit." Giovanna, so queenly, as if she had better things to do than picking berries and making hot homemade jams; better than finding unexplored beaches or unearthing broken terracotta vases in the hidden caves just under the hills; better than morning body surfing in the ten foot waves in the deep blue Sardinian sea; and better than wading with stolen kitchen knives through the cane fields to steal bamboo for our play forts and for our bows and arrows . . . as if walking her two mastiffs and learning German from the Bavarian swim coach in the villa next to crusty Mr. Duri's was more fun even than peeling open, frond by frond, Mr. Duri's palm tree!

When we were all still little, so little that our mothers still fed us

Nutella on bread every early afternoon for snack time, Giovanna had acquired, on account of her long hair and skinny legs, the much undeserved reputation of being beautiful. This went on for years, until Pietro called out that she was not only ugly but also a bitch, especially since she had taken to smoking. Even so, those afternoons that we walked the four miles uphill to Monte Nai for the disco dance for minors, the boys lined up to dance with her all the same. Giovanna had straight reddish hair like Lucia, and small maroon eyes that fixed intensely on a person. She had developed the peculiar habit of snorting hard enough to make the tip of her nose veer to the left. And the meaner boys, especially Pietro, said that the bouquet of whiteheads blooming periodically on the well of her chin was "clear evidence" that she wasn't a virgin. She was the only girl on the beach never to wear a bra, even though her breasts bounced when she ran, enough to attract attention from the "old people": the gardeners, the occasional, wandering, sphere-eyed goatherd. And some of the mothers even whispered about her father, the famous journalist Sobreo, and how he kissed Giovanna on the lips too much like a lover. But nobody ever said Giovanna was headed for "the bad finale." Mothers only muttered under a tight lip, sucking their breath through their teeth, that "the girl should wear a bra," and they walked away before Giovanna could stare them in the eye and laugh, even though they could slap us silly if they wanted to.

Giovanna was like a shaken fizzy water bottle, like when we held the thumb on the tip and pointed it at the boys if they acted stupid. She was the sticky spray, the icy cold surprise, the gooey sugar stain on our brown calves. When Giovanna arrived, things happened (including Fabrizio showing us his penis by moonlight after the bottle settled on his flip flop, and though bored even as he zipped and tugged and declared with a grin, "This is too big for you little girls," he nonetheless obliged, leaving us to contemplate in shameful silence how that sharp curve to the left may have inspired poets of days gone by to refer to their reproductive organs as bananas).

That summer Giovanna, who was in the seventh grade, had failed Drawing and History (Pietro Testa said because she was caught shirtless with a boy in the well of her high school stairs), and she had to go to summer "repetition school" in order to be able to move on to the next grade. When, midway through summer, she was finally absolved, Giovanna came in strutting, demanding to catch up on all the huff.

"Giovanna! You should have been there! Pietro dared Spirit and the lights went out!"

"Marzio, shut up! She didn't really say it exactly like that, not exactly, and..."

"No, no. It wasn't Lucia who started it! It was because we were talking about the girl who drowned who was found half nibbled by sharks..."

"Idiot! There are no sharks in the Mediterranean sea, and you're getting it all confused..."

Giovanna listened, her maroon eyes moving to the right and to the left, her nose veering with her regular snorts, an upper lip now and again disappearing under her tongue, but she said nothing until the end, until all of us had spoken by turns and deprecated Pietro Testa, his bad timing, and his big mouth, and praised Lucia and her fearful ways. We described in detail how, the next morning, her eyes rolled back in her sockets and the sweat covered her skin, even though none of us had been there to see it but Marzio, who couldn't be understood because he stuttered a little when he was excited, and if someone interrupted him he sighed and stuffed his thumb in his mouth and rubbed his head as if remembering all the hard knocks he had taken lately.

Finally there was silence. Giovanna snorted meaningfully. We heard the snot rolling back into her throat, and we secretly recoiled.

"And why, exactly, do we need to wait for Lucia?"

Collectively, we began to wonder if arrogance and skepticism weren't embedded in the mysterious genes of the natives (Pietro Testa was the only other Sardinian on this tourist-contaminated side of the island).

Giovanna scanned our faces.

"Anybody can be a medium," she declared, hands on hips. She scratched her chin and picked at a pimple. "Hell, I could be one if I wanted to."

"Noooo! Lucia warned us! You could call on the devil!"

Giovanna clicked her tongue and hissed, making a noise that the locals often made to signify that we Northerners of the peninsula had buried our common sense in the cement and asphalt of our sky-scrapered cities. She meant what she'd said plainly for years now: we were juvenile. We were gullible kids caught up in foolish endeavors, and when it came right down to it, we could "do the talk, but not the walk."

She turned back to her mastiffs, demonstrating their knowledge of her newly acquired German dog orders: *Platz!* (Sit!) *Ge Vek!* (Go Away!) The matter of the ghost was temporarily dismissed, at least in front of Giovanna, who would send the issue to an early grave by suggesting that we call on Spirit ourselves with a hand-drawn Ouija-style alphabet drawing and an ashtray for a pointer.

Even though all of us thought about it at our nightly gatherings on the porches of our villas, while the adults proceeded, oblivious, with their dinners, card nights, and Marilyn Monroe movie nights (only two villas actually had strong enough antennas to pick up the two state channels), we talked instead about Giovanna's demonstrations of her mastiff's identity crisis, and how she hunkered down on all fours for him, laughing when the confused dog tried to mount her through her thick bikini bottom.

It made us feel better to point out her slutty shamefulness because she often shunned us to hang out instead with those hated German tourists, whom we blamed for having mistaken Sardinia for their personal nudist beach and for the frequent forest fires that happened during the droughty summers. We had all noticed how, whenever one of those fires seared up another slice of hill, some bleached German investor would end up buying the burnt up land and building another villa. In the five years that we had frequented Costa Rei, we had grown from a spit-radius village to a sixty-five villa complex, and for this we blamed these harsh-speaking, sausage-loving people whom we had a duty to despise on account of what they did to Italy during World War II, even if our parents had barely been toddlers then, and even if our history books reluctantly acknowledged Mussolini had had something to do with it. But for Giovanna to prefer the company of Germans to us, for her to bask in the glow of their melanin-deprived hairless chests, for her to take up predilection for their sun-exposed genitalia was insult greater than we could bear, and we drank up bitterness with our sugared fizzy water, remembering her insults and enlarging them with our gossip.

For a while, and with Lucia missing, we were too demoralized to bring up the ghosts, and we focused our efforts instead on stuffing plastic sandwich bags filled with sand and water into the gas tanks of those ill-fated weekend dwellers whom we considered intruders, and on ripping up Mr. Duri's bougainvillea, and on taunting relentlessly a rather large group of modest Sardinian children whose parents had come on this side of the island to be gardeners and housekeepers to the richer cottage owners. On the outside we were a cheerful group of deeply tanned savages in fabric hats and Speedos, allowed to roam free with our parents' blessings (the older kids were trustworthy in their naïve adult eyes). But on the inside we were dangerously bored, gritting our sand-speckled teeth at Giovanna's betrayals and huffing around impatiently under Lucia's window.

At night, while the adults gathered in mosquito-safe kitchens, the clinking of the ice against their glasses fading proportionally to the rising volume of their laughter, we took to terrorizing the darkened home of the Sardinian pack because they had dared to attempt to infiltrate our bamboo play coves by spying on us, then ambushing us with wet scarab balls that became extraordinarily heavy when dipped in sea water and made an odd, splattering sound when colliding with our heads. We vowed revenge and obtained it at night, posting vitriolic poems of Pietro's creation that made rhymes with the most unsightly body parts of the Sardinians' oldest girls, and by smearing their windows, doors, and car windshield with tree sap and Fabrizio's own, lovingly donated cum juice.

Then we rang the doorbell.

And courageously ran.

This went on for some nights, until the weaklings betrayed their cowardice by turning to the vilest of all weapons: they complained to their mothers, who in turn complained to ours. There was a brief and angry congregation of the Twelve Mothers from those families who had first "settled" Costa Rei back in the twelve-cottage days. Though it was later rumored that all Twelve Mothers believed it was Pietro Testa's fault for being fat and needing to prove himself, the Mothers came to the consensus that we had all "taken up too much rooster" (we'd gotten too cocky), and to rectify this alarming development there was a vigorous raising and falling of the hands on our Speedoed butts with harshly uttered pronouncements on our state of delinquency, until we children confessed ourselves humbled and defeated, and we apologized, tear-faced, to our teeth-sucking, shit-grin-witnessing enemies. The Sardinians seemed satisfied, though they insisted on watching the spanking, and even asked for repeats. When they left, they glanced back over their shoulders, and by their whispers we suspected the feud had not yet ended.

For a while, things proceeded uneventfully; then, toward the end of summer, there came that fated night when it rained outside, and our behinds still ached with memories of our parents' spanking for another palm tree defiling. Lucia was back, quiet and frail like that freckle-dusted nose of hers that defied the aquiline-snouted legacy of her proud Roman race. She spoke again under her breath, and with a fist under the thick curtain of her hair. Pietro Testa was away hosing gas for his boat from the unsuspecting tanks of visitors. We were all angry at him, anyway. We rallied happily to his revolutionary calls against Mr. Duri's shrubbery, but we fiercely resented our mothers' anger on his account.

That night we were humble enough to lounge around in our living room, handling a card deck among us without any desire to play, and sampling an adult-like drink called Shandy that mixed our usual fizzy sugared water with a little drop or two of beer.

But Giovanna kept grinning at Lucia, though it took many of the Roman girl's skittering glances before Giovanna, as we Italians say, "spat out the bull frog":

"You should hear the talk around here, the way they build you up to look like you're a witch. These little kids think you've got the power to summon the dead. I have to tell you straight up, I don't believe in any of this shit. I think it's all power of suggestion. Me, I guess I'm like St. Thomas: I'll believe it when I see it."

Lucia wasn't slow to take the bait. She straightened her posture.

"Do NOT speak lightly of these things!" Her voice quavered for effect.

We were all smart enough to build on the opening: "Oh, please Lucia, please, you promised. We'll be good, we swear. We won't call up any bad ghosts. We want to see for ourselves. We want to experience Spirit. You promised us one day you'd do it. We've been waiting all summer! Would you rather we did it ourselves? If it's as dangerous as you say, isn't it better that you help us?"

"All right," Lucia relented. "Maybe it's better that I show you. But not a chain sitting. That's too dangerous. The spirits can sit inside you if you don't do it right. I won't do that. I will do a Ouija, just that. Because look at that girl," she said, pointing at Giovanna, who was grinning and snorting evilly. "That girl is a troublemaker."

We rounded up drawing paper and a small ashtray before Lucia could change her mind, and we warned Giovanna that if she was going to be *that way* she might as well walk in the rain back to her villa, or to her German friends and see what *they* knew about spirits. We drew the letters and the yes and no, and sat around the big dining room table with our fingers lightly resting on the thin glass ashtray while Lucia invoked Spirit with her eyes closed and her mouth set seriously in her face.

"Spirit, if you are out there, please send us a sign.

"Spirit, if you are out there, please let us speak to you.

"We mean no harm, Spirit. We only wish to ask you simple questions.

"Spirit, please reveal yourself; if you are here, let us know."

We held our breaths, as if breathing might scare away the ghosts, and we tried hard to keep our fingers light on the edges of the ashtray, lest we be accused of cheating. Only Giovanna grinned, now and again producing a cough that sounded terribly much like a laugh. Lucia threw her hands up, her long strands of hair flying behind her shoulders.

"I won't do it like this. When skeptics are in the room, only devils come."

"Oh, come on, Lucia, please. It's only stupid Giovanna."

"I can't help it," said Giovanna, both hands pressed against her mouth. "I'm laughing because I'm nervous!"

Lucia would not hear it. She kicked the chair back, and only because Giovanna grabbed her wrist and apologized did she finally agree to sit down and give Spirit another try.

"But no laughing," she warned. And Giovanna allowed a minute to let the giggles wear out, recomposed herself, and promised. No laughing.

Lucia directed our fingers back to the edges of the ashtray, and after a brief apology to Spirit, she settled back into a trance-like quiet, her eyes closed, but rolling rapidly under her eyelids. She again intoned as before: "Spirit, if you are here, send us a sign. Spirit, alert us of your presence if you are with us."

She paused for a long while, her silence broken only by a barely audible whisper, the utterance of something like, "It's here, I can feel the air changing."

Then the ashtray moved.

Only a little, but very abruptly. It shifted just below the starting point.

"Spirit, are you here?" Lucia asked. Her words broke up as she asked her questions. We understood what she said not because of each particular word, but because of our collective mood.

The ashtray edged slightly toward the "yes."

"I can feel it," whispered Lucia, her voice a frail reed. "A spirit is here, all right. Spirit," she said to the ceiling, "do you wish to speak to us?"

This time, the ashtray slid firmly to the "yes."

A chorus of questions exploded from our collective mouths; we all wanted to know if it was true, what was it like to be a spirit, what kind of spirit was it, where did it come from, and could Lucia ask it what it was like in the afterlife? And was it very, very painful to die? Was there really a God, and had the spirit seen Him? Could the spirit tell us the future? Would Marzio's farts smell as bad in that other world?

The ashtray began to swing, at first gently, from the yes to the no and back again.

"Too many questions," said Lucia. "One at a time."

The ashtray continued a slightly elliptic pattern between the *yes* and the *no* on our improvised Ouija board, picking up speed as we all fought over what the first question should be. The ashtray spun strongly enough that some of us lost hold of it, at which point it came to a hesitant halt, long enough for an accusation to fly: "Come on! Marzio's been pushing! I can feel him pushing from here!"

"Don't push. It confuses the spirit. It's like trying to put words into people's mouth!"

"I wasn't pushing! My finger wasn't even touching. Look here! Look! I have my finger above the ashtray."

Lucia shook her head and spoke authoritatively: "First and foremost, we must ask Spirit what his or her name is. Now stop, be quiet, and concentrate."

For a moment we settled. Lucia breathed meaningfully. Then, looking at the ashtray, and with a furrowed brow, she asked: "Spirit, what is your name?"

Giovanna laughed. We all, finally, heard her. It was evil, the way the chortles throttled her breathing, the way her spit popped against air in the back of her throat. For a second or so, Giovanna's chortle was the only sound.

"Stop it! Stop it!" Lucia gasped.

As if suddenly weakened by that cry, the ashtray edged slowly, painfully, toward the letter S. Then it climbed back up and around the yes/no circles to turn left toward the letter A. Giovanna snorted just as the ashtray turned downward and edged again, with somewhat greater decisiveness on the T, angling to crawl upward to the beginning of the alphabet, aiming for the A. Lucia shot up, her eyelids pushing back from her popping green eyes, her hands raised up to the sky: "Oh Lord and Little Madonna of Mine, protect us from this evil! Forgive us! Forgive us! Oh Lord, protect us from this evil presence!"

Lucia's full chest heaved with the weight of her droning, her eyes downcast at first, then popping open again, witnessing a terror we could neither see nor entirely understand.

Some of us littler ones kept looking from face to face for clues, wondering if it was all right now to take our fingers off the ashtray, even though Lucia had earlier warned us that to do so would piss off Spirit big time, not to mention weaken the energy flow. The older kids had pushed their chairs back, their hands in their laps, their faces turned eagerly to Lucia.

"What was that? What did it say?"

"It was trying to spell SATAN," someone whispered.

"Shhhhh," Lucia warned. "Don't even say that!"

The ohhhs of our freshly enlightened acumens died in our lungs, extinguished immediately by the chilled hush of fear. After all, we'd all grown up with Baptism, Communion, and Catechism, and we'd heard the S word hurled often enough at us from the pulpit to lose our milk teeth from chronic chattering.

"Spirit, rid us of this evil presence," begged our rattled medium. "Protect us from its dark influence. Even though we have called its presence upon us, we respectfully ask that it leave this house and that it not harm us."

Lucia cleared our hands off the table with a brief flutter of hers, and grabbing onto the hand-scribbled Ouija she ripped it in several pieces, reciting quick prayers and blowing on the broken edges each time before folding the pieces and ripping them anew. She invoked the Lord and Mary and Jesus and begged for their forgiveness, promising never to dabble lightly in such matters again. When she was done, and the Ouija pieces burned in a plate on the table, and when the ashtray was ordered covered in salt and then discarded, she drew a long sigh, her eyes closed and her chin over her chest, her hair draping around her like the painting of a Raphaelite Madonna.

After several moments in this memorable pose, Lucia got up and briskly dismissed herself. That was the last we ever saw of her. The night ended quickly after that: we gathered what was left of the candle stubs, the citronella spiral and its ashes, the glasses we had drunk from, the pencil we had used to draw our Ouija and various other accoutrements and dutifully cleaned up, as our mothers had taught us to. Then each returned to his or her respective home, shaken some, yes, but mostly just excited.

We did not yet know the dramatic and protracted epilogue to this story.

A month after our sitting, we will hear of the car accident: Lucia driving home toward Rome in her boyfriend's Fiat 500 way too late at night and way too drunk; how it will take almost an entire day before anyone finds her unconscious in the car; the two littlest boys of the group, Marzio and his best friend, Simone, will wake up screaming from nightmares for many nights; how each will ask his mother if Satan can really come and take a person's body; at our villa, where the sitting took place, dishes and glasses and plates will come flying from the kitchen cabinet where the fated and duly salted ashtray was replaced the very morning after the accident; how later we will vigorously proclaim it a coincidence to each other, saving our real fears for storytelling in years to come; three baby magpies will be found dead in the backyard that morning, each impaled on the sharp, needled limbs of an agave cactus; how we will ferociously blame the Sardinian pack we had previously tormented and their morbid sense of vengeance.

And we will blame Sardinians also for the strange noises that are heard at night, noises like a goat rubbing its horns against the wooden hurricane shutters of our bedroom windows, noises accompanied by prophetic whispers and by the ensuing scraping of goat hooves on the roof. We will say it was some disgruntled gardener who wanted work and found none, some unhappy shepherd embittered by the ostentatious sloth of the vacationers. We will even try to blame it on Pietro, who will stop speaking to us by and by.

But at the villa the night took over with its crickets and cicadas, with its tree frogs and its bullfrogs, and with the smell of hibiscus and oleander, and with the balmy scents of the sea. Sardinia's damp-and-dry slipped with us beneath the toasty sheets and blankets. It was cool and quiet outside, and we curled on our beds with the peace of heart of those who have earned their rest, with the sun still baking our skin, with the salt still saturating our pores, with the memories of the slapping waves and the hot fine sand and the jagged stones and pebbles still playing our bodies' senses like an action film's soundtrack. The ghosts of our recent Ouija adventure might have been gossamers even then, tingles on the back of our necks, but we felt protected by our beds and by the certainty of our adult parents returning home soon, bringing safety with their casual clamor of jingling keys and scraping shoes, slamming doors, and poorly restrained whispers. The light that seeped underneath our doors soothed us to sleep. We forgot all about the jolts and jerks of the ashtray and its awful intimations, traded it for dreams of frosty seas and air mattress battles and the glamorous body-surfing exploits we would undertake the next day.

The Walls of Gela

. . . .

Edvige Giunta

The Greek walls of Gela survive. Protected by glass, they suck the heat of the sun. My father stands by these walls, the bay behind him, open and eager. I watch him, silent audience, necessary audience. Then he begins to evoke ships, warriors, noises, blood, spears, the smell of war and fear and conquest.

Peoples who inhabited my island, Sicily: layers and layers of faces, of oppressors and oppressed, conquerors and conquered, invaders and exiles, betrayers and betrayed, faces underneath mine, strata of histories and stories that make up a past laid out in front of my eyes, momentarily blind. Sicans, Sicels, Elymians, Greeks, Carthaginians, Byzantines, Romans, Arabs. By the first century AD, at least seven major civilizations had inhabited Sicily. Normans, Spaniards, and others would soon follow. My father tells their stories.

My father celebrates his own Eucharist. His words become bodies, the bodies of those who thousands of years ago stood on this same ground where I stand today, a ghost, a shadow, without words of my own.

He is not a tall man—about 5′4″. He has been balding ever since I

. . . . .

EDVIGE GIUNTA is the author of *Writing with an Accent: Contemporary Italian American Women Authors* and coeditor of *The Milk of Almonds: Italian American Women Writers on Food and Culture.* She is Associate Professor of English at New Jersey City University.

remember him. But he stands so straight, his shoulders pushed back, his belly forward as he speaks of our town's ancient past. My father, the historian, shares only a few recollections of my childhood. These scattered remembrances document the fact that he was my father and I was his baby daughter. I hopped on his knees, danced on his belly, asked for ten liras to buy chocolate in Sicilian dialect: *deci liri u caccu.* His voice is soft, mellow, so different from the voice of the historian, the politician, the public figure, as he sing-songs, *"deci liri u caccu. deci liri u caccu."* I smile, sometimes snicker, my awkward adolescent self embarrassed by tales that hint at an intimacy of which I have no memory.

Where did the other memories go, the memories of all those other times he held me, played with me, rocked me to sleep? When my two sisters and I enter puberty, he mourns our childhood and clings to two or three memories of that time, fearful of our nascent womanhood. That ancient, fierce sense of honor, and that dread of shame women can bring upon the family, especially the men, saturate his ancient Sicilian masculinity. He claims with pride: "I am a nineteenth-century man." But we, his daughters, we are twentieth-century girls. We are quick, educated—bright girls, full of ideas and sense of possibility. We like to go out on our own, evade his watchful gaze. We defy him. And we are so in spite of him *and* because of him. As adolescents, we begin that escape that will bring each of the three daughters of Vincenzo Giunta to live far away from home—one in Rome, two in the United States. He will have American grandchildren. He will not understand their language. They will barely understand his. Did he know already we would leave? Did he dread it, even as he encouraged wild desires and aspirations for diplomatic careers that could take us to distant places to which he himself had never traveled?

In my memory, in my imagination, my father is a big man—always a grown man, never a young man, never a boy. His childhood is shrouded in silence, forgotten. He never speaks of it. But he compensates for this personal amnesia by becoming the repository of the town's memory.

Gelon, Caesar, Frederick. He knows them intimately. They sat at the same table, shared the masculine bread of power. But who were the playmates of the child Vincenzo? Did he play with his older brother, Rocco? The younger, Remigio? His cousins, Rocco, Saverio, Sascia? Did they play with his little sister, Edvige, my namesake, the "cripple"? What were his favorite games? Soccer? Hide and seek? Hopscotch? Was he punished for disobeying his mother? I do not know. My father's childhood memories are locked inside the dark rooms of his agoraphobic mother.

Two images begin to shape in my mind, contrasting and complementary, two sides of one wall. At times, they superimpose. Mostly they present themselves in juxtaposition, separated by a line of demarcation, sharp and dazzling, that signals the point at which two strains of my family history meet: my father, the epitome of intellectual force, and his mother, Nonna Ciuzza, the woman who spoke with assurance and disdain to her children, her grandchildren, and, rarely, her daughters-in-law—those young women who could not possibly be good enough to marry her sons, those sons she addressed using the diminutives of their childhood—Ruccuzzu, Vicenzù, Remì—even when they became middle-aged men with grown children of their own. Nonna Ciuzza, the woman who locked herself and her daughter in that house on Vico Marino for over fifty years, till she died in 1990. There they are. I am facing them: my father, whose voice rises as he talks politics and history to a handful of faithful listeners near the *piazza,* and my ninety-year-old grandmother, terrified of open spaces, who recites Foscolo's "Dei Sepolcri" in her secluded home:

> *All'ombra de' cipressi e dentro l'urne*
> *Confortate di pianto è forse il sonno*
> *Della morte men duro?*

How appropriate that this woman, who slowly but inexorably cut off her ties with the outside world and barricaded herself within the walls of her home, remembered this poem—one of those poems Italian students memorize in school—a lamentation over the tombs of great ancestors. She sits still, as straight as her crooked back allows, and recites, stressing each syllable, never missing a beat. Her eyes are half closed; the loose skin of her cheeks trembles with each utterance.

I am almost forty when I begin to realize how much these two figures—my father and my grandmother—and their excesses are entwined like the braids of a wicker basket. I don't fully understand at first to what extent one generates and sustains the other in a passionate, symbiotic relationship; this intricate relationship is not unlike the devoted hatred that connected my paternal grandparents for a half-century, preventing them from staying truly apart from each other, though my grandfather indulged in escapades—perhaps there were other women—that led him to live away from his home, away from his town, at one time for years. After my grandfather returns home, there is no reconciliation between my grandparents, but they spend the last years of their lives together—ten? twenty?—confined in the upstairs apartment of their house, their resentment seeping through the walls, their voices resonating in the rooms downstairs where no one lives. They will not sleep in the same bed, eat at the same table. They will spend days, weeks, months without seeing each other, but they will yell and curse at each other through the walls they share.

The house is theirs. It has two floors and a roof verandah. Once, I climbed the steps to that verandah, I think with my grandfather, and saw pigeons, lots of pigeons. That's all I remember. At some point, my uncle Remigio had some kind of office downstairs. I think it was a driving school. For a while, the house was full of people and their voices, though my grandmother and my aunt kept to themselves upstairs. Then, it was quiet again. Except when my grandparents fought.

Upstairs is where they chose to live: two large rooms, two bathrooms, and between the two rooms a small foyer where my grandmother cooked—there was no kitchen. Living downstairs would have allowed my grandfather some peace, some distance from those women who seemed to hate him—a sentiment he reciprocated. But he chose to live upstairs, in the room with the only door leading outside. Since my grandmother and my aunt never went out, my grandparents could co-habit without ever seeing each other—all they shared was a wall. The layout of the house enabled them to live together and apart. The two women never crossed the threshold of the door that separated their living space from my grandfather's because they didn't need or wish to. My grandmother was satisfied with her voluntary imprisonment, hers and her daughter's. She saw it as necessary, just, inevitable.

Every forced break from their life represents, for these two recluses, a traumatic event, a forced encounter with a world they do not trust and with which they do not wish to come into contact. My grandmother would tell the story of my aunt's injury over and over again, while my aunt would repeat a word, a phrase spoken by her mother, for emphasis or simply out of habit. When Zia Edvige was born, my grandmother became ill. It was an illness that to this day remains unnamed. I suspect it was postpartum depression. I know she was so sick she could not take care of the baby and, I presume, of her three little boys. They hired a wet nurse to care for baby Edvige. It seems that my grandmother came from a relatively wealthy family. My grandfather had made money in the twenties, selling tractors that modernized the local agricultural economy—the story goes that he was one of the first people in Gela to own a car. In those times, in any case, wet nurses were not uncommon. But this wet nurse's baby happened to develop whooping cough. My aunt caught it too and one day had a seizure; probably, she had had encephalitis. The seizure caused major damage to the right side of her body. Her arm became limp and twisted in spasms, like the ones that shook her body in frequent convulsions. Her right leg became a useless limb she dragged behind her. Her feet became forever trapped in awkward orthopedic boots. I do not know how old she was. She could have been a few months, one or two years old. This story, retold with ever so slight variations, was what defined my grandmother, the frame the old woman offered us so that we could understand her, and for my grandmother, there was no other story to tell.

She had denied her own milk to her first and only daughter. And now little Edvige was a cripple. And Ciuzza Giunta fiercely embraced her daughter's disability as if it were her own. She would not part from it, not even for a minute. And she would not part from her daughter. Ever.

The withdrawal from the outside must have been a gradual process. I know my grandparents traveled everywhere in Italy seeking doctors who could cure their daughter, to no avail. That was in the 1930s, when traveling was neither easy nor common. They went as far as Genoa, in northern Italy, probably a two-day train trip in those days. In time, the cause of my aunt's disability became mythologized. For a long time I believed she had polio when she was four. We knew about polio: I still have the round marks from the polio vaccine on my right arm, and so do my older sister, brother, and cousins. We attached a word, a disease that was familiar to us, to my aunt's story, a story that still remains, for me, full of questions. Nobody ever mentioned the word encephalitis, either because my grandmother did not know the word or because this word, so scientific, could hardly contain the magnitude of this family tragedy. *"La mia croce,"* my grandmother tells us, her head slightly bent toward my aunt. "My cross." When we get older, we, the grandchildren, scold her for this cruel appellation, but my aunt seems perfectly at ease with her role as her mother's torturous burden. In any case, she never dares to disagree with her, still a child at sixty. She just sighs, her chest heaving, her lips tight and turned downward, in resignation and disappointment.

The architectural space my grandmother and aunt inhabit mirrors their symbiotic lives, their isolation, and their refusal to allow anybody in, including my grandfather. The narrow balcony looking over Via Cairoli offers the only respite from the two women's seclusion. The balcony is very small. Only two chairs fit. A third leaves no space for legs. No geranium plants soften the gloom of the house, the hardness of the plain old tiles.

Daily, the two women reach out to the world and lower a basket below the balcony, dangling it in front of the grocer's open door on the street below. He leaves all his other customers and dashes out to collect the list of necessities my grandmother has scribbled on a scrap of paper with her antiquated, elegant handwriting. A few minutes later he runs out again and fills the still-dangling basket with the few items my father's mother and sister need for their survival: pasta, cans of tomatoes, milk, bread. Zio Remigio brings them meat from his butcher—nothing fancy, beef cutlets to grill on the stovetop; they do not have an oven. My father attends to their finances and brings the family physician when they are sick. Zio Rocco attempts to modernize their home, bringing them a radio, a television, or recording my grandmother's recitation of "Dei Sepolcri." My mother sends fruit and vegetables from our garden. Sometimes she sends over a special dish—homemade pizza, lasagna— but, out of spite, they do not touch her food. The grocer, the family, the neighbors, the town itself—they all become unwitting accomplices in the making of a life lived in seclusion. Their compliance makes it possible for my grandmother and aunt never to cross that line between them and the world, a line that gets thicker every day. Survival is the word that best describes these two women's relationship to the world, a world that, my grandmother taught my aunt, had betrayed them, a world that, they had learned, was hostile and ruthless. The laughter of elementary school children mocking my aunt before my grandmother decides to take her out of school—at six? seven? perhaps even as late as ten—gives her the reason she needs to seal herself and her crippled child inside that second-floor apartment on Vico Marino. How appropriate that they live on a *vico,* not a *via,* which is a street that stretches out in opposite directions. Instead, a *vico* has no way out: it's a dead end.

For years, they will sit in the one room where they spend their lives, a room divided into different living spaces by large, flowered curtains hanging from the ceiling and serving as walls: a sitting area, an eating area, a sleeping area, a closet space framed not by walls or wood but, again, by curtains hanging from the ceiling. Piles of things we were forbidden to see or touch barely peeked from behind the curtains. In this cluttered room, they submit willingly to a paralysis that is emotional as well as physical. My grandfather's room is instead sparingly furnished: a twin bed, a night table, a chair by the bed, an armoire, a small table, another chair, and a small cupboard. There must have been a refrigerator, but I don't remember one. Nothing ornate or elegant. Unlike the crammed room upstairs, the living room in the downstairs floor is spacious and uncluttered. It's what is called *il salotto buono,* the nice living room. Yet living room does not faithfully translate *salotto.* In Sicilian homes, a *salotto* is, or at least used to be, a room that was kept closed, though regularly and thoroughly cleaned, and was opened only for special visitors. A living room is a *soggiorno,* from *soggiornare,* which means to sojourn, to stay, and is used to entertain regular visitors. My grandmother and aunt's dwelling space upstairs did not allow for such subtleties: one room sufficed for all. Their *salotto* downstairs was conspicuous because its quaintness and neatness contrasted so much with its cluttered and shabby counterpart upstairs. A sofa, a couple of chairs, and a few scattered items of furniture testify to better times, times of wealth if not happiness. I cannot imagine a time in which my grandmother could have been happy. Gloom, not happiness, suits her best, though occasionally, when we visit her, she smiles and even laughs, her mouth closed, her body shaking lightly. I look at her expecting her to crumble to pieces any minute.

For my aging grandmother and her crippled daughter, every descent downstairs to the famed *salotto* was slow and painful; yet it offered a variation, desired and suffered, from the suffocating sameness of their days. The grandchildren ring the door bell and it takes ten to fifteen minutes for my aunt to come to the window, wave, walk to what used to be my grandfather's room, press the button that will open the outside door, and come downstairs with my grandmother if we have brought company: a rare friend, a fiancé for the official introduction. Downstairs is for select visitors: *estranei,* strangers, not necessarily people they don't know, but people who are not part of the family, not blood. My mother fluctuates ambiguously between the positions of insider and outsider. And so do I and my siblings: *"Vi voglio bene perchè siete sangue del mio sangue"*—I love you because you are blood of my blood. "I love you because you are my son's children," my grandmother would tell us with pride. That left me wondering, confused by what felt like both an embrace and a rejection. Could she forget we were also my mother's children?

Upstairs, three or four mattresses sit on the twin beds in which my grandmother and my aunt sleep. The beds are lined against the wall, the headboards against each other, almost conjoined. Every night the two women have to climb onto their beds, an ascent that must have been as uncomfortable as the descent to the rooms downstairs. My grandmother did not throw anything out and old mattresses were never discarded: they were simply piled up. She kept and accumulated valuable items and worthless objects, such as empty marmalade jars, tomato cans, rusted tin boxes of *biscotti* Doria. Once, when I was eight or nine, she gave me a plastic bag full of tomato paste and toothpaste tube caps as a gift, the only "toy" she ever gave me. I plunge my hand into the bag and stir the red caps, trying to hide my disappointment, while she smiles at me eagerly, expecting signs of enthusiasm. I look away from her face, from those eyes sinking deep into the crevices of old age, from those cheeks that hang on the sides of her face like empty sacks, from the hairy mole on the right side of her chin that she called jokingly *"lo spazzolino"*—the toothbrush—laughing at her grandchildren's thinly disguised attempts to avoid touching it when we kissed her. I always kissed the left side first, trying to avoid the contact with that excrescence of her skin. She would shove the repulsive *spazzolino* into my reluctant face, then giggle, amused with what she thought was a game.

Nonna Ciuzza's obsession for keeping went hand in hand with a need for acquisition of basic foods. She would purchase such foods in great quantity: bags of pasta, flour, and sugar; dozens of cookie boxes. Vermin would grow before my grandmother and aunt, who always ate frugally, could consume these obscene quantities of food, food destined to expire, like the money she hid, predictably, under her mattresses until my father persuaded her to trust a bank. My grandmother lived all her life in the expectation of a catastrophe of apocalyptic proportions. She made sure that she and her daughter would be ready to face it. She spent her life trying to keep the world outside at bay. After years, she finally agreed to have a telephone and a television, but those futuristic objects did not belong in a house ruled by its own rhythms, its own time. One day my father finds his mother and sister sitting in front of the blank TV screen, as if they are watching. "What are you doing?" he asks, surprised. My grandmother sighs, echoed by her daughter, and whispers that a man and a woman were kissing on TV. She had switched off the infernal machine to protect the chaste eyes of her daughter, who by this time was in her fifties.

They never receive us standing, though occasionally my aunt meets us limping at the door. They always sit, like twin statues, sometimes on two rickety chairs, sometimes on a bed that served as a sofa, covered with a faded flowered bedcover. They sit on the edge of this bed, in what must have been an uncomfortable position. Comfort does not befit them. They do not face each other in the light, but sit side by side in the dark all day long, until an occasional visitor opens the balcony or turns on the light. When I was very little, the two of them would embroider; they accumulated precious items for my aunt's dowry. The linen chest filled with delicate bedcovers, sheets, towels, tablecloths, napkins, curtains—none would never be used. My grandmother had embroidered "EDVIGE GIUNTA" onto a curtain. How little did this ostentatious object reflect the reclusive life of Zia Edvige. My father used to say that one day the curtain—which none of us grandchildren ever saw—should have gone to me, my aunt's namesake, but I always recoiled at that suggestion, horrified by the implication that I was the one most closely connected with Zia Edvige. At some point, I don't remember when exactly, the baskets that sat at their feet disappeared. Maybe my grandmother's eyesight was failing, and my aunt, of course, would not embroider alone.

My grandmother always speaks first. My aunt follows, echoing her last words or sighing, hands folded on her lap, her crippled foot coyly hidden inside the black or beige orthopedic boot peeking out from behind the good leg. Those sighs contain so many words, trapped like birds with clipped wings fluttering in uselessly open air. Occasionally, my grandmother offers a gift: a few coins, a box of stale cookies, decades-old chocolate wrapped in brown paper that says "Italian Army." This chocolate has lost its deep brown shade and has been taken over by the whitish streaks of time. She offers us candies that have been too long in a drawer and now stick obstinately to the crackling paper wrap, refusing to leave their home. Before we go to visit, my mother warns us not to eat anything she gives us. We accept the sweets, say thank you, and throw them out as soon as we turn out of Via Cairoli and onto Via Bresmes, after we wave goodbye to the two of them who still wave from the balcony.

For my college graduation, Nonna Ciuzza tells my father that she has a special gift for me: a pair of gold earrings. My father is pleased, painfully aware as he is of the discrepancy between my maternal grandparents' generosity and his mother's notorious avarice. This announcement causes great excitement in my extended family, as my grandmother never parts with anything of value. A few days after my graduation, which, of course, neither she nor my aunt attends, I visit them to secure my gift. Following the ceremonial congratulatory talk, my grandmother keeps silent for a while, then bends her head imperceptibly toward the curtain that separates the living room space from what we refer to as their sleeping quarters. My aunt, ever so receptive to my grandmother's silent language, gets up with a deep sigh and disappears behind the curtain. I hear her moving around, dragging the crippled leg and foot that both she and her mother refer to as *"la gambetta"* and *"il piedino"*—the tiny leg and the tiny foot—in that tragically infantilizing language Nonna Ciuzza and her children always used to describe my aunt. Her sons always use the Sicilian words: *'a iammuzza, u piruzzu.* But while my grandmother spoke Sicilian to her sons, she only spoke Italian with me, my siblings, and my mother. It kept the distance, marked the perimeter of intimacy.

My aunt comes back a few minutes later, holding a small, ancient-looking velvety blue box. My grandmother takes it from her daughter's hands, holds it in her cupped hands as if to shelter it from light, then opens it. Beaming, she reveals the delicate earrings that once adorned her young ears, her mother's, and even, she proclaims, her grandmother's. Pushing my face closer to the box to see better, I move my hand gently to touch my grandmother's first real gift. Snap. The box shuts and my grandmother says, "This is your gift." My aunt's hands receive the tiny box and take it back to wherever it came from. "I will keep this for you," my grandmother says. The gift consists in the brief viewing of the earrings.

Those earrings today are mine. After my father learned of his mother's preposterous gift, he did not say a word. This was unusual for him. Whenever we would complain to him about the two women's antics, he would laugh and say, *"Ma lasciatele perdere. Sono due povere pazze"*—let it go, they are two poor lunatics. He seemed to have made his peace with the grotesque, absurd ways of his mother and sister. But this time, he did not say anything. Later that day, he went to see her. I don't know what words he spoke to her, but when he came back, he had the earrings for me. I have never worn them. I don't know why. Perhaps I am afraid of letting the thin gold that touched my grandmother's and her ancestors' earlobes pierce mine. Perhaps this gift, so reluctant to leave my grandmother's abode, does not yet feel mine. But now they are with me, in the United States, locked away with other pieces of jewelry. One day, they will become my daughter's. I wonder whether she will wear them. One day a female descendant of mine will receive these earrings as a special gift and will ask her parents where they come from.

Nonno Diego, my grandfather, felt suffocated in the dingy, tragic home he shared with Nonna Ciuzza and Zia Edvige. So even when he broke his hip in his eighties, he recovered quickly, against everyone's expectations, although he did not undergo surgery because the doctors felt it was too risky at his age. Every evening—around seven o' clock in the summer, around five in the winter—he would go out, smelling of cologne, impeccably dressed: black suit in the winter, beige in the summer. Supporting himself at first with crutches, then with a cane, he would descend two flights of steep stairs with the help of one of the grandchildren enlisted for this important if not welcome task. Then he would walk on his own to Docente, the clothing store across from the Cathedral of the Madonna of Alemanna, and would sit there with other old men. The store was right next to Piazza Umberto, the town's main square, a mere five-minute walk from his home, although it would take my grandfather ten, fifteen minutes to get there. Watching the evening *passeggiata* flow by along the *corso* soothed his ache for life. For my grandfather, these daily outings were life sustaining, and he dreaded the cold winter days when he could not go out.

He sits there, looking so dignified, wearing his old-fashioned hat, saluting and saluted like a king. Older people say, *"buona sera cavaliere."* Many address him as *"parrì"*—godfather. My grandfather, though, was not a *mafioso*; he was a patriarch in the etymological sense of the word: *pater,* father, ruler. My father and his brothers and cousins remember him presiding at the long table where generations of them sat, his flask of wine at his feet, administering orders and food, love and terror. When he gets old, his children no longer listen to him in respectful silence. Their behavior toward him is marked by a mix of respect and resentment, derision and reverence. Now that he is old, he no longer rouses the old feelings of fear and deference, and his grown children retaliate, often dismissing him, flaunting the power that once was his. My older sister and I pass by Docente quickly, even cross to the other side so as to avoid the lengthy chat with him that he will inevitably demand if he spots us on the street. We fear that he will whistle to get our attention and thus embarrass us in front of our friends. Our adolescent dread of old age makes us ruthless: we turn away from our obligation and care little about his disappointment, which he never shows anyway. But sometimes we do stop by, hoping for the one thousand lire note he will occasionally offer. His fingers entwined around his cane, sunglasses on, he inquires about my mother, my little brother and sister, school. When we bend to kiss him goodbye, he smiles benevolently, still trying to exude authority through his slow and deliberate gestures, through his tone of voice, firm and loud.

My mother was my grandfather's captive audience. "Cettì, *ascolta!*" he calls out to my mother while she is busy at the stove, frying eggplants and meatballs and stirring tomato sauce, the bubbling of the pasta pot intermingling with the sounds of my grandfather's voice. He demands but also begs for that attention his children deny him. For a year or so, when I was eight or nine years old, my grandfather ate his meals with us, lunch and dinner, every day. Coming to our home allowed him to escape the solitary meals and the silence of his house, where his wife and daughter led a life so alien to his worldly taste. I imagine my grandfather eating in his one-room dwelling in Vico Marino, sitting on the one chair at the table that faces the cupboard. I turn away from that scene. His solitude must have been unbearable. But while he did not relish it, he tolerated it far better than his wife's and daughter's company.

One day he storms out after another proverbial argument with his wife, which occurs, as always, not face to face, but through the wall.

Their voices—my grandmother's shrieking, my grandfather's deep and raucous—bounce on the whitewashed walls, resonate in the house; their echo reaches the houses of the neighbors who are, by now, used to my grandparents' vociferous altercations. My grandfather yells to the two women that he hopes the roof will collapse on their heads. And indeed it does, a few hours later, while he is out. My grandmother and aunt are unharmed but hysterical, and my father tries in vain to persuade them that my grandfather couldn't possibly have had anything to do with it. Like my grandmother, I take curses seriously, and while I smile in disbelief every time I tell this story, I cannot help wondering.

In the evening, my grandfather brings us small milk chocolates wrapped in gold and red foil. We search eagerly in his pockets, always surprised by this bounty, unused to receiving gifts from our paternal grandparents. After this sweet ritual, we play cards: *briscola, sette e mezzo, scopa.* When we move to a new house—the two top floors of a five-floor building without an elevator—he comes only on Sundays; perhaps the flights of stairs are too much for him. My father picks him up around eleven o'clock in the morning and delivers him to my mother, then goes back to the town's center to talk politics and does not come back until lunchtime, around 1:30. My mother complies dutifully but occasionally becomes impatient and snaps, complains to her father-in-law that he is distracting her from her many chores, only to be reprimanded by him with a brief, sharp word or a stern glance.

My mother was attached to my grandfather, grateful that he loved her. Of the three daughters-in-law, she was his favorite. She keeps an old card on which he wrote: *"A Cettina, la migliore dei miei figl"*—To Cettina, the best of my children. This devotion pleased my mother, hurt as she was by the rejection of my grandmother, who treated her condescendingly at best. My parents had married in the midst of fiery opposition as soon as my mother had turned twenty-one: my father was a communist and my mother the niece of a priest. They had to obtain special permission from the bishop to marry in the church nine months after they got married in the town hall. Nobody from either family attended the wedding. A few weeks after their wedding, a distant relative came to Gela from a nearby town to bring a present to the newlyweds. Not knowing where they lived—few owned a telephone in 1955—she asked around where Vincenzo Giunta lived. Someone pointed her to Vico Marino, where my father had indeed lived until recently. The woman walks into the dead-end street, carrying the gift, and knocks on the door. A woman clad in black leans out the window: it's my grandmother. In response to the well-wisher's request to see Vincenzo Giunta and his new bride, Nonna Ciuzza proclaims: *"Mio figlio è morto"*—My son is dead.

My mother regaled us with these stories. We found them melodramatic, funny, absurd, and we could not understand how our grandmother could not love our gentle, soft, sweet mother, our mother so beloved even by my father's other relatives. And we could not understand why my mother would still want to have anything to do with her mother-in-law, why she craved a kind gesture, a word of appreciation from her.

For years my mother tried to please my grandmother, and when my grandmother died, she tried to please her daughter, never resigned to the fact that these two women could never, if not love, at least appreciate her. She worked for them as my father, his brothers, and their wives never did: cooked for them, washed their clothes, ran their errands, and always made sure we went to visit them. "I washed the staircase in her house, step by step, on my knees while I was nine months pregnant. She never even uttered a thank you!" my mother would recall resentfully, with that taste for melodrama that runs through my family. But my grandmother had only cutting words for my mother, though she usually spoke them politely. She would enunciate each word in Italian whenever she spoke to my mother, denying her the intimacy of dialect. Incapable of gratitude, she expected my mother to serve her, and so did my aunt, her daughter.

The hierarchy was already established when I was born: my mother laid herself down to serve as the foundation, the soil, upon which my father's strength could grow. She remained in the shadows, always there to support, stalwart like the stubborn Doric column at the *Parco delle Rimembranze*—the Park of Remembrances—that stands solitary, defying the elements and the merciless hunger of time that has already swallowed its sisters. My mother's strength never ceases to amaze me. "What's your secret?" ask those who have not seen her for some time, stunned by the fact that she always looks so serene, so young, her face smooth, with hardly any lines. She smiles somewhat bitterly. Sometimes she replies: *"Collere e dispiaceri."* Sorrows and worries.

By the time my parents got married, my grandmother and aunt had already established their life as recluses. Before my eyes is the image of two women clinging to each other in terror on the occasion of a rare and sporadic outing that could not be avoided: a hospital stay, a trip to the bank or the town hall where their signatures were required, or to the voting booth when my father ran in the elections. Never a wedding, a christening, a celebration, not even my grandfather's funeral: only dire necessity or obligation justified the breach of their seclusion. On my wedding day, my husband and I visit them after the ceremony for the obligatory photograph taken in the nice room downstairs, a room they had reopened after my grandfather's death for occasional visitors. My grandmother never allowed anybody to take pictures of her or her daughter, except on the occasion of a granddaughter's wedding. Then she claimed the photographs for herself. She could not allow her semblance or her child's to leave their house, as if in the unwanted contact with the outside world they might fade like ancient mural paintings uncovered after thousands of years.

When the downstairs room was reopened for my grandfather's funeral in December 1976, for the first time in years people flocked to my grandparents' house to pay their last respects to Diego Giunta. On the day of the funeral, my grandmother's ululating laments echo in the house, while relatives shake their heads and smile to each other know-ingly. One relative snickers in Sicilian: *"Si Decu Giunta 'ssi rrvigghiassi, murissi i spaventu!"*—If Diego Giunta were to wake up now, he would die of fear. The relatives and the townspeople respected my grandfather, and accepted, as my father and his brothers did, that his wife was mad—not the kind of madness that requires institutionalization, but madness as a word, a concept that would help them to condone, if not understand, the excesses that characterized the life of Ciuzza Giunta.

When the body is taken out of the house, her wrenching screams, echoed by my aunt's, can be heard blocks away and accompany us as we get into the cars to go the cemetery.

No church for my grandfather. An atheist to the end, he made my father promise they would not take him into a church after his death. And my father respected his wishes, in the midst of the hardly contained criticism of many family members. We drive away and leave my grand-mother and aunt behind in the room downstairs, the room for special occasions, weeping for the man they hated for most of their lives.

After his death, they dress in black, the color that suits them best. My aunt, who never even dignified her father with a stare, when she talks about him now refers to him as *"il nonnino,"* a warm, loving diminutive for *"nonno,"* grandfather. If anyone mentions his name, they both begin to weep, sometimes quietly, sometimes uncontrollably. For months after his death, every evening they sit at the sides of his bed, now stripped of mattress (probably piled up with the others), a worn bed-spread lingering on the old, shaky frame. On the bed, my grandfather's black suit lies, a stiffened weightless body with handless arms that stretch out toward the borders of the bed. His passport picture rests in place of his head, above the imaginary neck extending out of the jacket. In the evening, when my siblings and I, sometimes accompanied by my mother—never my father—go to visit them, we find my grandmother and aunt sitting like guardian angels at the sides of Nonno Diego's bed. We open the door, and our eyes encounter the gloomy sight of the two women immersed in their grotesque ceremony of grief. Once my father asks his mother how could she possibly cry for her husband considering that when he was alive all they did was fight. How could she cry for a man she hated? "He was still the father of my children."

It's January 1990. Nonna Ciuzza battles death. She has to stay alive. She cannot leave her daughter alone. She hisses orders to her daughter, who weeps quietly by her side. *Don't sign anything. Don't sign anything. Don't throw anything away. Don't change anything in the house. Don't ever leave this house.*

My father is so different from his mother. He is worldly, more like his father. The first college graduate in the family—in fact, the only one of four children to go to university, to have the discipline and the determination to do so—my father is smart, eloquent, daring, outgoing. My father the professor, the politician, the man with the big voice, my father the Marxist—my father knows how to tell a story to a crowd of listeners. He embraced his own father's passion for rule and, in trying to emulate him, surpassed him. He became the town's father, its historical memory, the one to preserve its ancient glory when the present was dissipating its eminent tradition, when the fumes of the oil industry had forever contaminated the same sky where Aeschylus's fateful eagle flew one day, so many days ago.

My father is an astounding orator, in the Roman tradition. Well-versed in history, law, philosophy, Italian literature, politics and, as I believed for a long time, in just about everything one can think of, my father is what you would call a born speaker. He can improvise a stunning lecture for audiences of one or one thousand. With his words he can evoke a battle that took place in the bay of Gela thousands of years ago or explain with extraordinary lucidity the philosophies of Plato, Hegel, or Marx. Give him an audience and I promise you, he will dazzle it. His words flow magically, his voice rises with passion and fervor.

And you sit there, in awe of this miracle. He knows language and wields its power well. He is a magician with words. And words rarely betray him. In my hometown everyone refers to him as *"il professore." "U pru-fussuri."* How many times have I heard people in Gela address him with that title? I was always *'a figghia do prufussuri*—the daughter of the professor, appellations resonant with respect and familiarity, part of our names, our identities, our lives in the town of my origins.

My father stands on the podium of the main square in my home-town while the naked bronze statue of Ceres on its pedestal hovers, enigmatic, over the heads of the crowd, made up almost exclusively of men. A political speech, a *comizio.* This is his space, physically and in-tellectually. He is a lover of open spaces, a public figure, always at ease surrounded by the crowd, the spotlight on him: orator, teacher, adept politician, even mayor for a time. The square is his mistress, whom he indulges, seductive and seduced. In this embrace, his figure, tall in my mind, emerges strong, like the warriors of Riace, his voice powerful, his tones carefully modulated, the Sicilian accent roughening his flawless Italian. My father is a lover of the agora: agoraphilia is his addiction.

My father's passion for the agora is such that he never wishes to leave it. He does not like to leave the town. A creature of habit, my father dis-likes traveling. Each trip represents a major disruption of his routine, a trauma to be avoided at all costs. My mother becomes the custodian of his precious, fragile equilibrium, while the children become both her al-lies and enemies, depending on whether they cooperate in maintaining it or work, unwittingly, to destroy it. As he grows older, his reluctance to go beyond the town borders becomes more and more pronounced.

Where do I stand between my father and his mother? I am an immi-grant, by choice and necessity. Desire, fear, curiosity, dissatisfaction, ambition: Which one has propelled me out of Sicily and catapulted me across the Atlantic? Perhaps all of them. I have traveled to places nobody in my family had ever seen. No one else in my family was in this country to meet me. I have left family behind, though over the years I have created and destroyed other versions of family. I leave when need or desire make it necessary. Only once in thirteen years have I experienced a sense of loss at leaving one of my American homes: an apartment with a porch in northern New Jersey. Sitting on the porch, I could see trees, touch the branches and leaves of one tree that hung over the fence. I could make believe it was Sicily.

I develop no particular attachment to the spaces outside the homes I inhabit. The palm trees of Miami, the beaches of the Hamptons, the heavy snow of Schenectady—they all blend into one landscape, a past left behind without regrets. Yet, while I wander from Sicily to Florida, to Long Island, to upstate New York, to New Jersey, changing homes ten times in thirteen years, I begin to cling to small spaces in the homes I inhabit. Shortly after each move, I reconstitute certain spaces: the black and white photograph of Sonia, my friend who died at twenty-seven of cancer, always in my bedroom; a colorful De Simone plate depicting the picking of oranges always in a visible corner; the silver frame with a photograph of my mother as a beautiful twenty-year-old on a small round table in the living room, surrounded by a blue and gold Limoges china box; two small silver frames with pictures of myself and my daughter; and a tiny bowl of Deruta ceramics, the *bomboniera* from my older sister's wedding, filled with small dried yellow rosebuds. Each new home becomes a modified replica of its predecessors. Miraculous parthenogenesis. But I never succeed in finding *the* home I crave. I never quite get it right.

I left home to become a scholar, a writer. But I am also a teacher, just like my father. I am, after all, the daughter of the professor. But I am also Nonna Ciuzza's granddaughter. So far away from what was once home, long after my grandmother's death, I find myself thinking about her, wishing she could answer my questions, that she could explain what happened to her. Was it a conscious decision to lock herself inside that wretched room in the upstairs apartment on Vico Marino? I wonder about the terror my grandmother and my aunt experienced during their sporadic outings. I wonder whether the space all around them—the streets, the people, the cars, the noises—felt like a prehistoric monster coming at them, merciless, unavoidable, about to swallow or crush them as they maintained a delicate balance on the space where their feet stood precariously: my aunt's crippled arm and leg twisted in spasmodic tension, her eyes petrified in terror; my grandmother's arm extended around her daughter's shoulder in vain protection, sharing and feeding her terror; my father behind them, concerned but impatient, his face turned away from that sad spectacle.

If I have indulged my father's love of the open space, like his mother, I fear every departure from home—mine and those of loved ones—even as I no longer know where home is. The two strains of my father's family, agoraphilia and agoraphobia, meet in me, in my wandering, my self-imposed exile, my dread of departures. Loss and longing have been following me ever since I left Sicily. And so every departure strikes me, heavy and inevitable, a sense of doom spiraling me down in the entrails of memory.

Nonna Ciuzza, buried in a grave nobody visits—my mother was the only one who ever brought her flowers; Nonna Ciuzza who did not leave me anything; Nonna Ciuzza who in the end did not get her wishes. After her death, Zia Edvige turned the house upside down, threw away all the old stuff, renovated the whole place, bought new furniture, and squandered the money—probably a few hundred thousand dollars—her mother had left her. What would she say? Nonna Ciuzza haunts me, like the gifts she unwittingly bestowed upon me, gifts I forget but that occasionally sneak up on me, surprisingly familiar, like old lovers with whom I never quite broke up, whose ghosts visit me unexpectedly and ask that I do not forget, that I tell the story, unrelenting.

I Denti Famiglia

· · · · · · · ·

PHYLLIS CAPELLO

There are those who dive into New York's treacherous harbor to end their lives. Not my Barese grandfather. Belongings clamped between his teeth, he jumped ship and swam ashore to start a new one. Good thing Francisco was young and strong, barrel-chested, his arms hardened by farm work. He married Bessie and they raised five children. My mother was their youngest. I was never told to which borough his strokes took him. Bessie liked to remind us she was American, a New Yorker, "born on the kitchen table," in a tenement on Bleecker Street, the Neapolitan part of Manhattan's Little Italy. Later, along with the many things he lost—family, country, language, customs—my grandfather lost his teeth, too. His tiny wife (she was barely four foot seven) had to cut the corn off the cob before she served it, the way you do for a child.

She told me the story only once—something about how he avoided Ellis Island, needed to marry a citizen. We were at a kitchen table in Brooklyn. It was crooked because the whole house leaned. My large family lived above her on the third floor; she kept us going. I was ten, her first

· · · · ·

PHYLLIS CAPELLO is a writer and musician. She is a New York Foundation for the Arts fellow in fiction, and her work has been published in many anthologies.

granddaughter. My mother was already sick. There was a new baby, another girl, two months old. I no longer know to which side the house leaned. I tried to keep the old stories whole inside me, learn what I could about the mysterious country from which we'd come, never tired of hearing about their lives there, how they'd reinvented themselves here. Frank went from farmer in a desolate landscape to merchant marine, fruit vendor, storeowner, and, finally, junk man. The other grandfather, a shoemaker in Sicily, arrived in Canada indentured to a railroad company, escaped during his first winter, walking over the U.S. border in nothing but his thin jacket. He sought shelter in the kitchen of a small Rochester restaurant and ended up marrying the sister of the owner.

Bessie was twenty-three; her younger sister had already married, so her father married her off quickly, sweetening the deal with an old truck. Frank got citizenship, a bride, and a Model T Ford. One day she told me the story of a princess who had, while looking for a perfect husband, spurned every man who'd come courting. Finding fault with every one, she commanded her royal baker to "make" her a man. She fell in love with her "King of Sugar and Honey," caressed him, took him out on the balcony one night to show him the stars, but she forgot him there. In the morning light she found him, liquefied by a rainstorm, and a perfectly beautiful princess died an old maid.

We did not always have a bed for each new child, or clothing appropriate for the season, but each Easter Sunday was an extravagant show. In completely new outfits we went to church and then made the maternal-to-paternal grandparents' house promenade, really a walk from southern Italy to Sicily, or from our part of the twentieth to another century entirely. Our part of Brooklyn, with its alleys, vegetable gardens, and churches, mimicked a small Southern Italian town. The avenue was our piazza; the barbershop and the shoemaker's basement were the men's clubs. Our clamshell-studded Mary niches harkened back to Demeter, but at the church the hands of immigrant women had worn away the Madonna's marble foot. They asked not for themselves, these women; their prayers were in hope that alcoholic sons would dry out, that emotionally fragile daughters would get well enough to tend the children, that a husband's lungs would be free of cancer.

Maybe Bessie prayed for me after those weeknight novenas when she kissed her hand and reached up to rub that marble foot so fervently. Perhaps she prayed that I'd be the one to carry on the old ways, look after things. You need strong young women, especially in a new country, willing to work doubly hard, to keep what's good in a family, ameliorate what is not. If that was the case, I failed her. I do not pray or cook, have family over once a week or even every holiday. I do not roast chestnuts on Sunday morning or take the first granddaughter on that small (was it uphill or downhill?) journey from kitchen to bedroom to uncover them still warm under the pillow. Not much is left of the old ways; all her hard work and all of mine have not kept them from unraveling. In houses that tilt things roll away faster than we can get hold of, though we wear away the surface hoping. Here we are, still in the intersection of old and new, swimming everyday between worlds, parcel in our teeth.

Sacrifice

· · · · · · · · ·

MARIA LAURINO

The geraniums sit in a large aluminum planter on the windowsill; their leaves pulsate like the beat of tiny hearts. The soft slap of morning air has awoken these plants of different stripes: the tender green-leaved young, the sturdy reddish stalks of the already bloomed, and shriveled petals, brown and hunched, that hang from stems like empty cocoons or garden bees humming silently. Each nervously awaits what's in store, fluttering, fluttering its little heart, supplicants to the wind. A pigeon swoops down for a breakfast snack and munches on some blushing flowered stalks. When will the fluttering stop; how much of the delicate plant will the pigeon destroy?

"Perhaps none of us are truly ourselves, it occurs to me, but only ourselves at a certain age. . . . We have no identity apart from our age," remarks the narrator of Tim Parks's novel *Europa*. To stare at the potted geraniums, the life cycle handed to me in a silver-colored planter, how can I not accept Parks's observation? If I were to define myself today at forty-five, no doubt I'd answer differently than twenty years before.

· · · · ·

MARIA LAURINO is the author of *Were You Always an Italian?: Ancestors and Other Icons of Italian America.* A former chief speechwriter to New York City Mayor David Dinkins and staff writer at the *Village Voice,* she has written for numerous anthologies and publications, including the *New York Times,* the *Nation,* and *Salon.*

There's an old parlor game about identity that supposes an alien descends from outer space to learn about the strange creatures that inhabit this place. In this close encounter of the therapeutic kind, the alien asks each person to describe himself with three nouns. When the scenario was posed to Lyndon B. Johnson, he famously declared: "I am a free man, an American, and a Democrat."

Simone de Beauvoir addressed the issue of female identity in her classic work, *The Second Sex,* stating in the book's preface: "But if I wish to define myself, I must first of all say: 'I am a woman'; on this truth must be based all further discussion."

Half a century later, after the feminist movement sought to erase discrimination based on gender, does de Beauvoir's assertion remain true, that who we are must begin with "I am a woman"? It's doubtful that women would offer the same response as LBJ: "I'm a free woman" sounds more like the line of a husky-throated divorcée with a scotch in her hand than a declaration of national and individual liberty.

When I worked at the *Village Voice* two decades ago, I would have answered "journalist" for the first noun, probably "American" for the second. But if I had honestly acknowledged the particular genetic, familial, and cultural blend that made me who I am, my response would have been: an Italian American woman of southern Italian descent who grew up with a disabled sibling. The answer probably disqualifies me from the parlor game's catchier format—and my response would need to change over time because the word "mother" is now essential to my identity.

Back then, however, I had no interest in motherhood and authoritatively claimed that if I had a child he would be in full-time day care so I could continue my work uninterrupted. I wanted to be autonomous, not bound to serve others, wishing for little more than a satisfying job and a room of my own. I had seen the wounds inflicted from too much self-denial delivering continual care.

. . .

"Could you hold my watch for me, pigeon?"

Pigeon, the girl bird, was Henry's nickname for me. It was the 1960s, when LBJ was president and suburban adolescents reveled in summer's freedom, playing leisurely games of softball after dinner around our cul de sac, running the bases while crickets hummed. On this evening, a rare event had taken place—the neighborhood boys had asked my brother to join them. Henry didn't have any friends on the block, but at least the Short Hills teenagers were nicer to him than the rougher-edged boys from Cranford, according to my mother, who wished to leave the working-class town as soon as my parents had moved there. In Cranford, my mother preferred that Henry stay inside after dinner because the neighborhood kids would routinely humiliate my mentally retarded brother, greet him with lines like "Hey, stupid."

Henry was eager to play ball, but always fastidious about his possessions, so he asked me to hold his prized Bulova watch. Happy to be the girl cheerleader, although anxious about how my oldest brother would be accepted, I sat on the curb and leaned my back against the telephone pole dug into our front lawn. On this balmy summer evening, I listened to the clatter of wooden bats hitting the pavement and the scratch of sneakers sliding toward the curb that stood for first base. I mindlessly stretched the gold-plated watchband, praying that Henry could catch the tossed ball and rooting for both my brothers, little accordion links in my hands, pull, press, pull, press, pull, press, pull . . .

Snap.

Could you hold my watch, pigeon? What did the pigeon destroy?

With little gold links resting in sweaty palms, I wished I could fly away to escape the circle of hell that I had inadvertently created with my own two hands. At eight, I was old enough to know that even minor events could have enormous consequences because my brother's mental retardation, coupled with mental illness, was a toxic combination. I knew how my brother raged against imperfection, until each nick, wound, or broken link could be repaired.

Before the game was over, I ran up the staircase, two steps at a time, to warn my parents about what I had done. My father shook his head in icy silence. "Oh my God," my mother moaned, already anticipating the ferocity of Henry's reaction. My carelessness had made the more-than-fair share of daily pain she experienced caring for my brother even worse than she could have imagined. I had expected their anger, but was still unprepared for the rage this incident would unleash in my brother. When I handed Henry the tiny links of his favorite possession, his face turned from bewilderment to anger. Turning red, he screamed and cursed at me like the man-child he was, out of control, flailing his arms, moving closer as my parents pulled him away.

I began my Pavlovian dash around the dining room table, the "Maria run," as my brother Bob labeled my routine response to Henry's out-bursts. Never knowing how to handle my fear, I'd circle round and round, the tiny mouse scratching the treadmill to nowhere, seeking relief in mere exhaustion. Finally my father, who could stand it no longer, jumped into the car to search for any repair shop that might be open in the evening. Miraculously, he returned with a new watchband, providing a temporary calm by closing the door on this crisis until the next one emerged.

"Think about your other children," my mother used to repeat aloud the advice of friends who told her it was best to put Henry away for the sake of the rest of us. When Henry was born in 1946, the era of early interven-tion, social workers, and consent decrees to ensure that special education children received proper resources didn't exist for working families. There were no national models of compassionate care but rather sinister stories about private pain, like our former president's mentally retarded sister who had been lobotomized decades earlier when the paterfamilias decided to permanently institutionalize his daughter to preserve the good Kennedy name. Americans had not yet been exposed to the shocking scenes inside Willowbrook; the response in the sixties was to shut damage away.

But my mother, who looked to the blessed Madonna as her archetype of maternal compassion and sacrifice, would never put her own flesh and blood in an institution. I'm not sure why she repeated her friends' admonition, perhaps out of sorrow for what Henry put us through. I was a child, too innocent to understand places like state mental institutions, and I retreated to my small room.

Thirteen years younger than Henry, I didn't know my brother in a gentler stage, the little boy with a patch over his lazy eye, prone to seizures and trying to navigate the larger world. When my parents lived with my grandmother, life was easier for my family because my brother had not yet experienced adolescence and its hormonal outbursts, and he was surrounded by cousins who enjoyed playing with him. But Henry entered my consciousness as an isolated teenager, and his irrational behavior caused a crazy anxiety in me.

For my mother, Henry's problems reinforced a lifelong guilt about a bad turn of luck—her doctor was absent from the labor room during a critical moment in my brother's birth, and like all parents, she questioned each decision that she made affecting her child's development. Should she have left my grandmother's crowded apartment in Maplewood, a town with good schools, to move to a house in Cranford? "The teacher said not to move, that he was making progress," my mother remembers half a century later.

My brother was placed in special education, and his "assignments" were humiliating, such as being told to pick up the other kids' garbage on the school grounds. He hated being in the "special class," words he repeated often, knowing that his uniqueness was not the kind that others coveted. When he eventually dropped out of school, my mother found an occupational therapy program that offered Henry the assembly-line privilege of placing pegs in holes. Unhappy and bored, one evening he mistakenly stepped off the train at the wrong station. The anxious search that followed proved too much for my mother, and she pulled him from the program.

Throughout each of these ordeals, one constant remained in the face of Henry's humiliation and defeat: my mother's unrelenting care of and devotion to her son. After years of my brother's sitting at home with nothing to do, my mother begged the personnel director at our local Saks Fifth Avenue to hire him as a maintenance worker. For a while, he thrived in this job, satisfied by the results of his hard work: sparkling glass shelves, lint-free carpets, clean-as-a-whistle windows. He left the house early each morning for his ten-minute walk to Saks, changed into a brown uniform that hung in his locker, and proudly wore a soft cotton shirt with the word "maintenance" sewn in a fancy script above the pocket. His boss, an Irish-American saint named Bill, watched over my brother as he pushed his heavy cart around the store.

"Hey, shop steward," Bill teased, and Henry beamed as Bill would affectionately pat the top of Henry's head and call him the boss.

But when Bill retired, replaced by a man who routinely picked on my brother, Henry lost his way. He became moody, wore his hair long, and because of a lack of coordination, occasionally banged the sharp corners of the maintenance cart into well-heeled suburban shoppers. Inevitably, he was fired and dealt a personal blow from which he never fully recovered.

And neither could my mother recover a life of her own. The constant attention that my brother required, along with raising two other children, cooking, cleaning, and reentering the workforce as a typist to help pay for Bob's college tuition ensured that my mother personified the opposite of a "free woman."

"You must have a really strong mother," a young woman at the *Village Voice* remarked to me one day as we stood by the restroom sink, the central place for girl talk at the paper.

Her observation, announced out of the blue by someone who didn't know me but seemed extremely intuitive about mothers, startled me and I fiddled with the faucet, unsure of how to respond. She was the shy and literary daughter of a well-known feminist who wrote novels and essays about trapped women like my mother. Finding my way through the labyrinthine world of New York City politics working with a macho gang of reporters, I regarded my ambition and determination as a reaction to, not the fruit of, my mother's steady presence.

"I don't know...." I mumbled and reached for the soap, momentarily washing my hands of the matter.

At the time I couldn't tell her, or myself, the obvious answer to the question—yes, I do—because in my new world strength through sacrifice was not a virtue applauded but a response considered both weak and stereotypically female. The place I worked, the vision I shared, was about achieving equality—girls just wanna have parity, don't they?—and sacrifice was interchangeable with martyrdom and subservience.

"You must really like to serve people," I once said to my mother, with the cruel indifference to her feelings of which only a daughter may be capable.

"Not really," she answered with a nervous laugh.

Sacrificio, sacrifice, spilled from the lips of Italian American women of my mother's generation like sugar poured into espresso, as they resigned themselves to sweeten life's bitterness, usually at the expense of their own desires. From a daughter's point of view, one whose mother stepped back allowing me to step forward, I had no use for this subservient role. It wasn't until I became a mother that I better understood how the sacrifice of one provides strength for the other, as well as the familial difficulties inherent in having a parent who claims most of the attention for him- or herself. And it was then that a feminism emphasizing rationalism, reason, and personal autonomy, but failing to probe the fundamental thread of human relationships—how the development of the child is shaped by the guidance, strength, and humility of the parent—felt terribly lacking.

My model of maternal care was greatly skewed because a finite period of dependency stretched into a lifetime—my brother's emotional behavior and learning abilities have stayed at the level of a young boy, so the burdens of dependency were never relieved. Those who have experienced daily the limitless demands of the disabled child are more sensitive to the giant holes in the American social service system, continually seeing how the world's richest industrialized country provides the least support to the young and needy. Philosophy professor Eva Feder Kittay, who is the mother of a profoundly mentally retarded daughter, set forth a political theory in her book *Love's Labor* to reconcile the conflict of dependency and equality in the lives of women. Kittay argues that equality-based policies have mostly failed women in both the public and private sphere—only a tiny number of women represent us politically, and whether working or at home full-time, women perform more than three-quarters of household chores and child-rearing responsibilities.

Indeed, if female identity is intricately tied to providing care, then a half-century later Simone de Beauvoir's declaration still rings true: "I must first of all say: 'I am a woman'; on this truth must be based all further discussion." Kittay has put forth a concept of equality based on the simple and profound truth that everyone is "some mother's child," a phrase that recognizes the "fundamental connection between a mothering person and the fate of the individual she has mothered," and whose iconic representation, she suggests, is found in the image of Christ through the suffering figure of Mary. Kittay rejects the notion of justice as individual, or based on the premise that each person has a conception of the good and competes equally for resources, in favor of a "connection-based" equality. Her formidable proposals point out the dilemmas of a feminism based on Enlightenment ideals and aim to shift the very language of Western thought from "I" to "we."

Kittay's theories reveal the intricate thinking of a woman, philosopher, and mother of a disabled daughter whose daily struggles have reinforced for her the reality that dependency and equality are mutually exclusive unless society offers resources for both the dependent child and the one who provides the care. By suggesting that the goal of a common societal good replace the credo of self-reliance, Kittay offers a theoretical rationale for paid family and medical leave, more flexible work time, and payment for dependency work—rationalized and routinized like worker's comp or unemployment—that would compensate mothers for their time caring for children or allow them to use the money for day care. Some of these ideas have long been adopted by countries to which conservative commentators refer as the coddled old Europe, and Kittay repeats the well-known fact that the (forever?) young United States is the nation in the world most capable of employing a public policy fairer to women and children, but also the most recalcitrant to do so.

"The encounter with dependency is rarely welcome to those fed an ideological diet of freedom, self-sufficiency, *and* equality," writes Kittay. "We have to use our multiple voices to expose the fiction and rebuild a world spacious enough to accommodate us all with our aspirations of a just and caring existence."

Women of my generation were raised on this diet, the lovely ideological truffle of having it all. So many of us found ourselves perplexed experiencing the emotional tug of balancing work with the reality of raising a child. The original feminist solution affirmed the model of male sovereignty by rejecting the caregiving role. These feminists became caught in the paradox of championing the rights of women while failing to adequately consider the needs of mothers and children. In her book *The Equality Trap,* Mary Ann Mason, now dean of the graduate school at Berkeley, explained, for example, how the National Organization for Women and the National Women's Political Caucus filed a friend-of-the-court brief in the early eighties *in favor of* the California Federal Savings and Loan after the bank fired a receptionist for taking a four-month *unpaid* maternity leave.

Fair is fair, the feminists argued; pregnant women should be treated the same as disabled men who under California law would not have been able to keep their jobs after a four-month leave. Similarly, courts created no-fault divorce in the name of equality, which left many middle-class women with children near poverty after the dust of the legal papers settled.

Feminist thought would evolve to question such concepts of liberal neutrality, but the fatal flaw in this early thinking about equality was the inability to reconcile the reality of dependency. The situation of a new mother cannot be compared to one of a disabled man. The California receptionist was requesting an unpaid leave to take care of her newborn, not herself, a selfless twenty-four-hour responsibility. Feminism, too, bought into the rhetoric of capitalism and rugged individualism, ensuring that American women as well as men can now work longer away from family than workers in the rest of the industrialized world do.

I used to think linearly, longing for the conclusive end of the sentence, a leap of faith that the future, not the past, offers the vital solution. But today my thought process feels circular, perhaps a crude version of Hegel's rhythm of history, that every idea posited needs also to be opposed. The feminist movement's historical and pivotal achievement was to create an antithesis to women's traditional subservience: autonomy against caregiving. Today's challenge remains finding a sustainable synthesis of the two.

My friend greets the mentally retarded man responsible for cleaning her neighborhood playground. He interprets her friendly hello as an entree into a longer conversation and stays by our side, unaware that the awkward pauses reflect a desire to talk among ourselves. It's the weekend of our twenty-fifth high school reunion, and my friend, recovering from a recent operation, has generously hosted a brunch for a few of us who now live in New York and Boston. We've left our crumbs on her dining room table and she rightly wants time to relax and talk while our children climb and slide. My friend tells the man politely but firmly that she's going to talk to us for a while. He quietly walks away.

Watching his head hang low, his eyes searching the ground with a well-honed loneliness, I know that I will eventually restart the conversation. I imagine injuries large and small inflicted by any person who has shunned this man or grown bored and irritated by his failure to recognize social cues. My childhood plays out before me: the memory of coming home one day from a supermarket with Henry, who lags behind me and walks fast to catch up. A man notices my brother's edges: crew cut, rail thin body, and fervent stare, and assumes that this figure threatens me.

"Is he bothering you? Do you want me to walk with you?" the man asks, cutting off my brother as he approaches me.

"No, no," I respond, humiliated that my trailing brother is confused for a dangerous man.

"What did he want, pigeon?" Henry asks a minute later.

"Nothing," I reply curtly, angry at everything: my brother, the man, suburban normalcy, and its stark absence in my life. So it is my nature to live in a city and carry on conversations with people who seem to be wounded sideline players in a life taking place before them.

A short time later, the mentally retarded man walks out of the playground's small equipment shed holding a navy rubber ball between his hands. Walking up to him, I ask him about the ball, the weather, any small talk that comes to mind. He has the worst set of yellowed false teeth I've ever seen. His upper plate lacks an adhesive, which causes his teeth to click and clatter each time his mouth opens, exposing the pink gums of a baby. The slipping teeth divert my attention from the conversation, for now I can only focus on these choppers as they dice words like a busy food processor and crumble sentences to meaningless letters. The man's hair is greasy, his uniform dirty, and he looks in desperate need of a scrubbing.

Yet he is some mother's son. Does she still exist? She must no longer be capable of caring for him or he wouldn't look this way. Who is his family and how worn have they become supporting a life that needs constant supervision and care?

Because Henry is my mother's son she takes him to the dentist for periodontal work to save teeth weakened by gum disease. Watching the man in the park, I think about my past frustrations with my mother's decisions, how she has seemed more concerned about addressing my brother's dental problems than the state of his mental health. But one is more easily fixed than the other, and as his mother, she must care for him, washing his hair and combing out the tangles, placing his freshly laundered clothes on the bed for each new day.

Being a mother who in her eighties still does not want to disappoint, she agrees against her own best judgment to fulfill Henry's wishes. She lugs a large ladder up the stairs to wash all the windows in the house because Henry finds satisfaction in dust destroyed and a job well done. She will also climb the ladder for him because my brother lacks the co-ordination to steady himself and he is prone to seizures. A few days later, a dark purple bruise covers her entire upper arm; the chorus of blood vessels that she ruptured by carrying the ladder frightens the eye and we tilt our heads slightly upwards when talking to her, not wishing to directly confront her vulnerability. In mothering Henry, she has always sided with her primal instincts, plumbing the depths of sacrifice's deep, dark core to the detriment of her own health.

In the heart of southern Italy, an impoverished eighteenth-century Neapolitan philosopher named Giambattista Vico sought to counter the values of Enlightenment rationalism, which he found coldly worshipful to the creed that truth is found only through the laws of science, and is ultimately antithetical to the textured layers of human experience and the symbolic ways in which people have viewed the world and expressed themselves. Man is doomed to misunderstanding, argued Vico, if instead of attempting to decipher the language and myths of the past, he uses contemporary social and moral values to imagine those who lived before. Vico's humanistic philosophy, little known throughout his lifetime and illuminated in the twentieth century by the brilliant Russian-English thinker Isaiah Berlin, suggested that history doesn't universally march toward progress, but rather evolves in cycles of cultural development.

"The myths and poetry of antiquity embody a vision of the world as authentic as that of Greek philosophy, or Roman law, or the poetry and culture of our own enlightened age—earlier, cruder, remote from us, but with its own voice," writes Berlin on Vico's theories. "Each culture expresses its own collective experience, each step on the ladder of human development has its own equally authentic means of expression." To Vico, there is no timeless natural law—a keystone to Enlightenment belief—and knowledge can only begin to be obtained by understanding nuances, examining how people used language, symbols, and poetry to respond to the desires, fears, brutality, and hopes of their day.

As inheritors of an Enlightenment vision of history, we optimistically assume that a vigorous and certain march toward progress continues, as long as barriers like ignorance and superstition are removed from its path. In some ways, America's myth of the melting pot extols this belief—that shortly after the early immigrants came here, they adopted the values and mores of the younger, stronger, ultimately more capable culture, and success was based on their ability to assimilate. The notion that people would no longer live by, teach, or pass along the values upon which they were raised was, of course, absurd, but nonetheless a fiction absorbed by the culture until only fairly recently challenged by the emerging voices of African-Americans, Latinos, and Asians.

But any hyphenated-American will feel, if attuned to the notes voiced by her relatives and ancestors, the pull and tug of these competing values. Italians, for better or for worse, think about personal sacrifice differently than many Americans, viewing it as they do through the prism of their particular culture and past. For impoverished southern peasants, life and sacrifice were synonymous, a daily fight for food and survival. Catholicism reinforced, as the mystery of the communion host dissolved on the tongue, that pain and suffering were inextricably bound to the hope of transcendence. Nothing was considered stronger or more important than blood ties, and honor was found in family responsibilities, not individual achievement. In some ways, the old world seemed fairer than the new in its call for sacrifice among men and women. At least men's hard manual labor and women's rigorous housework and childrearing balanced out more evenly than today's professional divide, in which fathers continue their office work and give up some former freedoms while working mothers end up handling most of the household work and child care.

My parents, in good southern Italian tradition, placed no limits on the sacrifices they made, or what they would expect of Bob and me. As we grew older, and the contrast in our abilities sharpened, my brother and I were denied the pleasures that eluded Henry. Henry, who loved cars and could name every model that GM produced, was not capable of driving, which meant that my brother and I couldn't drive in suburbia. Henry could not do well in school, so it was better not to acknowledge our academic achievements. "You know we're proud of you," was the most my parents offered.

Henry could not get married and have children; therefore my brother and I were denied both the pleasure and ability to discuss the future with our family. I would announce a boyfriend with the same trepidation my gay friends faced when they came out of the closet to their parents. Accepting my marriage was a complicated, heartbreaking struggle, as my parents clung to the past, refusing to admit that the only certainty in life is knowing that it will change, a reality that hit my mother with the cruel gust of a sudden wind tunnel.

My mother's sacrifice placed a tremendous burden on her, which will eventually be handed to my brother and me. But in the gray zone of life, in which two competing truths coexist, preventing a neat and happy ending, I have come to accept that no group home affordable to my parents could have delivered the same compassion and care to my brother.

My parents did the best they could within the limits imposed by their culture, religion, income, and what society had to offer them. The beauty and pain of parenting a child is tenderly laying the bricks of self-confidence, ability, and independence upon which he'll eventually walk, creating the steady foundation to leave the family who raised him. But what if the child is damaged? Someone must make the sacrifice and the mother usually approaches the altar first, and stays for the duration.

You must have a really strong mother, the feminist's shy daughter remarked to me nearly twenty years ago. Back then, I was incapable of understanding a fundamental truth of human relationships, that the sacrifice of one is the gift to another. A gift that American culture, fixated on personal achievement and unbridled prosperity, takes more and more for granted.

My friend, the poet and writer Wallis Wilde-Menozzi, moved to Parma, Italy, two decades ago with her Italian husband and their daughter. Her memoir, *Mother Tongue,* describes the cultural chasm she experienced between the values of her American birthplace and her newly adopted land. In a moving chapter on the death of her mother-in-law from cancer, she wrote about the decision of her husband, the chairman of the biology department at the University of Parma, to wipe clean his schedule once he learned of his mother's illness.

"He canceled all conferences. He decided he would give her medicine or baths or whatever was needed, day or night. He started cooking to tempt her to take a mouthful or two. His colleagues concurred. They left him alone or caught him during his kamikaze visits to his office. What is the distance between cultures? What is it like—that freedom that starts so early in the States—where a mother and father want you to become . . . to go. Why would it seem unnatural to give over an unmeasured amount of time to someone who is dying?"

Wilde-Menozzi has observed Italian behavior in a prosperous part of the land, where sacrifice may be a choice. She mused in a recent essay about a Parma grandmother, a psychiatrist and mother of six, who proudly reported on her three-year-old granddaughter's precocious insights: "Her little mind hums like a top. You know what she said? 'My mother was in your stomach. And I was in her stomach. And so I was a little bit in your stomach.'

"That beautiful continuity—that strong rooted space for the most basic and traditional links—is one reason Italy seduces in powerful and authentic ways," writes Wilde-Menozzi. "Human relations have as much space as work, and professionalism has different dimensions in terms of being a role. Family is not a sacrifice but an inevitable part of life, with its discomforts and adjustments, but also with its rewards of continuity, and the pleasure of knowing people through time, and having the right and privilege of taking care of them."

Sacrifice—a thorn in the side of reason, a balm to life's unfairness—is the very contradiction of sovereignty. It opposes values embodied in phrases like self-reliance, individual choice, and ownership society, ideas that dominate today's political discourse and the way we live. An engagement with sacrifice, the recognition that each of us carries an obligation to help the young, elderly, and needy, can serve as an antidote to a vision of equality fashioned on the cold, bottom-line mentality of the marketplace. To acknowledge that we are not free individuals but depend, and are sometimes dependent, upon each other is the essential journey of the human condition, filled with both joy and sadness. The decision to accept this with magnanimity, instead of laying it stingily in the arms of women, may be the fundamental test of those parlor game nouns that aim to declare who we are.

My Father's Music

· · · · · · ·

NED BALBO

On April Fool's Day, 1961, the dissonance of dueling accordions filled
my parents' Long Island kitchen. Peering down into the viewfinder of
an old Brownie box camera, its blinding flash about to burst, my
mother, Betty, captured the moment: her husband, Carmine, at ease in
slippers and clean gray plumbing uniform, his accordion resting on his
knees, swaying to the music while their only child joined in. Not yet
two years old, in red shirt and overalls, I clutched a boy's blue toy accordion like a rabbit by the ears. I can imagine how it sounded, the instrument falling open or closed, releasing its tinny moan no matter what
my father played. While leather straps helped him steady and guide
twin frames of inlaid wood, my dad's fingers flashed across the buttons.
The date, recorded in Betty's neat script in gold ink against black paper,
would have been a Saturday, but Carmine worked most Saturdays and
his clothes look freshly ironed. Already gray at forty-two, he wore the
same Clark Gable mustache that, through his life, altered just slightly
with the times. Perhaps it was Sunday afternoon, his one day off from

· · · · ·

NED BALBO received the Ernest Sandeen poetry award for his second collection,
Lives of the Sleepers. He is the recipient of grants in poetry from the Maryland Arts
Council, the Robert Frost Foundation poetry award, and the John Guyon Literary
Nonfiction Prize for "Walt Whitman's Finches: On Autobiography and Adoption."

work. He often wore his uniform when just relaxing around the house and in early spring wouldn't have had to mow the yard.

I know exactly what he played. All his life, my father's repertoire rarely changed, its core a group of songs he'd mastered in his teens or twenties, though in 1970, he added two new songs to his list: Hal David and Burt Bacharach's "Raindrops Keep Falling on My Head" (the theme from *Butch Cassidy and the Sundance Kid*), which was ubiquitous that year, and Cross and Cory's standard, "I Left My Heart in San Francisco," a city that Dad had briefly toured in 1944 as a G.I. assigned to the U.S.-occupied Philippines. Tony Bennett's version had sold over three million copies to lodge itself in the nation's collective consciousness, but in the eight years since its first release in '62, Carmine hadn't yet attempted his own rendition. Now, the moment had arrived. By the light of a lamp whose base featured a ceramic panther, he forged on, despite wrong notes, sometimes muttering *"Mannagia!,"* stopping for the night only when he'd mastered the main verse, the bridge a problem he'd reserve for tomorrow's practice.

By 1970, Anthony Benedetto, the son of Italian immigrants, had replaced Frank Sinatra as my father's favorite singer. Crucial to this rise in status had been Carmine's contrary nature, which bridled at honoring the superstar so many others said was best. "Bah! He used to be good," my father grumbled in old age as if oblivious to the breadth of Sinatra's recorded legacy, "but he don't know when it's time to quit! He sounds terrible now." Still, Carmine's eyes welled up when Sinatra died in '98, the skinny kid who crooned on radio for Tommy Dorsey's band now a generation's icon passing into history. Luckily, Tony Bennett was left, enjoying a new wave of success my father forgave when I informed him Bennett's own son had engineered it. This Dad appreciated: he liked stories of sons helping out their fathers. Otherwise, he'd find fault with any performer too successful, withholding adulation as if it were a point of pride to be the one soul not so easily won over.

. . .

With these exceptions, Carmine's songs reached back to an earlier generation, like the tradition of the diatonic accordion he owned, an echo of Italy kept alive in the enclaves of immigrant neighborhoods where history and heritage held fast. Photographs of Greenpoint, Brooklyn, during the 1920s, the years my father attended P.S. 23, show Model Ts, vegetable carts (6 lbs. of potatoes for a quarter), trolley cars on cobblestone streets, barrels of refuse, boys in knickers, cigar shops, shoemakers, banks, a girl (blurred) on roller skates. Women push their swaddled babies along in wicker carriages, while men in topcoats and fedoras stare grimly into the camera. The Old World did not let go. Block by block, Italians divided themselves—Siciliano from Napolitano, Abruzzesi from Calabrese—according to the towns or regions their residents had escaped, places of thwarted opportunity or strict conformity regarded now with tenderness and regret.

It was a borough in transition, urban in its main-street bustle but still a place of empty lots, potato fields, and unpaved streets, under construction in a decade when men could always find steady work connecting new housing to the city's sewer system. And so, at Tenth Avenue and 60th Street in November 1922, fourteen sewer workers stood under a supporting arch—seven with mustached, Italian faces—brandishing picks and shovels, proud of their masonry and labor, the photo's focal point the Irishman saluting at the center. Carmine's cousins, my father's brethren—men who labored in light and darkness—survive in the photos that have become one record of that vanished era.

And, everywhere, there was music. The U.S. had suspended civilian radio during the Great War, but afterward, business took the lead. Financed by Westinghouse, four stations were established, each in a major city, while the broadcasting boom that followed brought 500 more into existence. The turning point was 1922, when New York's WEAF ran the first radio commercials, and jazz of the pre-swing era found its first mass audience.

By decade's end, Rudy Vallee, the twentieth century's first crooner and forerunner of Sinatra, would sing in Italian and other languages through his trademark megaphone, the creative clash of a changing nation embodied in his material. These songs, too, were a source of what would become my father's music: the popular hits he heard as a kid, broadcast over radio, the romantic vocals and trembling brass that cut through static as he listened. But some of these hits derived directly from traditions older still, from sources updated or disguised, born in the homeland that Carmine knew only from rumor.

In reply to the usual question—"What are you?"—that all kids once asked each other, I'd say, "I'm half Italian and half Polish." My mother was born Elizabeth Gromatsky, and she never questioned her generation's ethnic rivalries: for her, anything Polish was best—the substance, no doubt, of conversations conducted with her mother, Stella, in the language that they shared. I would never learn Polish, Betty claimed, because my father was Italian; children could learn a language only if both parents spoke it at home. According to her, it was Carmine's fault that I grew up monolingual despite a smattering of swear words in both parents' ancestral tongues.

Still, Betty relented in other ways, acknowledging her husband's background. She admired his music and would, at times, even request a song if she was working in his vicinity while he practiced. She seldom actually sat and listened, but she enjoyed the trembling chords and calming mood of Carmine's playing. She'd simmer tomato sauce once a week, applying the wisdom gained in youth from some long-lost Italian neighbor who knew the ways of the Old Country. Proud of her meatballs and bronchiole, she recorded her culinary secrets in a corkboard recipe book from some Pocono Mountains weekend. Was it the weekend my father proposed, or a date important for other reasons? I know only that their engagement had lasted for two years, the wedding delayed because Betty's mother hesitated to welcome Carmine, biased against his Italian blood by her Polish chauvinism. In the Poconos, did Betty persuade him not to give up too soon? There are some questions sons and daughters shouldn't ask.

By 1964, we'd moved from Babylon, the village where Gugliemo Marconi had invented radio, transmitting his own voice to ships rounding the Great South Bay. Now we lived in Smithtown, in a colonial house too large for three, my voice echoing in the living room that we would never furnish, the polished hardwood floor a place to roll or slide. Carmine played in the basement or in the den just off the kitchen. I'd repeatedly request "The Woodpecker Song," my favorite, the tick-tick-tick of the bird's pecking mimicked by the rhythm, its cheerful tune descending brightly with each chorus. The song was an Andrews Sisters B-side in March 1940, but my father probably knew it from Glenn Miller's #1 single, which first charted a month later and held on for seven weeks. Or did Carmine know it from elsewhere? Like other hits of the era, "The Woodpecker Song" was born offshore, in immigrant music and traditions Americanized for radio. In the original Italian lyrics, nary a woodpecker appears. Instead, "Reginella Campagnola"— literally, "Little Country Queen"—offers a girl strolling at sunrise, riding a donkey into town, then returning home with gossip; its refrain praises her eyes, her voice, and the Abruzzo region. Harold Adamson's English lyrics sacrifice an entire world: the rural villages that immigrants cherished and idealized, the homeland that their children would know only from song or story. My father never mentioned knowing the Italian version. Still, he may have responded to the southern Italian flavor in composer Eldo Di Lazzaro's melody line. (An author of popular songs, Di Lazzaro grew up in Trivento.)

Slightly truer to its source is "The Butcher Boy": not the Irish ballad of the same title, but *"La luna mezzo o' mare"*: literally, "The Moon Is at the Middle of the Sea." In the English lyrics credited to Rudy Vallee—

I knew the refrain, the only lines Carmine consistently remembered—the title character relies on his profession to prove his fitness as a husband: he's gotta da lamb-chop, and da pork-chop. But, wait: the baker's boy has gotta da fruitcake, and a cheesecake, too, the use of dialect reinforcing Italian comic stereotypes. Whom should their intended marry? Unfortunately, she's fickle, her preference changing with each refrain, the listener left to smile wryly whenever she calls out, "Oh, Ma-Ma!" My father hummed along or sometimes sang a phrase or two—whatever he remembered on a particular day. The song portrayed a world where boys followed their father's lead, apprentices to the profession that defined their family's place.

But Carmine heard and understood the Italian version, too, which a wedding band performs in *The Godfather*'s opening scenes. On hearing the old man whose singing provokes such howls of laughter, my father would only say that the Italian words were "bad." Here, the daughter leaves the choice of husband to the mother. It's she who sings each verse, describing each man and his profession: the butcher holds the sausage, the fisherman his fish, the shoemaker his shoe, the gardener his cucumber, no doubt provoking sour looks from the prospective bride. Each alternative Mama offers seems as bad as the one before, with each man's prop a euphemism for his penis. Beyond bawdy comedy, the folk song offers a reminder: no matter whom the daughter weds, she can't escape her wifely duties, for, as Mama knows from experience, all men are after the same thing.

Still, romance, not sex, defined my father's store of songs. This was the age of Tin Pan Alley, when songwriters wrote to formulae but within those boundaries could express themselves with eloquence and range. The love song, then as now, cast its overwhelming shadow across the hit parade and Carmine's repertoire. "You're My Everything" debuted in the Broadway revue *The Laugh Parade* at the Imperial Theater in November 1931. On opening night, Jeanne Aubert equated "winter, summer, spring" with the beloved who was all these and, of course, the essential rhyme. The next year, Russ Columbo's version rose to #10. A star as popular at the time as Bing Crosby or Rudy Vallee, he died, perhaps accidentally, only three years later when a friend decided to show off an antique pistol. Born Ruggiero Eugenio di Rodolpho Colombo, the Camden, New Jersey, son of immigrants was a hero to his people. Carmine must have heard Russ Columbo, "The Romeo of the Radio Waves," even though he was only fourteen at the time the star was killed.

At times romantic longing showed up in strange places. Many first discovered "You Belong to My Heart" through Disney's 1945 film *The Three Caballeros*, whose protagonists are a Brazilian playboy parrot, Donald Duck, and a singing Mexican red rooster. Written by Mexican composer Augustin Lara, "Solamente Una Vez," or "Only Once," depicts exactly the kind of fleeting, brief encounter that reinforced the popular view of the Latin lover. Such men could awaken women to an erotic transformation. They were sensual, vaguely effeminate, yet, for these reasons, to be feared: a Mediterranean stereotype that encompassed Italians, too. But Ray Gilbert's English title shifts the emphasis instead to the singer's declaration of undying love: when the protagonist asks his beloved if she recalls "a moment like this," we know the answer must be yes.

Bing Crosby's version, backed by the Xavier Cugat Orchestra, reached #3 in 1945. Crosby was no Latin. Still, everyone did Latin songs; it was a genre that bands or singers were expected to explore, either as a change of pace or routine feature of their sound. Some performers of Italian descent deemphasized their roots, broadening their appeal by mixing Tin Pan Alley standards with strong, new songs identified with American urban culture. Thus, Frank Sinatra, the skinny 4-F kid that G.I.s once resented for distracting their sweethearts from the thought of imperiled boyfriends across the sea, filled out into the street-smart swaggerer of middle age, though his material and phrasing remained far subtler than his image.

I'd kneel on the basement rug, playing with Matchbox cars. With a faraway look, Carmine would gaze wistfully toward the ceiling—was he thinking of Betty, whom he'd serenaded with "You Belong to My Heart"? Upstairs, she dusted the house, made dinner, washed our clothes by hand; she labored over the flower beds, trimmed hedges, or paused for a cigarette. But as the bellows swelled and shrank, Carmine saw only the gathering stars, a million guitars strumming somewhere beyond my hearing.

Between songs, my father, too, would smoke, review what songs he knew, then pluck a number from the ether of his whim and memory. With a tilt of his head he'd resume, throw his shoulders into the task, squeezing air into hidden reeds while buttons clicked beneath his touch. He had no sense of measure, changing time signatures in mid-song, tapping one foot arrhythmically more as habit than as guide. Yet whatever song he'd work up remained consistent in itself, a hit transformed into some hummable, humbler approximation. In the Age of Swing, various artists would take their turn at the same song. If it had been a hit before, it might well ride the charts again. Or, if it hadn't, maybe some twist—a different vocalist or arrangement—would finally summon up the magic, sending it to number one.

But who were my father's audience? His siblings, wife, and I, and, decades back, Italian neighbors, friends, the G.I.s in his unit. Do any remember his renditions, offered freely with a smile, purely for attention and love of music? Today, in memory, I hear the songs as Carmine played them instead of the recorded tracks he'd meant to emulate. I recall, too, the dynamics, the rush of feeling in his performance where, for us at least, the rewards of art resided.

Accordions started showing up in the nineteenth century. Jesuit missionaries in China were introduced to the lusheng, a type of free-reed mouth organ that they eventually brought to Paris. Thereafter, this ancient "reed pipe" inspired the innovations that led to Europe's first accordions, harmonicas, and reed-based organs. A reed, composed of metal or cane, vibrates due to air flow, as when a clarinetist blows into the mouthpiece of his horn; an accordion, by contrast, conceals sets of metal reeds through which air is forced by the bellows' push-pull action. In 1860, as Italy struggled toward unification, the Pope's French allies brought along their accordions and concertinas. They caught on. Before too long, Italian production was established, and accordions like those we know became familiar. There are many variations in accordion design. During my childhood, Carmine played an organetto, a type of diatonic accordion from central and southern Italy: the *due botte* version offers two left-hand buttons for playing bass and ten on the right for playing melody.

The diatonic accordion, in any version, has its limits. The piano accordion's keyboard and use of "stradella" or "free-bass" buttons combine to offer a chromatic range over several octaves. By contrast, the diatonic versions play mostly major keys, in eight-note octaves that preclude all modulation. (Some modified diatonic versions offer limited chromatic options but remain awkward to finger, and, anyway, Dad didn't own one.) "The Butcher Boy" and "The Woodpecker Song" are cheerful, major-scale songs; by contrast, Hoagy Carmichael's "Stardust," my father's professed favorite, shifts into a minor accompaniment at the phrase "lonely night." But since only G major was possible in my dad's rendition, half of this "stardust melody" would sound less haunted than blindly hopeful. Unluckily, "As Time Goes By" suffered the same affliction: whatever passions had driven lovers throughout history or today, no listener could deny the glaring absence of F minor.

But my father didn't have a choice (or "cherce," he would have said: this dated form of a Brooklyn accent followed him throughout his life). Years before, on Humboldt Street, in his childhood single-family row house, his mother shut off the radio as everyone sat down to make music, command of their instruments uncertain but their enthusiasm strong. Their father, James, worked as a solderer for Worksman's Cycles of Ozone Park, building the Good Humor Ice Cream tricycles that rattled over New York's streets. The household he supported wasn't exactly prosperous but still included the upright piano around which so many families gathered.

Was it music they made, or noise, wrong notes and forgotten bridges common? What were the moments, locked in memory, to which they alone had access, siblings joined by experience, tradition, blood? Margaret, the eldest, could sight read and even played classical music, but at these sessions led most often with hits of the Roaring Twenties: "Side by Side," "Baby Face," or "California (Here I Come)," songs that recalled those happier, pre-Depression days. Next-oldest brother Mike would watch as Carmine and Joe joined in, at times trading their diatonic and keyboard accordions back and forth. Their sister Angie (baptized Archangela) witnessed Carmine's struggles, his broad fingers, accustomed to buttons, flubbing the treacherous black keys. "I can't get this one, give me the other one," he'd snap impatiently while Joe, ever the nudge, offered the semblance of support. "Oh, it's not hard—keep practicing," he'd goad his older brother, inwardly glad that Carmine's bass lines were clumsier than his own. The keyboard offered freedom, then, but also a challenge beyond my father: to coordinate melody and bass within a chromatic scale. But as soon as Carmine reclaimed the instrument he'd taught himself "by ear," he regained good cheer and confidence, if not the rhythm he never had.

"What would you like to take lessons on—accordion or guitar?" my mother asked in the fall of '65. We stood in the den where a large black-and-white Magnavox flickered, where I'd bang out rhythmic noise on a toy Mickey Mouse guitar, no doubt imitating some group I'd seen on *American Bandstand,* or the soundtrack of the Beatles' weekly cartoon. I knew this was an important moment. I could play accordion—"like Dad," she said, in case I'd missed the point, or I could learn guitar, if I wanted. Either way, I could decide. I'd never before thought of my father as someone I should emulate, but now my mother invoked him as if his influence would sway me, the only time in my whole life that I recall her doing so. She must truly have wanted me, this once, to follow in his footsteps. As the daughter of Polish immigrants who'd divorced during her childhood, and always anxious to please her mother, Betty had her own fond hopes: with lessons, I'd play even better than Dad, fill the house with polka music, and someday headline before her mother at the Polish social club in Hempstead.

But, partly due to Betty's influence, my choice was already made. My mother had taught me to read before I'd even started school, praised my drawings in colored pencil, maintained I'd one day go to college, and sent the message overall that I was meant for better things—the belief of all blue-collar parents ambitious on their child's behalf. Placed in a "home for girls" for some time after the divorce, Betty, a good student, didn't progress beyond eighth grade, while my father, a dyslexic long before the term was coined, struggled through grammar school until almost sixteen. His old autograph book reflects the indifference of his teachers: generic entries— "Best Wishes," "Success"—and Mr. Gottlieb's proverb, "Follow the Golden Rule not the Rule of Gold." No classmates seem to have signed, though his mother and Margaret did: "When you and I are far apart/Whisper my name to the Sa-ca-red Heart"; and "Love many trust few/Always paddle your own canoe." School wasn't the place for Carmine, but his dad had taught him to solder. After working at the Brooklyn Navy Yard before and after the war, Carmine became a plumber in the early 1950s, taking a job with an Army buddy who knew a licensed silver brazier could easily turn his expertise to this new calling.

There were unspoken messages, too, that made me feel less Italian. Growing up in the 1960s, I almost never saw Dad's family due to Betty's feuds over real or imagined slights. The worst meal she'd ever had, she said, was "alya oo"—Southern Italian dialect for spaghetti *con aglio e olio*—a dinner she couldn't even choke down on that night now long ago when Carmine had first brought her home to meet his mother. Why couldn't the women get along? Why did she fight with his sisters, too? Whatever the case, every Thursday, my father enjoyed his one night out, time he invariably spent visiting a brother or sister, four of whom had followed the same postwar migration to Long Island, but they did not reciprocate, and we three spent holidays alone, our large house oppressive in its emptiness.

In part, depression gripped my mother, who saw rejection every-where, even as she rationalized that others were merely jealous—of her well-kept yard, her figure, her husband's job, her son—but she was shaped, too, by the prejudices of a generation whose stereotypes of Ital-ians hadn't yet relaxed their hold. That generation used racial and na-tional epithets quite freely—my mother was proud of her "polack" background, my father sipped his "guinea red"—failing to make the leap that distinctions in ethnic origin paled beside the forces that claimed and homogenized their cultures. And so, my mother declared, I took after her side of the family, pointing out features she said were Polish, complaining vaguely of Carmine's quirks, little by little sending the message that although my father was Italian, for some reason I shouldn't think that I was, too.

In fact, I wasn't. I was adopted, a fact I didn't learn for years, but when I did, it explained a lot, including why we'd moved so often. Eventually, neighbors would notice that I didn't resemble Carmine and conclude I was too young to be this aging couple's son. Of course, Dad's family knew the truth at a time when most adoptive parents sustained the pretense that their children were biologically their own. It wasn't easy for Betty to drop the guard she kept up every day against the inqui-sition of neighbors or the chance remarks of strangers.

"I want to learn guitar," I answered. Betty asked if I was sure. And I turned my back, in a small way, on my father and an era.

Throughout his life, for long periods, Dad set the accordion aside, either because he was feeling blue or because he was just too busy. Laid off from his longtime job, an older worker without a pension, he worked (usually as a plumber) till the age of seventy-one. Years earlier, he'd watched as arthritis crippled his wife, and then he lost her to lung cancer a month after I went away to college. He sold our last house for too little, lived in various apartments, and never dated during the twenty-three years following her death. Although irascible at times, he saw the world with verve and humor; he was impatient with pretense and unfailingly self-deprecating. "You know, I'm dumb," he'd often say as if simply stating a fact, leaving me to point out all the ways he proved himself perceptive. Still, he struggled so much to read that he could hardly stay informed, a deficit that my own strengths only emphasized more keenly. He never said anything but must have wondered whether I'd have shared this weakness were I the birth son he and Betty could not have.

The third, and last, new song that I remember my father learning was a standard revived by the eight-track boom of the early '70s. By then, we lived in Brentwood, a blue-collar suburb near the South Shore, a step or more below Smithtown in property value and prestige. In June '67, Betty had moved us into a split-level ranch in a neighborhood where she'd already started to make friends. Things didn't work out, of course, and she soon regretted her decision. Our house, previously owned, was never right, or clean enough, as the realization hit that moving again was beyond our means. But we made the best of it. Soon, this home, too, was filled with music. One Sunday, my father, on a whim, connected his workshed record player to an outside speaker that he'd hung above the pool. Glenn Miller's woodwinds, tortured and tinny, suddenly floated over the yard as my mother looked up from her swim and Carmine laughed.

My father was ready for eight-track tapes and, with his brother's help, would have them. Uncle Joe, on disability from New York Telephone, had opened the J & B Discount Center in Farmingdale, Long Island. In toupee and leisure suits, he'd bounced back from his engagement to a seventeen-year-old girl whose father had threatened him with violence. His stock ranged widely, even wildly, from knock-off suits and cheap electronics to second-hand musical instruments, fad gadgets, and stationery supplies. He acquired, too, an inventory of bootleg eight-track tapes whose generic labels marked them as evidence of copyright infringement. A block from Uncle Mike's, the store served best as the brothers' hangout until Joe's reckless spending drove the business into the ground. In the meantime, he helped Carmine hook up an eight-track deck into his beat-up '63 Ford Fairlane.

Suddenly, Dad had a tape deck that played music I'd never heard— Al Martino, Jerry Vale, the latecomers of Italian crooners. Born a generation after Frank Sinatra and his Rat Pack, they owed much of their success to exposure on TV. But how long would the old tricks work? "Spanish Eyes," the signature song of the man born Alfred Cini, turns a Neapolitan ballad into a paean to Latin beauty, two stock Mediterranean types sharing a tearful "adios"; Martino's overdramatic singing, however, drowns the song in schmaltz. Also revealing is Jerry Vale's bitter anecdote of having failed to appear on Dean Martin's TV show. Having traveled across country only to be cut at the last minute, the former Genaro Vitaliano felt stung, humiliated, but he found no *paisan* in the star who informed him casually that guests were often cut when shows ran overtime. However justified, given the fee he'd forfeited, Vale's long-cherished grudge is one nursed by a secondary talent facing the privilege and caprice that greater talents believe their due. Even my dad considered Martino and Vale corny, though he was unable to articulate what he intuited. He loved the idols of his youth who'd defined the Big Bands' heyday; these would-be successors could never match their stature.

The tape we played most often when we ran errands for my mother, or when my father taxied me home from weekly lessons on guitar, had nothing to do with Italian music or the tunes my father played. It was, instead, another bootleg, the Mills Brothers' greatest hits, which clacked so loudly when it switched programs that my father and I would jump. The four original Mills brothers, black men born in Piqua, Ohio, had first gained fame in the early '30s through their exceptional vocal skills. Not only could they harmonize but their optimistic demeanor was perfectly suited to a nation facing the worst of the Depression. During World War II, they shot back to the top of the charts with "Paper Doll," a number one hit that eventually sold six million copies. The song's sheet music was popular, too, and underwent several printings in those years before an upright piano vanished from most households.

The Mills Brothers could bring to life even the most questionable material: their versions of "Opus 1," "Glow Worm," "Cab Driver," and "Mañana" are surprisingly appealing despite the low quality of the songs. Carmine, long indifferent to the Beatles, was glad we were finding common ground, that I'd stuck with playing guitar and now was even arranging standards. I didn't let on how much my lessons had come to bore me by that time or that I couldn't see myself performing the music that he loved.

One day in 1972, a tune still fresh in mind, the garage door banging closed behind him, my father, whistling, beat a path straight to his waiting instrument. I brought the groceries up to Betty, kissed her, then ran downstairs. Dad was back to playing accordion again. A few years earlier he'd acquired a Hohner German-style accordion with twin valves that reduced the challenge of playing bass. Once more in a musical mood, he'd been practicing every night, his right hand searching a single row of ten white buttons. We'd struggled, at times, to collaborate. Our instruments were at odds: a guitar that played the "real" chords, that changed keys as the song required, versus the diatonic accordion with its inherent limitations, to say nothing of Dad's unorthodox sense of rhythm. But that day, effortlessly, fingers confident and quick, he played a verse from the Mills Brothers song we'd come to most enjoy. The bridge required a change of key and strayed quite far from the recording, but Carmine's return to the main melody was clear and clean. It was the last song I remember him teaching himself by ear: "Standing on the Corner, Watching All the Girls Go By," a tune he'd known for years but had never before attempted, the endless sea of songs that filled the world and the airwaves holding possibilities beyond his reach. Only years later would I suspect he'd lived the song in Greenpoint, Brooklyn: a young man with brothers or friends glancing slyly at girls who passed, some nights playing on the stoop to draw them closer. When had the instrument he owned passed from playing Italian songs to the popular music of the Swing and Big Band era? And who would play it when Dad was gone—when his generation had died out? These were questions that I never thought to ask at the time.

Italian organ-grinders had faded from New York in the '20s—old men in rumpled clothes who wore their contraption on a strap, endlessly rotating the crank that played its predetermined program—and, in a few years, the Italian accordionists, too, would pass away. True, other hands had played the instrument as well—African or Cajun, Irish or Quebecois—and would form their own traditions: kaseko, zydeco, or conjunto. And there would always be revivalists, grandsons and granddaughters of Italia, keepers of photographs on which the ink of forgotten names had faded—those who'd seek out ancestral villages, learn the language, discover the music, perhaps retrieve and try to master that dusty gadget in the attic.

That day he learned the Mills Brothers' song, I still thought myself Carmine's birth son. The question "What are you?" hadn't yet taken on unwelcome implications, causing me to hesitate between the history I'd believed and the uncertainties from which I'd long been sheltered. Not yet cast into doubt about my home or heritage, I was indifferent, like any other self-absorbed American son. Italy was a far-off country, one I'd probably never see, whose inhabitants and ways had hardly touched me. When that inheritance was lost, I didn't feel differently—not right away, at any rate—but such knowledge lay at least a year or so ahead. For the moment, I knew that I loved my father whose good mood was contagious, and to hear him playing again only confirmed that I'd loved his music, however limited or imperfect, oddly paced, fraught with mistakes. And so, as before and after—when he practiced a new song, or when memory failed in later years—I helped by singing along, leading him through that exacting bridge, back to the verse, my father smiling as he swayed.

Sources Consulted Include:

Berner, Thomas F. (1999). *The Brooklyn Navy Yard.* Charleston, SC: Arcadia.

"The Diatonic Accordion." Available at http://www.accordionheaven.com

Epstein, Dan. (1999). *20th Century Pop Culture.* New York: Quadrillion.

Grudens, Richard. (2000). *Jerry Vale: A Singer's Life.* Celebrity Profiles.

Ierardi, Eric J. (1998). *Brooklyn in the 1920s.* Charleston, SC: Arcadia.

Laredo, Joe. (1992). *Liner Notes to Al Martino: Capitol Collector's Series.* Capitol Records, Inc.

Laurino, Maria. (2000). *Were You Always an Italian? Ancestors and Other Icons of Italian America.* New York: Norton.

Malpezzi, Frances M., and William M. Clements. (1992). *Italian American Folklore.* Little Rock, AR: August House.

Pierce, Max. (1999). "Russ Columbo: Hollywood's Tragic Crooner." Available at http://classicimages.com.

Pulling, Sr. Anne Frances. (1999). *Babylon by the Sea.* Charleston, SC: Arcadia.

Valentine, C. Irving. (1951). *The Art of Playing Hohner Diatonic Accordions.* New York: M. Hohner.

Washington Square

· · · · · · · · · · · · ·

CAROL BONOMO ALBRIGHT

I heard my mother's chair scrape the floor. She had moved the stool she habitually sat on closer to my father.

"Your mother has to register as an alien . . . she has to go to the post office to register," my father pressed, " . . . by January first."

My parents were in our small, neat kitchen, whispering. They sipped their espresso from the robin's-egg blue demitasse cups. My mother used the little pot with its slender spout that she turned right side up when the water boiled, making the blue and yellow gas-flame minuet to the last droplets of the overflow. The pot's metal was shiny against the stove's black burner. My father's chair backed against the storage closet with the pencil sharpener screwed inside, and where a narrow length of pepperoni always hung.

We lived in a modern apartment building that had been gutted and renovated from an old tenement, south of Washington Square Park. The building was no longer a walk-up but had an elevator and central heat—not a combination kitchen stove-heater with auxiliary gas

· · · · ·

CAROL BONOMO ALBRIGHT, the editor of *Italian Americana,* teaches Italian American Studies at Harvard University Extension School. She has published fiction, reviews, literary criticism, and journalism, and is the coauthor of *Republican Ideals in the Selected Writings of Joseph Rocchietti, 1835–1845.*

heaters—tight windows that didn't rattle with every breeze, a modern layout with an entry hall rather than the railroad flat model with its no-wasted-space efficiency, no privacy, no aesthetic considerations.

Our building, with my mother's clean kitchen, sat in the middle of an Italian immigrant neighborhood where we shopped for sausage and ate American mashed potatoes. It was a neighborhood that had housed artists in need of cheap housing and local color since the 1930s. Directly north of us was the old "American" enclave with families like the Rensselaers in their brownstones overlooking the park and Eleanor Roosevelt living in a mews off Fifth Avenue. My mother was not insensible to the differences between the neighborhoods. She was highly attuned to the mores of each and tried to negotiate an identity somewhere in the middle of the two. Without re-alizing it, she staked out her identity within this "in-betweenness."

I overheard my parents as I stood by the bookcase in the living room. Late afternoon light on this warm October day seeped through the large windows, illuminating the paintings of a wind-tossed sailboat and two still lifes. Our baby grand piano stood in the corner, the Sheaffer ink I had spilled earlier in the day on the ruby and blue Kermanshah rug mercifully blended into its medallion pattern. My grandmother, who lived with us, sat by the window, knitting.

My parents' whispering excited me: my overhearing them meant I would be privy to their hidden adult world. But I was hardly prepared for a revelation about my own grandmother. Their whispering signaled to me that being an alien was not a good thing. The word itself sounded so dark and foreboding with its echo of the Alien and Sedition Acts we had studied in school. The easy association and confusing connection of alien with sedition—like day and night, following each other in-evitably—made me shudder.

An alien? How jarring that word sounded—so un-American. This was the first time it occurred to me that my grandmother might be less American than I was since, to my mind, she was as American as I: she lived in America, had worked in America, paid taxes, obeyed its laws.

I blew my nose. Nana's crocheted edging on the borders of my hand-kerchief scratched. My dear sweet grandmother who had taught me to knit and whom, in my hubris, I had tried to teach to write, was now being labeled an alien! As I stood by the bookshelves, I felt shame about that stigma and stared now with sullen distaste at the complete set of Mark Twain's works. Connecticut Yankee, indeed! I pushed against the book, hoping to blot it out.

All these thoughts, swirling inchoate in my mind, made me feel scared that something terrible would happen to my grandmother if she didn't register on time. I wanted to hold tight to her even if she was this alien, speaking only Italian, wearing her black dresses and straw hat with the smashed cloth flower perched atop her head at an odd angle to accommodate the wispy, white bun. At the same time, this latest reve-lation froze me and made me forget how much I enjoyed her long sto-ries in rhyming couplets in her Calabrian dialect, the Easter bread she baked with strips of dough braided over the imbedded hard-boiled eggs, the fried *struffuli,* the word sounding like a rush of wind blowing from the north, and which my mother referred to as honey balls in front of Americans.

I pulled out the book I had been looking for when I overheard my parents' whispers, *The Autobiography of Benvenuto Cellini,* bound in brown cloth with gold lettering and decoration. My parents had bought books like this through the mail—whole sets of Dickens in their black and red bindings, Twain in cream and red, and world classics for my brother and me to read. I fingered the gold-edged pages.

Cocooning myself into the overstuffed chair, my back and head rested against one velvety, broad arm and my legs dangled over the other, wobbly and loose from such abuse. I didn't stop to smooth out my crumpled skirt, but instead bent over the book with its photos of Cellini's beautiful gold work and sculptures. Cellini experienced no confusion about who he was or how his origins fit into his present life. He had certainty, the comfort of his sculptures, of definite things like these books, printed about an Italian life that made for wholeness. I dropped away from my confusion into his world.

Cellini's first name, *Benvenuto,* he wrote, meant "Welcome." Although we were American, we were also Italian. My parents' struggle was to feel welcomed as Americans. For me, an American identity wasn't enough. George Washington's false teeth and cherry tree and the Puritans and Pilgrims seemed bland compared to Garibaldi's dashing figure and Dante's journey from hell to paradise.

I sank down deeper into my chair as the silence enveloped me. On the page the words flowed in front of me about Cellini's belief that it was "much more honourable to have sprung from an humble origin," and to have laid "a foundation of honour for my descendants, than to have been descended from a noble lineage...."

The rattle of the ragman's cart broke the stillness. Glancing down to the cobblestones below, I saw the Jewish ragman with his gray beard and faded wagon making his weekly trek from the Lower East Side onto our street in Greenwich Village. This day slabs of cardboard, rags, felt, and bits and pieces of stuff, too dirty to know what they were, fell off the wagon. His head pointed down as he maneuvered the cart from behind. Today the wagon was piled so high the ragman couldn't possibly stop to rest without toppling half its contents. The wagon wobbled and teetered, but the ragman had melded with its wooden handles. He shuffled down the street while Studebakers and buses skirted round him, another alien, I supposed, wandering among these streets and strangers.

My grandmother, who hadn't heard my parents' whispers, craned her neck now toward the window, and noticed the ragman too. "I'm glad," she said, "that no one in the family had to work in a rag factory... they were dirty places." *"Sporca,"* she repeated, "dirty." Her brows knit together like the yarn on her needles. Leaning against the window sill, she stood up, her corseted figure unbending from just below her bosom to the top of her thighs, her thick stockings taut and smooth on her thin legs. She slipped the knitting into her basket and readied herself to do an errand, her black-heeled oxfords moving quietly across the rug. She was still in her familiar world, her daughter in the kitchen, her granddaughter at her side where she could reflect that her family lived better lives than she had.

My mother called me to peel and cook the potatoes for supper. I stopped reading about Cellini's parents' courtship—how his father "soon became sensible to the charms of Lisabetta; and at length grew so deeply enamoured that he asked her in marriage." Reluctant to stop reading altogether, I brought the book into the kitchen with me and placed it, pages splayed down, on the table. My father had become enamored of my mother at a wake. They met south of Washington Square Park at Parrazzo's Funeral Home, where the southern Italians of Greenwich Village held their wakes. Blonde, fair, with high cheekbones, my mother had a serenity in her hazel eyes that made you want to know more about her. My father had slicked back auburn hair, an aquiline nose, and a wide-open smile.

My father always said, "Your mother and I met at a wake and it's been one long funeral ever since."

"He has a sense of humor, your father," my mother would add.

My mother, who strained against her own confusions with two identities, served mashed potatoes almost every night. She bought the story, prevalent at the time, that Italian cooking wasn't healthy. She educated herself in American cooking ways as best she could, writing to Metropolitan Life Insurance for their cookbooks of healthy American recipes which their actuaries, no doubt, determined would make you live longer and their company more profitable. Along with mashed potatoes with—by my mother's lights—their nourishing milk and gobs of butter, we most often had steak, which was my father's alimentary paradise, like the *Cuccagna*-land Italian peasants dreamt of, where it rained ravioli and macaroni rolled down mountains of cheese. When the mood hit her, my mother made upside-down cake, its brown sugar syrupy and glistening against the yellow pineapple.

"What's it mean," I asked, moving Cellini's autobiography out of the way so no food would smudge it, "that Nana has to register?"

"Shush," my mother hissed. "We don't want anyone to know." She took the steak and Swiss chard, along with the fixings for salad, out of the refrigerator. Looking straight at me, she stood rigid for a moment, holding the food tight against her chest, her face stony and white. "It's something we don't talk about... don't say anything to anybody," my mother cautioned. The walls of the long narrow kitchen seemed to be closing in on her and me.

My father pulled me to his side and hugged me. "It just means that people who aren't citizens have to let the government know they're here." My head shot backward: it had never occurred to me that my grandmother wasn't a citizen. I couldn't move, however, from non-citizen to alien with its echoes of menace and strangeness.

Each of my parents had a different way about them. Though my father could barely string together two sentences in Italian while my mother was bilingual, and whereas my father loved steak while my mother loved garlic and oil on her *scarole,* my father was not at odds about his identity. He solved his duality by retaining his Italian roots but living materially like an American: he took my mother to Bermuda for their honeymoon. Photos show them both nattily dressed, relaxed, confident. My father's business success made him an American and gave him entrée into an American lifestyle. For him it was as simple as that. Although my mother shared this lifestyle, she pursued an elusive American acceptance. It was my father who was comfortable enough with who he was to want to move to Riverdale and my mother who refused to leave her neighborhood, fearing the loss of her community and not fitting into the new one.

My father was expressive and open. I rarely asked my mother about her past. She equated her poor immigrant beginnings with inferiority and she sometimes enhanced details to make her family—and herself—look better off than they were. Such embellishments made me distrust a lot of what my mother said. They went against what I knew in my bones, beyond language. My father, with similar beginnings, told us heartrending stories of his poverty: how a man in a bowler hat came upon him, at around age five, crying on a stoop because his hands were frozen from having no woolen gloves and the man "threw me two bits." What did that man with his bowler and quarter represent to my father? Was it this coming together of clothing, money, and warmth that began his self-definition?

Another story involved his working as a delivery boy for six months. "The boss fires you after that," he'd tell us, "'cause he'd have to give you a two-bits raise—*a week*. One day I was riding on the subway delivering the guy's brooms, brushes, pails—so many, I had to pile them on my back. A guy on the train said to me, 'What's the matter, kid? The horse die?'" Now that he had his own business, he could laugh heartily, a note of triumph in its ring mixing with suppressed tears.

I dropped the potatoes into the boiling water. As the water sputtered, I began to think about all those nameless immigrants and their descendants. I had learned a lot about the immigrants' day-to-day lives from overhearing conversations as my mother gossiped with acquaintances while I accompanied her on errands. Like their work stringing tags, a thousand for twenty cents, a whole family gathered around the table after supper, slipping a short piece of knotted string through a hole in a price tag, then looping the string into another knot. Workers in a dress store attached the tags to the garments and wrote the price. Or the 10,000 hard candies the women wrapped in cellophane each day at the candy factory, day in and day out.

My mother created a kind of American fairy tale about herself. But in her own uncertainty, she created not one, but many identities. One of the many names my mother gave herself to become American was Maggie. I could tell when someone had met my mother and their relationship by how they addressed her: Peggie for early school friends, Maggie for those she met through work, Margie for her later friends, Margaret for her family, and in the neighborhood itself they referred to her as Mary Pickford because she looked like the silent film star. Nicknaming was common in our neighborhood: Fat Louise, Skags, Frank Ketchem-up. "Michelina Guerrieri," my mother used to say. "I wanted to die, to hide under my desk and never come out when the teacher called my name for the roll at school."

Once when I was five, right before Christmas, I was playing in the little park by St. Anthony's Church that my grandmother had taken me to. Impinging on the play space, an elevated crèche was filled not only with life-size statues of Jesus, Mary, and Joseph, but also half a dozen sheep and cows as well as the three Wise Men and their camels and a gang of angels and shepherds. We kids, nonetheless, raced around in the diminished space. While I caught my breath from one of the recent contests we had devised—whoever ran the length fastest from the farthermost cow on one end to the shepherd on the other won—the other children's father approached me and asked, "Are you Mary Pigfoot's daughter?" His handsome face, cocked to the side, smiled down at me.

"Yes," I answered, gulping for air. I knew my mother was known by some such name, though I knew nothing about the film actress.

"I've known your mother since she was your age," he added with a tinge of wistfulness.

Being known as Mary Pickford must have been the greatest fairy tale of all for my mother to live in. Mary Pickford, I later learned, was not just a movie star—that should have been enough to affirm my mother's being fully American—but was America's Sweetheart. Her every move was photographed and reported upon. Even after she divorced Douglas Fairbanks and married Buddy Rogers, that didn't displace her from the hearts of America.

My mother's resemblance to Mary Pickford went beyond the neighborhood. When we ate out on Sundays—we habitually frequented

Schmidt's Farm Restaurant somewhere in Westchester County, where my brother and I always ordered the turkey dinner—the waiter for that Sunday always asked if my mother was Mary Pickford. My father, afterward, would say to us kids, "Do I look like Buddy Rogers?" But he chuckled from this attention his wife had received.

My mother's sweet smile made you forget she was ambitious. Before she was married, she was the first Italian hired as a secretary by Reo Cars uptown. She spent her improved salary—she had worked in the candy factory on Eighth Street for two years while attending secretarial school at night—on watercolors at the annual art exhibit in Washington Square Park; a little fox stole, the kind that was all heads, beady eyes, and paws; tickets for the theater and musicals; and vacations when she rode horses.

As the light outside the kitchen waned, I continued to read Cellini's autobiography, now in a more desultory way. I looked up from my book when I heard my grandmother shut the front door. She had just returned from picking up a bottle of milk for tomorrow's breakfast at the dark, narrow store around the corner, run by a poor woman with elephantiasis, whom my grandmother patronized as often as possible, stopping to gossip in Italian. I watched as Nana removed the bottle from her dark cloth shopping bag. Before placing the bottle in the refrigerator, she shook it to mix the milk and the cream, clotted on the inside of the cardboard top.

Now in her straight-backed chair by the window, Nana fingered her rosary. She spent a lot of time praying at home or in St. Anthony's dark, lower church with its flickering candles in their red glass containers and six life-size statues on either side of the altar. Though my grandmother lived in America, she was, unlike my mother or me, untouched by it. I now realized that she could have just as easily been living in China, so little was she involved with America's larger rhythm: she lived in our Italian neighborhood, she spoke only Italian, she rarely exposed herself to anything but her Italian way of life.

Now she looked at neighbors returning from work or hurrying back from a last errand of the day. On the roof across the street, the man who trained pigeons to fly in formation locked them in their cages for the night. A sliver of moon rose above the bricks and cages and stars shone, luminous, in the darkening sky while the Swiss chard my mother was cooking in oil and garlic sputtered along with its fragrant vapors.

I stayed in the kitchen, thumbing through the Cellini autobiography, reading about his grandfather's saving Benvenuto, at age five, when he clutched a scorpion in his hand. And then the next time I read about his grandfather, it was for his funeral. I heard the steam hiss and watched it sneak out through the cover on the pot of potatoes.

How terrible, I thought, to lose someone you love so much. I slipped into the living room to look at my grandmother sitting quietly by the window and couldn't imagine life without her. I hoped this alien registration business would bring her no harm and that it would quickly become a story she would turn into a comedy as she often did with the little tragedies that beset her in America.

I checked on the potatoes, poking them with a fork. When my grandmother and I spent time together, there was quiet and calm. We made things and lived out who we were in the making. She and I often spent our time together with her showing me how to knit or how to fry *zeppoli*. Or I watched her drain the spaghetti, adding watered-down ricotta to it and sprinkling that with Romano cheese and black pepper for lunch. She prepared a little bowl for me, urging, *"Provala, provala"*—Try it, try it—pleased as I slurped up each silky strand. At dinner, I watched her ladle spirals of my favorite, *strindini,* whose curlicue shape delighted me, into my portion of chicken soup. Now as I stood by the kitchen door watching her, her black rosary beads clicked in a regular rhythm, soothing my soul; her Ave Marias whispered in our quiet house. Only my mother, her dark green apron tied loosely at the waist, chopping the Swiss chard in the kitchen, and my father turning the pages of the *World Telegram* broke the silence.

. . .

The next day was Saturday. As I dressed for my friend Martha's twelfth birthday party, I fretted about my grandmother's alien status. But Martha's party that afternoon on Washington Square North helped me forget about it for most of the day. Away from my mother, I knew who I was. When I returned home, my mother gave me another reason to fret, but it wasn't about my grandmother's alien status.

"So what was their brownstone like?" my mother asked.

Every time I went to one of my American friends' homes for the first time, I had to report back to my mother about what their apartment looked like, what condition the furniture was in, and what kind of a housekeeper my friend's mother was. Martha's living room was large and square with high ceilings and tall windows overlooking the park. Sparsely furnished, the space was dominated by a dusty baby grand piano. The piano bench and a few wooden chairs were the only other furniture to speak of.

My mother chortled in disbelief when I finished my report on Martha's home. "They didn't have any furniture in the room?" my mother continued. "And no rug? Just the bare wood floor? Was it polished at least?"

It gave my mother such joy to hear that most of my American friends' mothers were not as good housekeepers as she that I'd add colorful details about these women, to enhance my mother's gloating. She particularly loved hearing about Sheila's mother's unproductive attempts to keep their Tenth Street brownstone with its worn furniture clean against the onslaught of three rambunctious boys. The tired furniture and Sheila's mother in an unkempt housedress evened out the equation of my mother's being Italian. And thus she established herself at the head of her self-created hierarchy.

"No, it was sort of scratched up and dusty like the piano—well, not as much dust as the piano..." I trailed off. These offerings to my mother made me miserable with disloyalty to Martha and her family, whom I admired and who brought me into a world of art. We girls at the party—my classmates at St. Joseph Academy: Judy, Tonya, Sandra, Joan, and I—had a lot of fun. Her mother played the piano and we all stood around and sang songs and her father was so nice . . . he laughed a lot and joked with each one of us, making us feel special.

Martha's father was a modern artist. A few weeks before, Martha and I had been allowed to take the Fifth Avenue bus by ourselves uptown to the Museum of Natural History. As the red bus lumbered along the congested street, we talked about art. She told me, "Modern art represents something about the thing you're painting."

"What d'you mean? Give me an example."

"Well, say the artist puts in a lot of seashells like the ones we saw at the museum. It might mean he's feeling free like he's on vacation at the beach or maybe if he puts cat's eyes in a painting, he's saying something about the character of the person, like they're catlike in their walk or stealthy. Something like that."

"Hm-m, I see what you mean. Is that the kind of painting your father does?"

"Sort of."

All my American friends lived north of Washington Square Park. My one Italian friend lived, like me, south of the park, as most of the Italians did. The park acted a bit like a Mason-Dixon line, those north living and believing one thing, those south another. And there was some merit to each of them and some falseness and rigidity. The park sometimes acted as a bridge for me between these two worlds and sometimes as a moat that separated one part of me from the other.

I liked both ways of living and believing. At home I spoke Italian with my grandmother, played "Santa Lucia" on the piano, and read about Italian artists. With my friends' families, I sang "Turkey in the Straw," discussed art, made amateur movies with my father's eight-millimeter movie camera, and went to museums. From Martha's family

I learned about modern art, and I liked Tonya, who was creative in her writing like her father, a children's author. I marveled at the courage of Judy and her parents, who escaped from Nazi Germany, first fleeing to England, then gaining entry into America. They were people from a larger world than mine. I viewed my journey in America as one toward this larger world.

In my own small, intimate country there was the warmth of my relatives, and having my aunt and godmother and my married cousin nearby, and eating all our special foods, and having my grandmother live with us, and hearing her speak in Italian, and listening to opera, and having all the storekeepers know us by name. My mother's immaculate house, with her artwork on the walls, her Oriental rug in the living room, and her piano in its alcove, was central to her world, where we lived in the complicated certainties and confusions of her making.

She believed that a beautiful and clean house was the most important thing after feeding her family a balanced meal à la the Metropolitan Life Insurance Company recipes. These were things she had not experienced growing up. She was happily scandalized when I told her that Sandra's mother read while I played at her house in the One Fifth Avenue residential hotel where they lived and that she ordered a lunch—a creamed chicken dish with toast points—from the hotel for us girls at Sandra's birthday party.

Late afternoon of the following Saturday we started off on our weekly errands. As we left the store of Virginia, the owly eyed delicatessen owner with the silky falsetto voice that broke into trilling laughter, my mother told me about the *fattura,* the potion-maker from the Lower East Side who had clients in all the Italian neighborhoods, she was so good. I finished chewing the paper-thin slice of Genoa salami that Virginia had given me. My mother told me the *fattura* was able to put her son through law school on her earnings. This Italian world wasn't completely strange and alien to my mother! It was useful in bringing an American living to a *fattura's* son.

"Once," my mother said, "my cousin Mary in White Plains went to her. Mary's husband Frank was very sick. They were newlyweds. He was almost dying because the blood was constricting in his veins. Mary told the woman how worried she was about Frank . . . Mary thought the girl Frank jilted to marry her had put the evil eye on him. So the *fattura* gave her a potion to put in his coffee and told her not to worry . . . and that Frank loved her and he'd get better—and he did. That woman was very powerful."

I asked my mother if she really believed that the woman cured him.

"Oh yes," she assured me, "that woman was powerful—not like the ones today. Your grandmother isn't as powerful as she was. Nana can't set bones like that woman from the Lower East Side—"

"Is Nana going to register as an alien?" I interrupted, unable to keep quiet any longer about what was on my mind.

"Yes, it's the law," my mother sighed. Then she continued her train of thought, not lingering on this subject she found so filled with shame—*vergogna,* as my grandmother said, a word that sounded so much more like the feeling my mother held buried within her. I took some deep breaths, my chest expanding in short, quick bursts.

"The women of today," she continued, clearing her throat, "the *fatturas,* aren't as good as the old ones." She was as firm in this belief as she was that mashed potatoes every night were good for her family. My mother would stay in this world, nestled in her immigrant neighborhood, while I would eventually venture beyond the bookshelves in our living room.

If one part of my mother invented herself as an American, another part of her was still deeply attached to the ideas of my grandmother's world. Despite my mother's efforts to be American, the Italian-pagan ethos of my grandmother exerted an unconscious pull on her. My mother held firmly to certain beliefs: you should eat American food, keep a perfect house, educate your children. Your daughter should accompany you on your errands to learn how to do things.

We continued our shopping, stopping at Jimmy the Butcher's. When we entered, the sawdust on the white and black tiled floor hushed our footsteps. Each of the three Pacelli brothers, all with their thick black hair and black eyes, stood behind his own butcher block. They wore white aprons flecked with spots of blood. Each butcher had his own set of customers and, even if one of his brothers was very busy, the other brothers would never wait on a customer not their own. My mother used Jimmy.

"He was good to me during the war," she told me, which meant that he saved meat for her when shortages occurred. "Sometimes he even sold me meat when I didn't have any ration stamps left." The last statement hung in the air, the silence reverent with my mother's thanksgiving: she still frequented Jimmy's store despite the new Grand Union around the corner.

I angled my way in front of the customers who lounged on the chairs' wooden seats with curved-wire backrests while others stood, waiting their turn. I snaked past Palma with her black cloth shopping bag, frilly leaves of celery spilling over, to watch the gleaming knives speed across the fatty edging of lamb chops or slice across a flattened piece of calf's liver, dark as blood, soft and slippery as silk.

Jimmy, the shortest and oldest of the three brothers, pushed his head forward from his neck and hunched shoulders, like a turtle poking its head out of its shell. He recognized us with a quick nod and a slight upturn of his mouth, his piercing black eyes blinking nervously. After whacking bone and meat with his cleaver, he trimmed the pork chop. He swept the scraps of fat and bone off his block with one quick motion, wrapped the meat, grabbed a black crayon, and marked the price in large, careless numbers.

"Hello, Margie," Jimmy breathed, his eyes darting up from below his black eyebrows. He looked down quickly. "What can I get you today?"

"How are you, Jimmy? I'd like some braciola. A pound will do, half a pound of chuck steak, and a roast of beef—about three pounds."

On Sundays we ate Italian—mostly: my mother and grandmother prepared the sauce, rolled the braciola with garlic and parsley, formed the meatballs, fried the sausage, stuffed the artichokes, mixed the salad—and my mother cooked roast beef. But no mashed potatoes were made that day.

With smooth, elegant motions, Jimmy cut the beef into thin slices for the braciola. When he reached for the chuck, my mother added, "I'd like it ground, please." I watched as he put it in the meat grinder, the beef squeezing out in long pink strips dotted with bits of white, first coming straight out, then flopping over like so many useless puppets. Jimmy swiped at the holes when the grinder stopped extruding beef, gathered the strands into a ball, and laid it on the paper. Then he readied the roast.

"Thanks, Jimmy. That'll be all for today."

Dusk was falling quickly. We walked toward MacDougal Street and passed the pork store where, hanging in the window, fatty, short salamis glistened next to lean, long ones. The slightly vinegary odor of the cheese store wafted our way before we passed by, its round *scamorze,* hanging next to the *cacciocavallo,* caught up in a little knob of cheese on top. In its window, the coffee store displayed the map of Italy's boot, made out of the beans it sold freshly ground. The fruit and vegetable men moved silently, covering for the night their produce, which they displayed on sidewalk stands while the Raffettos locked the door of their ravioli store. Then came the barn where the police horses used to be boarded, the air there still pungent. We passed the poultry store, but didn't go in. The chickens, tight in their crates, were quiet now. The early evening air was cool. The fireflies drifted down from Washington Square to the thumbnail park on Sixth Avenue, their glow against the red brick buildings as intense as the stars on a clear night. The wind came up, licking the leaves, swirling the street debris and cloth scraps in ever faster and tighter circles, rattling the cellar door and the bakery's window until lightning flashed and rain swept across the store fronts. We ran to our door.

Upstairs my grandmother sat hunched over her knitting in her chair by the window. My father, having shed his suit jacket, relaxed in his blue velvet chair, which my family and I always vacated when he was home. Loosening his tie, he read about the Dodgers' chances next year—always next year—in the World Series. Cellini lay hushed in the bookcase, waiting to talk to me again from centuries past, the first of many books I would read down the years about Italy and the Italians.

The Names of Horses

. . . .
ANNIE RACHELE LANZILLOTTO

My father wants to give them all away. The men are coming over to take a look. One man will take two. The other men at least will take a look. There is no coffee in the house. My mother is leaning out the window reeling his clothes in just ahead of the rain. The clothesline squeals as she reels it. Sock by sock she unpinches and drops into the brown plastic basket on the kitchen table and the basket fills. I am feeding Blacky. He pushes the nipple of the baby bottle out with his tongue and looks for her with his mouth he looks, but days ago she slinked away, curled up in the light coming in through the screen door, curled up like days do and dust—beneath the radiator Penny lay down in that diamond cut-out of sun there patched on the floor. She had six pups two weeks ago. Every day since she's moved less and less. Now only parts of her move. Her tail for instance slithers out of the diamond onto the cool dark floor, and her fur—when the hall door is opened, her fur lifts with the wind, and her eyes—as I feed the puppies she is too weak to feed, her eyes follow my hand to their mouths, then fall away. With the day the sunlight stretches across the floor and she, toward the back of

. . . . .

ANNIE RACHELE LANZILLOTTO is a writer and performance artist of Barese heritage and a fellow of the Rockefeller Foundation's Next Generation Leadership Program.

the staircase. The stairs there lead nowhere, spiral up into the ceiling. My father had that way closed off years ago. I toss circles of meat at her, things she used to jump for. I touch salami to her tongue and it drops. I walk away. I come back. It still lies there. The sun has climbed the underside of the stairs.

My father wants to give them all away before they're named but each I've named already I've whispered their markings into their little twitching ears: Blacky, Spotty, Whitey, Rusty, Patches, Shep. Blacky's all black like his mother black with a white streak up the belly to the neck, and a white tip on the tail as if the tail had been dipped in paint. The others look like Bow. Bow is the shepherd dog outside the white house down the corner. They keep Bow on a chain they call a choker. Whenever anyone walks by, Bow shoots out as if the lengths of chain will never end but chains do, and Bow gets yanked back up into a twisted leap and chokes. That's why they call that chain a choker. I count on that chain for my life I count the years I count the links I count the rust, one day that chain is gonna break and Bow will fly right out over that little white wall two cinderblocks high and land dead in the middle of our street just as Greengrass in his white hot rod is burning rubber round the corner onto St. Raymond's from Zerega the way he does without looking. We live on a one-way street named after a saint. This is the Bronx. You learn your lessons early. Greengrass is the neighborhood boy to be feared and Bow is the dog on the block to be feared and Bow and Greengrass fear one another. Greengrass with his terrible motor and Bow with his ears swiveling just ahead of the roar.

If he wanted to keep them he would have named them all by now. He would have given them the names of horses like he nicknamed us, taken a binder down from one of his two shelves lining the kitchen-long wall, spread the racing forms out over the kitchen counter and let each paw drop onto a name. "You name what you keep. You keep what you name," he says sitting at the kitchen table, sturdy maple and oval, where he carves circles and arrows, numbers and underlines through his loose-leaf paper with pencils the size of his cigarette butts, resharpening the lead tips with a steak knife.

The houses are almost touching. The alleyways are thin and filled with argument. The backyards are crisscrossed with laundry from second and third story windows. My mother's clothesline is the grandest on the block, spanning our cement yard from her second story window out over my basketball court way out to the pipe my father rigged atop the roof of his garage. At night her clothesline swings empty in the moon wind until morning when it begins its daily rounds from window pulley to garage pulley, her world to his world all over again.

My father comes and goes at all hours. He is The Heatman, known as the only serviceman willing to go anywhere in the Bronx and Harlem at any hour whenever a boiler breaks and the people need heat. He keeps a cut-off lead pipe the size of a baseball bat under the driver's seat of his van. For service calls he carries the pipe in one hand and his toolbox in the other. I've heard stories of him using both. His hours are unpredictable. He can come back home at any time. I know when my father is home by the opening screech of the gate. The front gate he kicks in the wire gut like a dog. His entrance is recorded in a scar whitening the cement by each entering sweep of the gate. The screech of the gate is louder than the squeal of her clothesline. A simple cry of friction sending squirrels into trapeze feats leaving branches in their wake. The puppies all huddle in their box. An arc scratched for good in the sidewalk.

He pulls his van up the lip of the driveway and throws it in park just beneath her window, "CAW-FEE!" This time she ignores him. This time there is none, and she knows he knows there is no more. This morning he wouldn't give her a nickel, "No, not fi-cents," he'd said on his way out to work, afraid she'd go to Frank-n-Joe's, where Frank or Joe or even Li'l Joey might squeeze her hand as she slid the five pound bag over the counter to be ground, and slip her a thin slice of salami to tuck inside her cheek to chew on the walk home. "It don't make sense," my father had said, "if they went giving salami out to everybody they'd be broke in no time."

"CAW-FEE!" he yells up at her window, almost singing. This is his salutation to her. Coffee is the main currency between them. She yanks the rope. The sun and rain come down together. She yanks the rope. The puppies huddle in their box. She yanks the rope and the basket fills. There is no coffee in the house. His shorts by the crotch she rips off the line. "CAW-FEE!" She yanks the rope. She yanks the rope. The knot catches the groove of the pulley at the far end over his garage. She pushes the rope out the other way. She yanks the sun. His shirts come down together. She yanks the rain. The green shoulders clamped to the line march in the air, their arms swinging, falling, swinging toward her, elbows bending. And the basket fills. "CAW-FEE!"

"You know there ain't none," she yanks, "there's no milk, there's no sugar. If you want, give me money. I'll go to Frank-n-Joe's. You know that." The garage door he hoists up like a great white sail. Black gaping holes, the clean-cut lips of so many copper pipes stacked into pyramids stare out of the garage, taking aim at him from head to foot.

"Hey You!" he shoots up at her.

"I have a name!" the words spit out of her defiantly down at him. His worker Willie-boy is with him. Somehow this protects her. "I have a name!" she says again. And I hear a trumpet call.

"Hey Meatball!" he calls up at her, laughing out his mouth.

"I have a name!" Her words hang in the air, damp, with pinched corners. The drums are not far off now, and the men lifting their knees in unison. Although I've never seen my Daddy marching, I have seen the men he has killed in his eyes. He looks at them sometimes as if those men are standing behind my eyes. They hide in the shadows in the creases in the gray matter in my father's brain. They come out when he tells me lullabies about a white horse on a mountain then the mountains turn to hills and he drifts off into silence and then there are explosions out the roots of trees. I avoid going to bed at all costs. Sometimes

I awaken to him standing at my mother ready to strike. I stay up as late as I can every night. My father and I play poker with circular chips he cut carefully with giant silver scissors from the labels of Gold Medal quart milk cartons. We play until eleven o'clock, then we watch the evening news and I fall asleep, but I get up again at one-thirty and we watch "Alfred Hitchcock Presents" and "The Twilight Zone" and the tension in my body is matched by these stories. In one episode a prop-plane with red markings on its wings crash-lands into a house, ripping in through the living room walls and landing next to the couch; the woman living there has a past connection with the pilot, he's been lost since the war, and she's been waiting. This is the episode I want to re-play night after night: the lost soldier who crashes into the living room, bringing his war right to the couch. I see my father as a young marine my father is circling overhead my father can demolish the plasterboard that surrounds our rooms at any moment now. As I sit facing the tele-vision set I run my fingers in the patterned terrain of our sea blue liv-ing room rug, I see my father in Okinawa and Guadalcanal in that sea blue. The walls can split any time now.

Willie-boy stands half in the garage and half out, the rain darkening his shirt in spots. "Hiya Mrs. Lancilotta," he calls up, taking care with each soft sound.

And before he can even finish, she says, "Willie! Call me anything but that!"

"Okay Miss Ray," he says, widening his eyes and wrapping his lips around his teeth to hold back from smiling.

My father is walking around the back into the house. There are two gates and three doors my father has to pass through to get into my mother's kitchen, our fort. The first door is a screen door, never locked. The second door leads into a small foyer where Penny lies. The third door has a diamond-shaped window through which we can see his head a split second before he plows into the kitchen, uproots the *Daily News* out of his back pocket, and tosses it at the table. Then he begins to shed.

One boot scores the heat pipe, the other the wall. My mother scratches her head, concentrating on where things land so she can find them later when he says he doesn't know where anything is, and where'd she hide them. He tracks to the bathroom in damp socks, pressing water out each step. I follow him close behind. I watch his every maneuver. I'm careful not to get in his way. Everyone is in place: the puppies in their box, Mommy at the kitchen sink, Daddy at the bathroom sink, Penny in her shadow. He leaves the bathroom door open. I watch. He dunks two fingers in the can of grease solvent. His hands chew it, blackening the sink. Handcupfuls of hot water splash his face, head, up his nose, neck, ears, gargling like a drowning gorilla all over the mirror and walls. The black never comes all off. Knuckle skin, palms and underneath his nails are black etched with oil stains built up over twenty-three years. Indelible. There are roadways in my Daddy's hands. A whole map. He points to the markings and tells me he knows The Bronx like the palm of his hand. "Never get that grease off," he says, "they don't make a soap that can take the grease outta these here hands. This is the history of New York. We built this city, each brick, each ice, each coal, every frame of sidewalk."

Twenty-three years is how long he's been in the business and the marriage and that's how long the war's been over. "We fought for peace. There's been no peace since," he reminds us, singing war-era tunes: "You made me love you. I didn't want to do it. I didn't want to do it." He aims this song at my mother but it feels aimed at me too, for without her there'd be no me. He laughs as he sings. When he sings, it is a refusal to talk, he sings loud and ignores the rest of us. He towels his whole head furiously and finger combs his hair through with Vaseline hair tonic, getting wet at the crotch from leaning against the sink. He walks back into the kitchen with the big white towel around his neck like a muscular peasant shouldering a dead lamb. He taps a new pack of Lucky Strikes on his wrist twice fast, rip-cords the red cellophane band with his teeth, spits it out onto the floor and pulls a cigarette out with his teeth. My mother's eyes follow the red cellophane band as it floats to the floor.

"I get any calls!" There is little question in my father's voice.

"No, I don't think so." There is a tentativeness in my mother's tone of voice. This provokes him.

"What do you mean you don't think so! It's yes or it's no!"

"What am I, your secretary?"

My father laughs. That's not a good sign. It means he's running out of words.

Willie-boy comes in, and stands in the doorframe, half in the kitchen, half out, ducking a little to fit under it. His hands are in his pockets. My father jokes that it's a habit from years of Willie thieving. My father walks past Penny and steps down to the basement ducking his head as the stairs spiral down.

Willie asked my mother if she'd save some more of his earnings each week so as to be sure he wouldn't gamble it away.

"I'll tell you what, Willie," my mother says, "I'll bless your money." She takes his dollars to her Bible. She layers the bills in between the pages of the big colorful pictures of Moses walking through the Red Sea bed. "Now your money's blessed," she says to him discreetly and with conviction, "now it has to go to your wife and kids."

Willie nods, "That's just where it's going Miss Ray, that's just where it's going."

My father stomps back up the stairs. The phone rings. I run to it, climbing on the stepstool to reach it. The voice asks for Joe. I cover the mouthpiece as he has trained me to do since the business is run out of her kitchen, and I whisper-shout, "Daddy, are you home?" The voice on the phone laughs. My father takes the phone, exhaling a gruff laugh.

"Sure," he says into the phone, "right six," he says, "come on over for coffee. Right. I'm here. Right. Sure bring hoodycall." He hangs up and takes a sandwich of folded money out of his front pocket. He opens up a soggy twenty, and hands it out toward Willy, the bill's edge woven around his thick middle finger. This bill he doesn't fold into a tight little square hidden in his palm the way he hands me money, no, all flat open and showy like the American flag they just stuck into the moon. "Ga' head, Shine, go on down the corner and bring back five cups of coffee and buy yourself an egg cream."

I always thought Shine was the most beautiful last name you could have in the whole world, and of all people, I was glad Willie had it. His bright flat open hand and long fingers received the green bill and crawled back into its post in his front pocket and his smile broke loose on him. He had a smile on him Willie-boy did. He tried to contain it, pulled the corners of his mouth down, bit at his bottom lip, but once out, his smile was like an ice-cream sandwich stuck in his dark head. I loved Willie. He bought me presents when I was sick. When I was bedridden with mono, he brought me a hand puppet with one character from *The Wizard of Oz* on each finger, Dorothy holding Toto, Tin Man, Scarecrow, Lion, and the Wicked Witch. When Penny was nowhere to be found last week, it was Willie who said, "They go somewhere they never been before, somewhere special when they're ready to give birth," and true enough my mother found Penny in her bedroom up on the blue chair that folded out into the bed where I sleep. Penny wasn't allowed there, and my mother chased her away. She went back to her dark cave hallway off the kitchen. Her whole body started bucking as each puppy covered in slimy juice shot out of her. Penny licked each one of them clean as they fumbled around blindly sucking the air as if swimming to find the surface: six puppies one slimy mass changing shape as they jockeyed into position each on a teat. When she had no more life to give suck to, she bit at their necks to pull their mouths from her. Willie brought in an empty cardboard box from the garage and settled the puppies underneath the kitchen window. The puppies' collective mission became to climb over one another to stretch for the top of the box, to try to get back to their mother. She retreated to join her shadow on the floor next to the radiator.

Willie takes the twenty and walks out the back door and ducks through a hole in the fence to go get the men coffees. My mother bends down to pick my father's clothes up off the floor. She tosses them down the basement steps like unwanted fish back to sea. She takes the brown basket full of dry clean clothes and tosses it down the basement steps. He walks out whistling the same tune he was singing. My father's whistling has a whole dictionary of meanings. This particular whistle means my mother doesn't exist and should stay out of his way. He bunks into her as he exits, as if she's a piece of furniture he has to walk around. She leans against the great white refrigerator and slides to the floor covering her eyes with her hands. I pull at her arm to get up. She walks directly to his shelves as if something is guiding her. His shelves are the only place in the kitchen that's off limits to the rest of us. His shelves of binders. She grabs at the binders and one falls open to the floor. His binders are full of horse racing statistics. His system. His hours and hours of thoughts and strategies. His gambling with our lives. His "one day my horse is gonna come in" promises. Hours of his hand-written notes and scrawls surround the names of horses. Some of the names are crossed out. Other names are heavily underlined. There are words written thick in the margins, like SCRATCHED. JOCKEY CHANGE. SLOPPY AT THE START. She grabs at them, her hands do the thinking, her hands grab a bundle of a hundred tickets held to-gether by a rubber band. I know it's a hundred. I help count them at night. Money. It is all money spent, she thinks as she grabs a fistful of pages. She goes to her window. She does what she knows how to do. She grabs the wooden clothespins. She snaps a page onto the clothesline. She pushes the rope. She rips more and more pages, clothes-pinning them to the rope, pushing them out over the yard into the soft rain.

"Here," she shouts, "here's where all the money goes. This is what he does. This is where he disappears. This is where he goes. This is where all the money goes." She pushes the rope. My father looks up at her and laughs. Then all the men there laugh. She shouts the names of horses down onto them, as she pushes his pages out over their heads, "LOST BOY, BREAKINMYCHANCES, MOONRISE. How much did that one pay?" She pushes the rope. "SURVIVOR'S GLORY, THER-MOMETERRISING. Here's the milk." She pushes the rope. The sun and rain come down together. "NOTMYPROBLEM, BONE ALONE. Here's the sugar. MERCURYSSON, EMBRACEABLE. DOCTOR'S ORDER, CALLITMADNESS, SORRYLOU, ITHADTOBEYOU, Here's all the coffee you want!!! Hey you! Here! You want coffee!" She grabs a pack of ticket stubs and flings them out all over the men standing in the yard. The stubs flutter and whirl down onto the wet cement. There is a different color for each race each day of the week. Stubs from Belmont. Stubs from Aqueduct. My father has years of stubs. My father always says never throw away a racing stub.

He looks up at her, "That's some stunt, Lilly," he murmurs under his breath. "Snake. Cow. Bitch." He laughs. Then all the men there laugh. And the troops seem not far behind.

I hear Blacky yelping. I tilt the box. I reach down through all that softness. Blacky is nowhere in the box. I follow the sound. I race to the hall. Blacky is in Penny's mouth. The radiator is silent where she lies. Penny is pressing Blacky's head against the iron bars. I clap at her till she drops him.

She closes and latches her window then the shutters, then slides down the wall to her shadow on the floor. She swallows her tears in the back of her head as if the tears do not exist if they do not exist, but mountains from ground shells and time. I lift Blacky to her neck and he licks. She passes her eyes over Penny's wilted belly then her hand. She calls our family physician, Dr. Riciardi. While she's on the phone with him, her hand passes over Penny's belly and stops quietly over one spot listening like a hand reading a Braille, she bows her head. "I'll be damned," she says into the phone, "there must be a seventh still in there." She instructs me to run down the corner to the drug store on Zerega and St. Raymond's to buy "CN," the disinfectant. "Go now," she instructs, "and get the money off your father." She pushes my birth name out of her mouth, the one short syllable she was forced to don on me in honor of his mother, the one short syllable to compensate for the long last name. "Ann." A. N. N. I filled into tiny boxes letter by careful letter on school exams. I wished she said, "Annie." When she says Ann I get worried. She sounds distant, formal. She never wanted to name me that, but it was his choice. His mother.

I kneel by Penny and shout, "Open your eyes!" but if salami didn't move her, I thought, forget about it, words ain't gonna do what salami can't.

I run out the back door, down the steps, up the alleyway to the back of the house where the alleys open up into backyards back to back two by two up and down the whole block in a row, separated only by a wire fence gut high that the neighbors talk across at the corners where four backyards touch beneath the fencing; where you can see that they really all are one, although each has been painted a different color that provides distinction all along the edges; where the trees hang fruit over the property lines and in September drop them; where in one corner Penny and Gigi and Lucky Two Balls nose each other where their tails join their bodies, and in the other corner Penny and Cocoa the giant poodle would.

I run down the block past Bow. Bow runs out at me and gets twisted up in the air and chokes. He barks through his choking like he's underwater. At night Bow is kept in his backyard off the chain. Seven fences away from Penny, seven fences he jumped to get to her. "He raped her twice," my mother says, "in the puppies you can see his markings clearly."

I don't need money, the guy down the corner store knows who my father is. I pull the murky brown bottle with the red letters CN off the shelf and the clerk nods at me and tries to hand me a paper bag, but I have the bottle by its neck and am out the door running back up the block, past Bow still barking. My father is carrying a big black piece of wood out of the house wrapped in my mother's new plaid comforter inside my blue plastic rowboat. Black wood like a cut-out of Penny. I shout her name. Her pink wood tongue is out the side of her white wood mouth. My father says, "Maybe one we can keep," and the back doors of the green work van slam shut.

It was the presence of this already dead one inside her that made Penny die. That was my understanding of it. She fed her puppies till she died. Then we took over with baby bottles. Five times a day we fed the puppies Similac. A whole box of puppies soft as dandelion flowers. I'd push my nose into the fur of each of them and just breathe there. They smelled safe to me. Blacky we kept. I'd bury my nose in Blacky's fur. I sat on the kitchen floor and pushed the nipple of the baby bottle in his mouth and let him suck. He smelled safe to me.

My Mom sprinkled the CN ritualistically everywhere Penny had lain, as if a magnificent power was present in that one bottle of liquid, as if she was blessing the dog's presence, and releasing her at the same time.

Behind the tomato rows we found six holes dug deep like for planting. Six holes Penny had dug to bury her just born. Penny knew she couldn't take care of them, she knew she was dying. My mother strung the tomato stalks up into the light with leftover yellow wool tied to sticks. We watched the globes turn green for weeks and grow to orange pink rose then red then red then red red red.

It is the smell of CN now not of death that I remember. CN was sweet. Awful. Sweet.

Dagos in Mayberry

· · · · · · · ·

PETER SELGIN

> *Columbus discovered no isle or key so lonely as himself.*
> —ANONYMOUS

One rainy evening not long ago in New York City I attended a reading and panel discussion featuring Italian American authors. I went because I'm a writer, and also because—though it's not something I'd given much thought to—I am what some people call Italian American. And though I enjoyed the readings, the discussion afterwards disturbed me. At some point in their lives all of the panelists had felt discriminated against as a direct result of their Italian background. As they told stories of jobs denied and promotions withheld I listened with a mixture of unease and outrage, but also with bewilderment. It had never occurred to me that I belonged to a persecuted minority.

In the small Connecticut town where my twin brother, George, and I

· · · · ·

PETER SELGIN's work has appeared in *Glimmer Train, Missouri Review*, the *Literary Review, Bellevue Literary Review*, the *Sun, Northwest Review, North Dakota Quarterly, Rattapallax, Salon.com*, the *Chicago Sun-Times*, and *Newsday*. His novel, *Life Goes to the Movies*, was a finalist for the James Jones First Novel Fellowship, and his story collection, *Bodies of Water*, was short listed for the Iowa Fiction Award. He lives in New York City.

grew up, we were called all the usual names and treated to the customary crude jokes (Q: Why is Italy shaped like a boot? A: Because they couldn't fit all that shit in a sneaker). But to me those jokes weren't acts of ethnic discrimination, but part of being a boy among boys, which is to say *persecuted.* Had our ethnicity not furnished them with a handy means for doing so, our peers would have found other ways to torment us.

This, at least, was how I had always looked at things. Now, though, sitting at that symposium listening to those speakers, I started to wonder if maybe all my life I had been naive—or worse, in denial. As the stories of prejudice mounted I grew so uncomfortable I finally grabbed my umbrella and stormed out into the pouring rain.

It had been raining all day. As I lurched into the dark, drenched street my anger toward the four panelists rose to a fever pitch in my blood. The absurdity! The paranoia! The entrenched, perverse solidarity! They reminded me of a support group I once attended for people with inflammatory bowel diseases (in my thirties I suffered from ulcerative colitis). As the veterans introduced themselves and elucidated their ailments I couldn't help noticing the relish with which they inventoried their symptoms and their surgeries, displaying them like medals, dropping names of doctors and procedures as if they were celebrities in a gossip column. This was no support group, I remember thinking; this is a fan club. I never went back.

As I splashed my way to the subway I concluded that all these Italian Americans crying discrimination would likewise never be "cured" of what ailed them. They were too obsessed with it, intoxicated by their illness.

I realize now that this was an unfair assessment. But I was angry. The panelists had upset what had until then been at a kind of equilibrium, like a smoldering but benign volcano. Worse, they made me feel as if I'd had a disease all my life without knowing it. At forty, suddenly I was being forced to confront my ethnicity, something I'd never really confronted before. As I stood dripping wet on the subway platform I wondered,

What has being an Italian American meant to me? Has it been a source of pain, or pleasure? Has it helped me, or hurt me? Or hasn't it mattered?

The small Connecticut town my twin and I grew up in was called Bethel. Think of Mayberry, RFD, television's version of Anytown, U.S.A. There was a brick town hall with an ice-cold water fountain and, next door, a greasy spoon named the Doughboy, after the lichen-colored statue on the town green. There were two barber shops, Patsy's and Chris's, each with a revolving candy-striped pole. At Mulhaney's variety store for a dime you could buy a fudgesicle or creamsicle from the freezer case, which opened to exhale a cloud of frost in your face. Add the dreary ruins of a half-dozen abandoned hat factories, their cold brick smokestacks upthrust into the low New England sky, and voilà: my hometown.

When my parents moved to Bethel in 1957, Bethel had a population of just under 8,000. Though some residents commuted to New York City—two hours away by train—most worked in the local factories and stores. My father was an exception. He was an inventor, his laboratory a crumbling stucco shack at the bottom of our driveway, which rose up a steep incline after passing under the swaying manes of six huge willow trees. Everyone in my family called it The Building, as if it were the only standing structure in the world, let alone in Bethel, Connecticut.

I loved to visit my father there. After school I'd jump off the bus, charge under the willow trees, and knock timidly on his door. I'd find Papa working in a cloud of dust at his typewriter, or at the drafting table, or wiring a circuit, smoke from his soldering gun rising in arabesques up into the blinking fluorescent lights. If especially lucky I'd find him behind the lathe, the metal-darkened fingers of one hand curved over the smoothness of the spinning chuck, his other hand manipulating an array of dials and levers, like the engineer of a locomotive, guiding the bit that sliced through metal, spewing out steamy turnings—"curlicues" George and I called them—of aluminum, copper, and brass.

This was my father whom I would not have traded for all the fathers in the world. Though he was born in Milan, you would never have guessed it, since he spoke better English than Walter Cronkite, albeit with a faintly British accent—mid-Atlantic, someone once called it, conjuring an island-sized nation halfway between Europe and here, with its own flag and customs. Its chief export commodity: eccentric fathers.

My father's was no ordinary immigrant's trajectory. He first came to the States at the height of the Great Depression, in the mid-thirties, when he was twenty-two, having spent many youthful summers in England, where he embraced that country's culture and language. He earned his Ph.D. in engineering at Harvard, then took a job with what was then the Bureau of Standards in Washington, D.C. On a trip to Italy he met my future mother. A flurry of romantic letters across the Atlantic led to their engagement and to a provincial Italian girl's brave migration to a new world with all its uncertainties.

My parents struggled. Though my father's secure government post could easily have led to a cushy job with Westinghouse, Sylvania, or IBM, instead he quit to go it alone as an inventor, freelance. With our pregnant mother he set out in search of a house within traveling distance of New York, one with an outlying structure my father could convert to a laboratory. Less than a year later, with my brother and me just a few months old, they relocated to Bethel. To my knowledge they were the first Italian immigrants ever to have done so.

I've painted a picture of the town. Now I'll paint one of my parents. Another '60s TV show comes to mind. In *Green Acres,* a white-haired Eddie Albert played a patrician and pompous corporate executive turned gentleman farmer, with Hungarian actress Eva Gabor as his thick-accented, dimwitted, Park Avenue-via-Budapest wife.

My father was no gentleman farmer, but technically he did work on a farm. In its previous incarnation The Building had been a black market farm, selling poultry, eggs, butter, and other contraband items rationed during World War II. And no, Mom wasn't Hungarian, or dimwitted, but her northern Italian good looks were every bit as stunning as Eva Gabor's, and her accent was as thick and pungent as the Genoa salamis Papa brought home from Manganaro's Italian import store on Eighth Avenue.

And like Eva Gabor, Mom was a fountain of glamour and flirtation. She smiled for the paparazzi in her head, and seeded just about every male who'd venture into the bridal boutique where she worked with a heart-throbbing crush. She married my father because (she claimed) he looked like Charles Boyer. But her Charles Boyer turned out to be something of a slob, a man who wore the same ratty sweater and stained pants day in and out, with his zipper yawning half the time. Papa was as oblivious of appearances as my mother was concerned with them. Mentally she still lived in the land of *bruta figura,* where appearances were, if not everything, close to it. She and my father were oil and water. He was pedantic, rational; Mom was dramatic, emotive. Mom was all instinct and innuendo, Papa all logic and intellect. That he was fifteen years older and twice divorced only added to the disparity. Occasionally, in the midst of one of their perpetual clashes, George and I would turn each other and mouth the words "Green Acres."

In a town like Bethel it didn't take much to stand out. That our parents were foreigners helped, but that was just one of their eccentricities. As I've said, our mother was ravishing, a combination Sophia Loren and Anna Magnani, with Magnani's long nose and burning eyes and Loren's sculpted Egyptian lips. She was far and away the most exotic and alluring woman in the town, which might have been cause for envy and the malice that usually goes with it, had her foreignness not exempted her from the grind of Bethel's vicious rumor mill. Thanks to that accent Mom could get away with almost anything, including being glamorous in a town where glamour was as alien as a bottle of *Strega* or an Alfa Romeo. Both sexes were drawn equally to her. UPS drivers spun off their routes to drop by and visit her. Like sharks smelling blood my schoolmates circled her, gathering round the black Chambers stove in her kitchen where, while stirring up a batch of *Bolognese,* she'd regale them with tales of Tripoli, Libya, where she was born, and where she'd zoomed around town on the back of her crazy brother's *Lambretta,* and plucked ripe figs and dates off palm trees, and had a pet monkey.

And though in many ways her opposite, still, my father was no less attractive to my pals. Sometimes he'd hire them to work with me in his laboratory. We'd sit side by side at a bench in The Building, me and one of the neighborhood kids, sorting nuts and screws from a big cardboard box. In the background my father's radio played—static, mainly. Smells of orange rind, solder smoke, and flatulence perfumed the dusty air. Every so often my father would let fly a dithering curse or a thunderous fart. My friends got a huge kick out of Papa's farts and curses, his explosive *fucks* and *dammits* and *shits,* his trumpet-herald flatus; their faces would turn red as they'd tear with laughter. They loved Papa's gadgets too, his Color Coders and his Mercury Switches, his Rotorless Motors and Thickness Gauges. They couldn't get over the fact that he was an inventor, like Thomas Edison. Like Henry Ford. Like Leonardo da Vinci.

Until I was twelve, being the son of Italians was all *sugo* (gravy). I assumed that all of these fine eccentricities were part and parcel of my parents' being Italian. I pitied the other kids, who had nothing to compare. Their fathers wore dull suits and worked dull factory and office jobs. Their moms cooked ravioli from cans with bloated winking chefs on the labels. They failed to grasp that *real* Italian dressing came out of two bottles, one called oil (olive) and another called vinegar (red wine), and not from a single pear-shaped bottle labeled *Kraft* or *Wishbone.* While we were weaned on watered-down *vino rosso* they drink Kool Aid and cow's milk with dinner, which they called "supper" and which they ate at an absurdly early hour—six o'clock—and which featured such ghastly items as raw cucumbers and radishes (for not having to eat radishes alone I'd have cherished my Italian upbringing).

When it came to food, I counted myself blessed. It tugged at my heart to see my friends' mothers turning can openers on tins of Dinty Moore stew or Campbell's Cream of Cheddar Cheese soup: supper. Not that my brother and I minded that sort of fare; in fact we welcomed the rare diversion of hot dogs and baked beans or corned beef (though at bean casseroles I drew the line). Still, my friends had to eat this crap *regularly*, except, that is, when they'd come to my house for dinner, in which case they would be treated to mom's spinach lasagna drooping with mozzarella and/or drowning in béchamel sauce, chicken *cacciatore* or *risotto ala Milanese*, thin-pounded cutlets of veal coated with flour and fried lightly in olive oil, sprinkled with parsley and served with sunny yellow lemon wedges. For dessert: a *crostata marmalata* (jam pie), ornamented with a filigree of sweet buttery crust, and mom's glorious *tiramisu*, or—better still—her *zabaglione*, soaked with enough *marsala* to intoxicate an army, as if Mom's looks weren't intoxicating enough.

But the most intoxicating part of dinner was the conversation, if you could call it that: the endless jokes, puns, insults, and arguments that flew around the dining room table, with no one spared. Guests had a choice: they could join the melee or sit there and take it.

For the Rowlands, the parents of my best friend Chris, it was too much. While at their dinner table the closest thing to a conversation was "pass the butter," at ours "Shut up!" and "Fuck you!" made as many crossings as the *Queens Mary* and *Elizabeth*. One advantage of having an Italian mother: we could swear to our hearts' content, provided we did so in English. Our father, who loved to shock the puritanical and faint-hearted, would tell terrible jokes, off-color ones usually, the more embarrassing the better. Once, having delivered himself of a real stinker, my brother and I simultaneously burst out with a loud, "Pig!" Dinner over, the scandalized Rowlands cornered our mother in the kitchen and said to her, "How can you let your children speak that way—to their own *father!*" To which she replied that we *always* called our father "pig," that it was a term of endearment, that each of us had his or her animal moniker: George, who loved the water, was "fish," I, with eyes too big for my skull, was "tarsier," Mom (for no apparent reason) was "monkey," while Papa, less opaquely, was "pig." This explanation didn't satisfy the Rowlands, who never accepted another dinner invitation from us.

Was the Selgins' outrageous dinner banter likewise a product of Italy? Was my father's tasteless ribald humor as much the fruit of his nationality as our mother's good looks and succulent cooking? If so, all the more reason to embrace my origins.

But there were other reasons, like growing up in a house filled with books and paintings, mostly my father's. Like his hero, Winston Churchill, my father was a Sunday painter, and a good one, too. His oils covered the walls of our house. Those surfaces not covered with paintings were taken up by bookcases sagging under the weight of volumes in English, French, German, Italian—all the languages my polymath father spoke. And though I had barely cracked a book in English, just having all of those books around me filled me with a sense of sophistication. It was like growing up in a library, or a museum. By comparison my friends' homes—and by extension their lives—seemed empty. True, Lenny's WWII veteran dad had painted his bedroom ceiling with tromp l'oeil cloudy skies and dangled model Mustangs, Spitfires, and Messerschmitts in a permanent miniature dogfight. And though this had its charms, still, it lacked the snob appeal of growing up among paintings and books.

And already by age ten or so I'd become something of a snob. Of course I didn't see it that way. But I did believe that the Selgin family had something special, something those other all-American families in Bethel lacked. It wasn't just that my parents were from Italy, that small, boot-shaped country across the ocean. It was something broader, deeper, something with implications greater than the curly hair on my head, the color of my eyes, the food I ate. Somehow, by virtue of who we were, the world's boundaries and horizons were stretched wider. Our house on the hill was a little closer than other houses not only to that other country across the sea, but to the rest of the world.

Already, though, the other side to having Italian parents—the side that wasn't all bookshelves and béchamel sauce—had begun asserting itself. For every eccentricity that filled me with pride and delight, another caused me embarrassment and suffering.

Take my father's bicycle, his rusting Raleigh three-speed. Every day of his life, winter and summer, until he was well into his eighties, Papa pedaled that Raleigh to the post office and back. I can still see him now, in work-stained shorts and black kneesocks, his calf muscles as big and boxy as toasters. Sometimes he'd wear his beret, a black one speckled with multicolored lint. Often the school bus would pass him by along his route, with me and George on board, and then all the bus windows would fly open and a dozen heads would pop out shouting, "Hey, there, Mr. Magoo!" Our father would smile day-dreamily and keep pedaling. As for me, I would witness none of this display; I'd be too busy cowering in my seat, waiting for the humiliation to pass. What self-respecting dad rode a bicycle, let alone in black kneesocks?

Just as humiliating were those trips to the swimming hole, the muddy one under the railroad trestle behind an abandoned hat factory where Bethel dads brought their kids to fish and swim. Unlike all the other dads in town, ours refused to jump into the water. Instead he would wade in ever so slowly, inch by embarrassing inch, rubbing palmfuls of brown water over his pale sagging shoulders and sunken chest, wincing and making faces like he was being tortured. Having already jumped in ourselves my brother and I would shout, "Jump, Papa, jump!" To which my father would reply, "I'm sorry, but I can't; *I'm too old.*" I equated the word *old* with Italian, and wished my father were American. If he'd been American he would jump—like Burt Lancaster in *From Here to Eternity.*

Papa wouldn't throw a baseball, or a football, or any kind of ball, or a Frisbee. He "loathed" (his word) athletics. He wouldn't watch us play baseball, never mind take us to a game, which may explain why my brother and I were so lousy at sports, and at defending ourselves, too. On a monthly basis we'd get our noses bloodied. Bobby Mullin, who went to St. Mary's, punched our clocks regularly for being atheists, another eccentricity we picked up from our father.

Still, though I had begun to see the drawbacks of being an immigrant son, I never saw myself as the victim of prejudice. If I didn't fit in it was my own damned fault for having the wrong parents, or being born in the wrong country, or both. Rather than blame the neighborhood kids who taunted and teased and bloodied me—the same kids I once pitied—I started to envy them. I envied their fair straight hair and pale, squinty eyes; their skill with a baseball bat or a hockey stick; their ability to throw a pass and dribble a basketball. I envied the ease with which they blew bubbles with their gum, and whistled through their fingers, and spat between their teeth. I longed to be truly one of them—as I'd begun to see that I was not. I wanted to score their goals, hit their home runs, shoot their hoops. I longed to be a *true* American, to cut off my European roots and replant myself in fresh, loamy New England soil, to trade my mother's drunken *zabaglione* for a thick, hearty slice of all-American apple pie.

Paradoxically my supremely egocentric and unpatriotic Papa had long since disowned his own country. Having left Italy in his twenties, he never looked back; he left behind everything connected to his homeland: his language, his religion, his accent, even his name, which he changed from Senigaglia to Selgin, one of his less successful inventions, its supposed virtues being lack of obvious ethnicity and ease of pronunciation (in fact almost everyone gets it wrong; the "g" is supposed to be soft).

"You are the only Selgins in the world," our mother often reminded us. I found it hard to believe. How could there be no other Selgins? It was as hard as believing that in our huge stamp collection—two albums and an overflowing shoebox—there was not at least one one-cent magenta British Guiana stamp worth sixty thousand dollars. On my first solo trip to New York City, when I was sixteen, at the enormous library with the giant lions, I sifted through three dozen fat phone directories, intent on disproving my mother. There was indeed one other Selgin in the world, living in some dusty ghost town in New Mexico, first name Margaret. One of my father's two former wives.

Among the few things my father didn't leave behind in Italy was his mother. She lived with us in our house, in her own "apartment" on the ground floor. To me she was simply "Nonnie." Though she supposedly spoke ten languages, English was not one of them. Visiting her, I would be forced to speak Italian. As an incentive she would feed me a bowl of her delicious "homemade" rice pudding, served with a tantalizing swirl of raspberry syrup and a maraschino cherry on top. In time I would discover that the rice pudding came from a can. Still, it was delicious.

Nonnie's apartment was its own cramped museum filled with trinkets and doilies and Japanese fans, smelling of mothballs, lilac perfume, and fried foods. She would recite to us from an ancient leather-bound volume of Dante, its pages foxed and gilded, or from the *Aeneid,* the syllables falling from her papery lips along with the dust from its pages. She taught me the legend of Romulus and Remus, the twins who, suckled by a she-wolf, went on to build the City of the Seven Hills. On her windowsill Nonnie kept a miniature bronze of the famous Etruscan statue. She would point to the tiny twins under it one by one and say, *"Questo e Giorgio, e questo e Pierino"* (This is George, and this is Peter). It tickled me to think that in a past life my brother and I had founded Rome.

Until we finally crossed the ocean to see the real thing, our grandmother's dusty apartment was as close as I had come to Italy. As far as I know, my brother and I were the first ten-year-olds from Bethel ever to set foot in Europe. My mother being afraid of planes, we were forced—*forced!*—to travel by ocean liner. Before docking in Naples, the *Queen*

Anna Maria pulled into Lisbon, Portugal, where—my mother having worked her considerable charms—we were granted an audience with Italy's deposed king. From Naples we rode a fast train to Rome, and a faster one to Milan, where Uncle Sergio met us. Our uncle turned out to be every bit as crazy as my mother had described him, but older and with no *Lambretta*. He walked with a limp and wore faded brown and gray clothes that made him look like he needed dusting.

As far as George and I were concerned, Uncle Sergio was pure joy. He had all the advantages of an adult—including a gold pocket watch and a Kodak Instammatic camera—and none of the drawbacks (including a sense of responsibility and shame). He wasted no time teaching us every Italian *parolacci* (swear word), including some we didn't already know. The three of us never stopped giggling. Sergio was sixty-seven years old.

Everything about Italy thrilled us. The little cars that looked like dachshunds on toy wheels; the coffee called *cappuccino* with a fun layer of foam on top; the ice cream called *gelato* that was so much better than American ice cream (especially *nocciola*—hazelnut). *Chinotto* was brown and bubbly and looked like Coke or Pepsi, but George and I found it superior; we found everything in Italy superior. Water was served in tall green bottles with filigreed labels and carbonation, and beat hell out of American water. The trains, the trees, even the birds, all seemed somehow better. So did the clay tile rooftops, and the old shutters in all the old windows, and the sounds the church bells made, heavenly enough to make even a ten-year-old atheist want to fall to his knees and pray, almost. Every place you looked there were spewing fountains and naked statues, paintings, sculptures, and *cortiles*—courtyards with cloudy willow trees like the ones that ran up our driveway, painted on stucco walls.

From June to September we took in all the major cities and sights, as far north as Bergamot on the Swiss border, then back to Naples to catch the ship home, with two Italian bicycles we'd nagged our mother for stowed in the cargo hold: George's cherry red, mine lime green. As the

Queen Anna Maria pulled away from the dock my brother and I cried, something we hadn't done when we sailed out of New York harbor.

When we uncrated those bicycles we were the envy of the neighborhood, the first Italian ten-speeds ever to grace the streets and sidewalks of Bethel. *Legnano,* said the decals on the frames. *Campagniola,* said the S-shaped appendages called derailleurs. The neighborhood kids, they couldn't get over all those gears. "What are they all for?" they wondered, scratching their heads, but didn't need much convincing to be persuaded that ten gears were better than three.

The bicycles were too big for us; we had to wait a year to reach the pedals. During that time appreciation turned to envy, and envy to resentment, and resentment to malice and mischief. Fool that I was, I let Wesley Conklin "hop on" my bicycle for "just a sec," only to have him pump away down Wooster Street with me in hot pursuit. I chased him all the way into town, past Mulhaney's variety store, past the Doughboy and the town hall, through the middle school parking lot, past the ruins of hat factories. As dusk settled I sat on the front steps of Wesley's house, waiting with sore legs and burning tears for him and my *Legnano.* Finding me there, Wesley's parents took pity on me and invited me in for "supper": Campbell's split pea soup and a salad of iceberg lettuce and cucumbers. With *Wishbone* dressing.

A few days later it happened again. This time Sean Deifendorf took off with my bike. I called up his parents to lodge a complaint. The next day at school Sean and his older brother Keith cornered me in the lavatory and beat me blue.

By the time George and I started high school each of us had had our bikes stolen no less than a dozen times. Finally we gave up and bought cheap Schwinn replacements, with chintzy chrome chain guards and saddles with fat springs under them, bikes no one would bother to steal. The *Legnanos* went into the garage to gather cobwebs and dust.

As I pedaled my piece-of-shit Schwinn around I felt the eyes of the whole town upon me, watching me, laughing at me the way those kids on the bus had laughed at my father on his rusty Raleigh. For the first time I tasted the alienation that would hound me for years: the sense that I didn't and would never fit in, that I was both too good and not good enough, unique, but also somehow inferior, incongruous. If there was prejudice at work here it cut both ways. I convinced myself that my ostracism was the product of envy, and took it as a back-handed compliment. Yes, I was bitter, bitter and scornful and full of false pride, riding high on my mental *Legnano,* my scorn a substitute for dignity.

Still, I refused to surrender, to get down off my ten-speed attitude. Instead I clung to what I defined as my "uniqueness." Since I liked to draw and was good at it, and since artists were known to be alienated, I declared myself an artist: a label which, in my own mind, trumped all other labels. I went to art school, wrote novels and plays, and scraped by as an illustrator. When I could afford to, I traveled to Italy, where I pretended to feel at home, something I'd never felt, really, in my own country. I married a woman of Sicilian descent, who shares my love of anchovies and *vino rosso,* and who's an artist like me. And I considered myself reasonably happy. I still do.

Still, there is that familiar sense of displacement that follows me everywhere I go, along with an ache of loneliness, the kind that most people probably feel when they stand at the edge of a pier looking out to sea. I can't even say that I mind it, really. Or maybe I've just grown used to it. Maybe I'll never achieve what the Portuguese poet Fernando Pessoa called that "distinction of spirit that makes isolation seem a haven of peace free from all anguish." Perhaps the only country this Dago from Mayberry will ever feel at home in is the country of Solitude, that uncharted island halfway between Italy and the United States of America, a country the size of a hyphen.

But I am not an Italian American any more than I am an American, or an Italian. I am the American-born son of parents born in Italy, rife with their eccentric, egocentric, displaced genes. Maybe others see me as an Italian American, but I don't. I see what I see in just about everyone: an amalgam of where we've come from, who we are, and—maybe most important of all—what we choose, or refuse, to be.

I Heard You the First Time, Daddy

· · · · · · ·

RITA CIRESI

My father was a man of fruit and vegetables. From four A.M. to four P.M. he trucked wooden crates of produce out of my uncle's distribution warehouse in downtown New Haven, Connecticut. He came home smelling like all the green and brown and red things pulled up from the earth and plucked from vines and trees, whose American names I did not know until I set off for college: *escarole, rape, carciofi, radicchio,* and *fiori di zucca.* Like the famous portrait of "Summer" painted by Giuseppe Archimboldo, my father seemed to have a cucumber for a nose, apples for cheeks, cherries for eyes. His teeth, which he rarely brushed, were indeed an open pea pod, and his sweaty work clothes gave off the odors of grapes and melons, figs and mushrooms, chestnuts and corn cobs, plums and pomegranates.

I knew that the cheerful heads of cabbage and bags of gnarled Yukon Golds he delivered to the Yale University cafeterias eventually became cole slaw and potato salad; I also knew that the spinach and tomatoes and mushrooms he trucked up to the back door of New Haven's *pizzerie* became toppings for the delicious *apizza* for which the city had become famous.

· · · · ·

RITA CIRESI is the author of five award-winning novels and short-story collections, including *Pink Slip* and *Sometimes I Dream in Italian.* She directs the creative writing program at the University of South Florida.

But just about everything else about my father seemed a mystery to me. For instance, I did not learn his given name until after I had swilled my first alcoholic drink (a concoction of Smirnoff vodka and strawberry Kool-Aid that my boldest sister dared me to drink) and after I had smoked my first nauseating cigar (a fat green Dutch Masters that this same sister commanded me to puff all the way down to the nub).

My father's first name always had been a source of confusion to me. My mother, a former Army nurse, referred to my father strictly in the third person. "Here comes The Dad," she said, with tight, grim lips when my father's truck lumbered up our steep, crumbling driveway. "The Dad is here" was indeed a dire announcement. It meant we four Ciresi girls had to glance up from the fuzzy black-and-white television set—where we were glued to reruns of *Dark Shadows* and *Gomer Pyle*—to actually acknowledge our father's grunt of hello. It also meant that for the rest of the long Connecticut winter evening, my mother would holler in my father's half-deaf ear, "The Dad! You want some ravioli? The Dad! You want some ice cream? The Dad! You want to snore all night on that couch or you want to go upstairs and snore in your own bed?"

For a long time I operated under the mistaken impression—as did every telephone solicitor who called—that my father's name was Gooey-Peppie. Our electric bills (and phone bills and gas bills) still came addressed to my grandfather Giuseppe, who had died years before I was even born.

I also went through a phase where I thought my father's first name was the same as his last name. "CIRESI, CIRESI!" loud male voices bellowed into the phone when I dared to answer it. Sometimes the caller would add, "YOUR FATHER!" I knew this rough command was not as rude as the shouts of the boys on the playground at school: "Your mother!" "No, your sister!" "No, your twin sister and all your girl cousins and your bitch of a dog, too!" Still, I often wondered why these guys who so curtly demanded the ear of my father never spoke with the sort of gentility I heard on my oldest sister's ALM Method language-instruction tapes. In the segments that dealt with proper telephone manners, one heard civilized Italians—*real* Italians—clearly enunciating vowel-rich dialogue such as: *"Pronto! Chi parla? Vorrei parlare con il direttore, per favore."* Translation: "Hello, who's calling? I'd like to speak with the manager, if you please."

The Italian American men who called for my father said neither please nor thank you when I hollered back at them, "AH-SHPETT-AH—HOLD ON!" I loathed rousing The Dad from his deep snoring slumber on the couch. *Somebody's on the phone*—to my father—meant *Somebody was calling to tell us somebody else was dead.* I always felt just as relieved as my dad did—no wake to attend, no need to suit up for a funeral—when the voice of one of his cronies came through on the other end of the line to cheerfully holler, "Yo, Ciresi!"

"Yo!" my father hollered back. "Cheech! Hezzadeech, Sawzeech!"

(Translated into somewhat purer Italian: *Ciccio, che si dice, mia salsiccia?* and into coarser English: Hey, Fat Frankie, what's going on, ya sausage-head?)

There were, of course, variations on this *Francisco-Salsiccia* theme: "Yo, Rosso-Red!" "Yo, Tony Boy!" "Yo, the Great Michele!" "Yo, Ugly!"

The Dad didn't seem to know anyone who had a normal American name, like Tom or Bill or Dick. Every single fourth cousin or we-go-way-back buddy of his had a nickname that got rung like a stuck doorbell. For instance, when we visited the Long Wharf Food Terminal, where my Uncle Augustino (better known as Zio Augie Doggie) operated his produce business, we found my father wheeling wooden crates of cauliflower and Boston lettuce over to the massive trucks idling along the loading docks. My father stood on the metal platform and shouted down at the beef man and the cheese man and the banana man and all the other man-men who worked at the terminal: "Yo, Shorty! Yo, Lucky! Yo, Moo Cow! Yo, Pecorino! Yo, The Cat!"

On weekends my father met his buddies at a downtown lunch counter for coffee and an English muffin slathered in butter. These cronies were The Judge (who as far as I could tell had never worn a black robe), The Doc (who probably had never delivered a baby), and the Rabbi from Napoli (a big question mark here). My father knew brothers called Itch and Scratch, and Twins named Tony Boots and Tony Shoes, neither of whom owned a Thom McAn store, but who were a barber and a keychain salesman respectively. From his days in Panama—where he sweated out all of World War II playing poker and smoking cigars and guarding the canal—my dad had Army buddies known as Three-Finger Tony, Bulldog, and Pirate. Among his cousins, my father counted a Carlo who was a Chaz and two Stefanos who were known as Hey, Big Steve! and Hey, Little Steve! when they weren't known as Stevie Hot Dogs and Stevie Bananas. The guy who painted our house every three years—driving a Sherwin-Williams–splattered woody station wagon with seven rickety ladders sticking out of the back—had the smooth cheeks of a baby's butt, which earned him the ridiculous name of Coolie Face Mac.

We only found out the real names of these men when they died and my mother carefully clipped their obituaries from the newspaper using her fanciest pinking shears (which imparted a festive air to death). So Fazool-and-Beans went down into history as a Bruno, Windy the Fart as a Massimo, Booger a Placido, and 2 x 4 a Cosmo.

Sometimes people close to my dad called him "Tah-dee." Frightened that my father would have to die before I knew if he spelled this name "T-o-d-d-y" or "T-o-d-d-i-e"—I took it upon myself to ask my vodka-swilling, cigar-smoking sister, "How do you spell Daddy's name?"

"S-a-l," she said, "v-a-t-o-r-e."

"Whuh?" I asked.

"His name is Salvatore."

"So how come nobody calls him Sal?"

"What are you, *stoonod*?" my sister asked. "Then people would know."

"Know what?"

She leaned forward, snapped her Juicyfruit gum between her crooked teeth, and conspiratorially whispered, "Know that he was *Sicilian.*"

For a long time I thought my off-the-boat father—and all his off-the-boat friends—had nicknamed each other in an effort to seem more American. But then I realized they were just putting their own spin onto the age-old Italian practice of using diminutives like *-ino* and *-etto* and fatten-me-up endings like *-one* and *-accio*. My dad's Giuseppes (who would be Peppes and Beppinos) became instead Spaghettis and Toothpicks. His Rosarios became Fat-Froggys and Big Cheeses.

One of my dad's most famous renamed characters was Curly the Paper Boy. Curly delivered the *New Haven Register* around four-thirty P.M. every evening. The problem was, he started his delivery route on the south side of Fourth Street. We lived on the north. Which meant my father walked up and down in front of the lace-curtained living-room windows, jingling his change and reporting on Curly's very slow progress. "There goes Curly," he said. "Curly's at the Barones' house. Curly's at Esposito's. Curly's at Casa Scalese. Curly is . . . Curly is . . . Curly is on our side of the street now." Until finally we saw Curly's tight black Sicilian curls appear directly in front of Casa Ciresi and my father hollered, "Curly's here! Yo, Curly! *Che si dice,* Curly, howzzit goin'!" Curly hurled a rolled copy of the *Register* at the front door. After my father had retrieved the paper, he turned around and told us—just in case we had missed all the excitement—"That was Curly."

My father's urge to repeat the names of his friends and relatives not once, not twice, but so many *molte-volte* that we wanted to stick our big toes in our ears, became known in our family as "The Shecky Greene Syndrome." The official terminology for my dad's say-it-again-Shecky-ism dated back to an infamous Saturday in 1973 when my father—who loved to "go to the horses"—tuned our flickering black-and-white Zenith TV to WTNH, Channel 8.

"Hey, Reet!" my father called out to me, although I sat right at his slippered feet. "C'mere, Reet!"

"I'm right here, Daddy," I said. "I heard you the first time, Daddy."

"Lookee here! It's the Kentucky Derby!"

I had inherited my dad's love of the races. I thrilled to the glamorous characters found at every track: the midget jockeys in their United Nations-colored silks, the elegant thoroughbreds with high tails and brushed manes and snorting nostrils, and the society ladies in wide-brimmed hats and flowered dresses and locked jaws who perched in the boxes holding their opera glasses in their white-gloved hands. I wanted to be such a lady some day. But alas, I also wanted to be one of the horses. And one of the midget jockeys. Yet I knew I could not be any of them unless I were reincarnated (a no-no for us Catholics).

So I was sitting right there, watching my father tightening the tin foil on the rabbit ears so the TV would get better reception, when The Dad pointed to one of the horses being corralled into the starting gate. "Hey," he said, "there's a horse here named Shecky Greene. Shecky Greene, remember Shecky Greene the comedian on the *Ed Sullivan Show?*"

I remembered. And so I squinted at the fuzzy TV screen, half-expecting to see a short Jewish horse dressed in a tuxedo and cummerbund. Holding a microphone. Curling back his lips just like the famous talking horse on television—Mister Ed—to say, "But seriously, folks!" *Tonight, appearing live, from his famous act at the Riviera Hotel in Las Vegas,* Shecky Greene the horse would disparage his mother-in-law. Poke fun at the other faggoty geldings with their long hippy hair. Drive his car into the fountain of Caesar's Palace casino and say, "No spray wax, please!"

My father decided this equine phenomenon was not to be missed. So he began summoning my older sisters. Unfortunately I had three. So sisters A, B, and C all got summoned individually. "Yo, Anna Marie! There's a horse here named Shecky Greene! Yo, Rose Mary! Come see the Shecky Greene! Yo, Jo-Jo-Jo! It's Shecky!" Getting my mother into the living room involved a few more sheckies. "Marie. Marie. MARIE, whattareyadeaf or what? Come on in here. There's a horse here named Shecky Greene!"

By now we all had more than gotten the point. Right here in our crowded living room—crammed tight with a player piano with the rolls removed from its guts, a sagging avocado green three-cushion couch, a ripped maroon vinyl recliner taped with black duct tape, a flame orange armchair, a mustard yellow wing chair, a wooden rocking chair that looked like it belonged to Ma Kettle's grandmother—right there in our flea-market living room was a certain member of the equine genus named after a famous Vegas comedian, SHECKY GREENE.

My sisters and I looked at each other with dismay. For this was just the Derby. Ahead of us lay the Shecky Greene Preakness. And the Shecky Greene Belmont—a race that went on for a grueling full three minutes. How would we survive the Triple Shecky Crown without doing the unthinkable: telling our father, "Please, Daddy: *stai-zeet!* Shuddup, already!"

Fortunately, Shecky Greene lost the Derby. To one of the most famous horses of all time: Secretariat. As we left the living room (leaving behind The Dad to bemoan the outcome of the race), I whispered to my sister, "If I ever start *shecky*-ing like Daddy, shoot me."

Thirty years later, Shecky Greene (the horse) has probably gone to the glue factory. Shecky Greene (the comedian) is dead of cancer. Paperboy Curly has probably hunkered down in Sun City Center, Florida, in some double-wide trailer park. My father is eighty-nine years old. And I am a writer, doing what writers do to avoid doing their real work. I am sitting on my dirty dog-slobber-covered couch perusing not the Curly-delivered *New Haven Register,* but the *Tampa Tribune* (delivered by someone named Tammy who lives in Zephyrhills, whom I have dubbed "Zephyrhills Tammy").

Unlike my father, I never look at the sports page. But today the photograph of a gleaming brown horse catches my eye. "Hey Bee Bee," I say to my daughter Celeste. "Bee Bee. Bee Bee. Lookee here. The horse who won the Kentucky Derby is called Smarty Jones!"

My comment elicits only a bored adolescent yawn.

So I say it again: "Smarty Jones!"

"I heard you the first time, Mommy," she says.

She may have heard me. But I am not done repeating it. Even though I have vowed never to *curly* or *shecky*, I like the sound of *Smarty*, which reminds me of those beloved pastel-colored sour candies of my youth, and the cropped tones of *Jones*, a beautifully bland all-American name if ever I've heard one (never mind its Welsh origin). So I say it again. "Smarty Jones!" And again, with a British accent: "Smah-tee Jones requests the pleasure of your presence at high tea—oat scones shall be served." Followed by a Texan accent: "Got me a hoss here named Smarty Jones that oughta rustle up a few hundred cattle." Then with a Boston accent: "Smahtee Jones pahked his cah in Hahvard Yahd to take in all the ahtwork."

Over the next few days, I cannot let Smarty Jones go. My daughter gets an A on an algebra test and I tell her, "Great job, you Smarty Jones!" My golden retriever catches the tennis ball for the twenty-fifth time in a row and I tell him, "You are *such* a Smarty J.!" One of my students turns in a paper with his own last name, Barnes, spelled wrong at the top. *No Smarty Jones are you!* I feel like writing in his Barn-margin. By the time the Preakness arrives, I have *smarty-ed* and *jones-ed* so much that my daughter informs me, "You're getting just like your father, Mommy."

This is second in insult only to "You're getting like your mother." But what do I care? My beloved S.J. wins the second race!

On the evening of the Belmont Stakes, my husband and daughter drag me out to dinner. It is their downfall that they choose to dine at Red Lobster—which has at least four TVs posted above the bar—and *my* downfall that we arrive during 2-for-1 Happy Hour. After one too many a Bloody Mary/Bloody Mary, I hear the Belmont bugle blaring. I rush up to the bar. And it is there, peering over the shoulder of a fat guy downing Stolichnaya, that I watch Smarty Jones lose the third and the longest and the toughest race of the Triple Crown to a horse whose name I cannot even remember.

"Birdstone," my father later reminds me. "Yup, Birdstone. Birdstone took the prize. Birdstone was the one. Birdstone stole the crown from Smarty Jones. Smarty Jones. Smarty Jones!" His gray eyes grow wistful. "How'd you like to have a nice, American name like that?"

Bitter Herbs?

· · · · · · · · · · ·

Sandra M. Gilbert

The Spices of Life

A few days ago I started to write a piece that I was going to call "The Spices of Life," and it was of course going to be a culinary memoir and one that, like so many works in that overworked genre, would be full of contradictions—savory with celebration though salty, too, with some of the sorrow that often flavors memories of menus past. What I find myself writing, though, is more elegiac than I'd expected it to be, not just salty but bitter with what I think I recognize as the alienating taste of loss that accompanies cultural displacement, the mouthful of bitter herbs that immigrants swallow as they journey from the known to the unfathomable, from the table of the familiar to the walls of estrangement.

Beginning the writing again, I've put a question mark after my new title, hoping that as I remember more deeply, the bitter will turn sweet, or at least bittersweet. "You had a happy childhood, Sandra," my schoolteacher-mother used to say in her most authoritative classroom voice when she read some of my poems. "So why must you be so *mor*bid?"

· · · · ·

SANDRA M. GILBERT has published seven books of poems, most recently *Belongings*, a number of books of criticism and anthologies, and a memoir, *Wrongful Death*. Her latest book is *Death's Door: Modern Dying and the Ways We Grieve*.

And it's true that as a child, raised in times and places that must have been at least intermittently harsh for my elders, I rarely recognized the tastes and scents of loss. I thought the flavorings were always happy, frequently festive.

But I myself was often sad, for reasons I couldn't understand, as if now and then I too had dipped into a dish of bitterness.

Tarragon

In the summer of 2002, I was in the kitchen of David's Paris apartment—"my" kitchen, in a way, because although David, my *bien aimé,* is the sole owner of the place, I've organized all the stuff in the *cuisine*—and David was napping in the bedroom around the corner, and I was making—what was I making, some sort of chicken salad maybe, or a sauce for fish?—but when I opened a new little vial of dried *estragon* and held it to my nostrils, its aroma flooded out and into and all around me, and just as if I were Proust, I was overcome. Tears pricked at my eyes, not, like Marcel, for a town unfolding its roads and roofs out of the past, but for just one person: my mother—Angela Maria Caruso Mortola, dead at 97 in January 2001—who seemed to me to spring like a genie from that small bottle. She alone, or rather she and her long, lonely life in Jackson Heights, Queens: her widowhood; her isolation; her ambivalent loyalties to Sicily, the land she barely remembered; and to America, the country whose company she so much longed to keep.

It's sometimes said that we know our ethnicity and its history through the foods we inherit from our families, the scents and savors of what was once the quotidian. And certainly we hyphenated Americans have produced so many recipes for and of nostalgia that any memoirist must now fear her ancestral kitchen can no longer yield much more than kitsch: *Nonna*'s marinara sauce, *Zia* Teresa's inimitable *polpette,* or for that matter Grandma Molly's gefilte fish.

But my weepy memories of my mother were different. My tears didn't well up, as I sniffed the *estragon,* because I was reminded of some *specialità* of hers. Rather, they came because she mostly couldn't and didn't cook, not at least during her thirty years of marriage to my father. When, throughout the more than thirty-five years of solitude she endured after he died, she was obliged to cook for not just herself but for me and my family on our intermittent visits to New York, tarragon was the rather unlikely herb she chose to use as seasoning for most salads, soups, and sauces—maybe because, along with oregano, it was one of the first dried herbs to appear on the shelves of supermarkets in Jackson Heights. So the distinctive, not especially Italian (but instead rather Frenchified) aroma of tarragon perfumed all her "company" meals, though by "all" I mean just a few concoctions that she labored over: a quite nice preparation of breaded (and herbed with tarragon) chicken cutlets, a kind of veal stew with a light (tarragony) sauce, and a salad of (tarragon-flavored) marinated artichoke hearts.

To be sure, my kitchen-phobic mother came from a Sicilian household with quite a culinary tradition, and there were many family stories centered on food, most notably, perhaps, the tale of my father's trial by sausage. The son of a Russian mother and a Niçoise father whose ancestry was ultimately Ligurian, my father wasn't really used to things Sicilian when he first came a-courting my mother. So the older sister with whom she lived felt free—indeed, obliged—to test his love. It was New Year's Eve, and she offered him a ferociously hot sausage, along with whatever else she'd prepared (the story doesn't include the menu, though I could reconstruct it if I had to, but never mind). All innocence and love, the skinny young man who was destined to become my dad bit right in, for this was long before the days when you could buy a package of standard issue hot Sicilian sausages in your local Safeway, and he had no reason to be suspicious.

Thinking it was just an ordinary sausage, he took a *big* bite. And manfully chewed as tears came to his eyes.

"Sandrina, we *knew* he really loved her," my Aunt Frances would assure me, with each telling of this tale.

"You should have seen Uncle Al's face," a cousin would chime in. "But he never said a word!"

And my father, listening, would beam and flush with delight, even twenty years later.

Maybe my mother was daunted by the complexity of a culinary heritage that included trials by sausage along with magnificent *pasta infornata* (the family name for what, I later discovered, was also called *lasagna*) along with miraculously orange *arancini,* the incomparable Sicilian rice balls whose recipe is, I suspect, genetically transmitted to a select few citizens of Persephone's island. Or perhaps, as a proto-liberated woman (a flapper and a free spirit, she always told me), she scorned the humdrum drudgery of the stove. Or perhaps—a corollary of this—she thought cooking would turn her into a stereotypical Italian mama, redolent of garlic and olive oil and *basilico.* Because in our two-bedroom, gray-carpeted, genteelly furnished Jackson Heights apartment, with its "Duncan Phyfe" table and chairs, its quasi-Regency sofa, subdued Chinese prints, and Lowestoft lamps, my father cooked and she mostly washed dishes or scrubbed floors, tasks that, oddly enough, seemed more *simpatico* to her than hovering over the stove.

Well, there was at least one distinctively Sicilian dish that she did now and then make for me. When my father went off by himself to a meeting of the local Democratic Club or the Society of Civil Engineers, she would once in a while assemble a dish she remembered fondly from her childhood: *escalore in brodo,* with spaghetti. This was a preparation my father heartily disliked, and so, for that matter, did I at that time, though now I can vaguely appreciate its merits, or what its merits would have been if my mother had cooked it with more true Sicilian abandon and less would-be-WASPish restraint. Done right, *escalore in brodo* might mean sautéing lots and lots of crushed fresh garlic and maybe a little hot pepper in good rich fruity olive oil, then adding big handfuls of rinsed escarole, squeezed almost dry, to the garlicky oil and sautéing some more, and finally uniting the vegetables with several quarts of broth into which, after a while, one would introduce a half pound or so of cooked spaghetti. The whole would then be served piping hot with lots of freshly grated parmigiano, romano, or pecorino. And many traditional cooks would probably also dress the dish up with little meatballs, some white beans, and/or some slices of cooked Italian sausages, hot or mild.

But it pains me, now, to write these words, remembering as I do that my mother's humble and conflicted version of this recipe was usually as bitter as it was watery—not enough garlic! overcooked escarole! not even a bouillon cube to simulate chicken broth!—even while it was the most elaborate effort she made in the kitchen, at least until Daddy died and, for thirty-five years, she took up tarragon.

Of course, my mother didn't really need to linger alone in Jackson Heights for all those years. When my husband and I moved to northern California with our three young children two years after my father succumbed to the long-term aftereffects of boyhood rheumatic fever, we urged her to join us, first in the little Sacramento Valley town of Davis, then in more sophisticated Berkeley. Installing herself with, or near, her daughter (I was an only child) would have been the old-fashioned Sicilian modus vivendi for widowhood. It was what her sister Frances did when *her* husband died, and what all her sisters-in-law did when *their* husbands died. But to my determinedly "modern" mother, with her memories of free-spirited flapperhood, such a solution was utterly unacceptable. Just as she'd scorned the aromatic *Italianità* of the Sicilian ghetto in Brooklyn where she grew up, she renounced the role of aproned *Nonna,* nor did she want to seem to depend on me, her professorial daughter, despite her all-too-often-reiterated pride in the academic achievements she had herself trained me for. No, she too was a professional—a retired schoolteacher, a would-be clinical psychologist, an avid reader of the *New Yorker* and the *New York Times Book Review,* a theatergoer, a restaurant connoisseur, a would-be independent woman-about-town. No pantry theatricals for her, no perpetual second bedroom in someone else's home, and no diminished quarters around the corner from the daughterly Big House either. She would manage on her own, thank you, like any other up-to-date American.

And for a while she did. She had a few friends nearby, and, for maybe a decade, a number of relatives. But gradually the friends moved away, south to the sunny retirement homes of Florida, or west to be near *their* kids, and gradually, too, the relatives who hadn't already moved in with their children began to die, until my mother, surviving into her late nineties, was left almost entirely alone for the last fifteen or twenty years of her life, except for our intermittent visits: alone and still stubbornly refusing to budge from her "beautiful" apartment, the gray carpet, the lyre-backed chairs, the elegant lamps, the shadowy Chinese prints.

Perhaps it was then that the scent of tarragon became, for me, the perfume of her loneliness, the scent of a solitude into which only the voices of successive *Late Show* comedians brought something resembling company. For my mother passed her nights with Johnny Carson (of whom she said "he's my best friend") and then Jay Leno (though she didn't think him a worthy heir of Johnny) as well as a series of news announcers whose tidings of urban violence filled her waking and sleeping hours with dread. Yet paradoxically, it was in these last years of widowhood that she enthusiastically rediscovered the ethnicity she'd so roundly repudiated as a young woman fleeing the Sicilian ghetto of her girlhood. Indeed, in these years she kept a file of clippings from the restaurant reviews that ran in the *New York Times* and would take us excitedly to Italian restaurants recommended by Mimi Sheraton or Ruth Reichl, places whose proprietors treated her with exactly the deference due the *nonna* she now was but had never (she thought) wanted to be. And in another of life's little ironies, she repeatedly congratulated me, my husband, and our children for our attempts to replicate not just her sister's and mother's Sicilian recipes but even my paternal grandfather's Niçoise-Ligurian achievements in the kitchen.

Oregano

My father's father was an artist *manqué*, born in Nice, who had, he said, come to the United States from Paris toward the end of the first decade of the twentieth century to study, of all things, painting. Like Rick in Humphrey Bogart's most famous role, who claimed that he'd gone to Casablanca to "take the waters," Grandpa was obviously "misinformed." So he became first a waiter and then the co-owner of a restaurant on Franklin Street, in the heart of New York's market district. As I recall, his establishment was what T. S. Eliot would call a "sawdust restaurant with oyster shells," a lunch or supper place for truckers hauling vegetables to town and for buyers or sellers of produce. Well, to be frank, I don't remember oyster shells, but I do remember a black and white ceramic tile floor sprinkled with drifts of sawdust on which stood tables surrounded by what would no doubt now be extremely expensive, authentic, early twentieth-century bentwood chairs. And in this form the restaurant prospered for more than thirty years. But chairs, tables, and sawdust alike vanished into the shadows of history when Grandpa and his partner decided to "modernize" the restaurant in 1948, replacing the old accoutrements with shiny new linoleum tile floors, "leatherette" banquettes, and chrome-edged vinyl-topped tables, the best that mid-century America could offer, so that the place looked like a vintage Hopper.

Then there was a labor dispute: the longtime, old-fashioned waiters didn't want to join some union or other that tried to organize them, the union threw a picket line around the restaurant, the truckers—all, of course, card-carrying Teamsters—wouldn't cross the line, and so the restaurant itself went the way of the bentwood chairs, the sawdust, and the old black and white ceramic tiles. Grandpa and his partner declared bankruptcy. The only money left to Grandpa's family was what my grandmother had saved from her household allowance. This was in fact a decent sum, for my Russian-born grandma was raised in the ways of

French thrift. As a girl, she lived in Paris, where her mother worked as a housekeeper for the Orthodox priests at the Cathedrale Alexander Nevsky, so when Grandma and her husband emigrated to America she built herself a fairly substantial bank account through patient domestic calculations. Yet Grandpa was as unmanned by her money as by his loss of the restaurant, never recovering from the calamity that had left him, as he evidently felt, utterly at the mercy of his wife and of his daughter, my father's unmarried sister, who together kept the household going in something like its former prosperity, Grandma with her savings and her thrift, my aunt with a dreary job as a personnel manager for General Electric.

Throughout this complex history, however—whether his restaurant succeeded, faltered, or failed—Grandpa kept on cooking. When he was in the money and when he was out of it, he managed his personal kitchen, perhaps more than his professional one, with such dexterity and dedication that in my family he founded a patrilineage of cooks, passing on recipes not just to my father (who kept sauces simmering in our Jackson Heights kitchen) but also to my husband (a non-Italian who replicated some of Grandpa's recipes better than I did) and my son (who learned them so well from my husband that he became head chef in his own family).

If the aroma of tarragon is the perfume that evokes my mother's solitude, the scent of oregano—mingled with odors of garlic and inhaled through clouds of cigar smoke—conjures Grandpa's kitchen, both its early prosperity and its late defeat. Over the years I've written often, even obsessively, about this kitchen, from which regularly emerged enormous and intricately festive meals to mark the turnings of the seasons. Our New Year's supper featured a rather Americanized baked ham but one that was garnished with Grandma's own mellifluous version of *salade russe,* side by side with Grandpa's stuffed mushrooms, *caviar d'aubergine,* and—*pièce de résistance!*—lobster salad. And then there was a spring menu of roast lamb accompanied by Really French flageolets (they were canned and my aunt bought them at Bloomingdale's gourmet grocery) and completed by a cake topped with strawberries macerated in some brilliant combination of liqueurs in which Grand Marnier played a prominent part. But best of all, the cycle of the year was crowned by a Thanksgiving dinner, joyously followed in just a month by a Christmas feast, centering on a roast turkey stuffed with Grandpa's inimitable spinach-mushroom-sausage stuffing.

I don't remember what my grandparents served for dessert at Thanksgiving. Pumpkin pies were certainly alien to them so perhaps we had one of my Grandpa's splendid crèmes caramel, a golden ring of custard lapped in bittersweet burnt-sugar syrup. And I know that Christmas dinner never ended with pumpkin or mince pie though it sometimes theatrically climaxed in blue flames flickering over a plum pudding and sometimes in a luxurious Mont Blanc of puréed chestnuts happily married to whipped cream.

But the stuffing with which Grandpa lavishly garnished his turkeys was the sine qua non of his cuisine, the dish for which he was and still is most famous among our extended network of family and friends. And it is the dish that now tells me how deeply Ligurian he was.

My grandparents, Amedee Mortola and Alexandra (Sasha) Zelensoff, had somehow met and married in Paris. Like so many children of immigrant families, I haven't a clue how and where they came together, nor do I know exactly when and where they wed. I did learn, not long ago, that my father, Alexis Joseph Mortola, was born in the 17th arrondissement of this city where I now spend a good deal of time, but of the life the family lived in Paris I know nothing beyond my grandmother's tales of the "Russian Church" (i.e., the Cathedrale Alexander Nevsky). Yet of course the family's Gallic connections are evident in their menus—the *salade russe* that we actually called "Russian salad," the *caviar d'aubergine* always described to me as "eggplant caviar," the various marinades of artichokes and mushrooms and roasted peppers that you can buy from most French *traiteurs*. My grandparents' vast lazy Susan was always heaped with *hors d'oeuvres variés* that included these and other succulent starters for an overture to every feast, although the course itself was often metonymically described as "the lazy Susan."

But though Grandpa was called "Frenchy" in the New York market district, and Grandma's domestic frugality was no doubt fostered in Paris, and the French army tried to draft my French-born father when he was eighteen (the United States Congress had to pass some sort of special resolution to save him, as it evidently does in many such cases), and my aunt Louise, despite her servitude at G.E., had a Master's in French literature, and although until World War II cut Americans off from pleasure trips to Europe the family went at regular intervals to visit relatives in Nice and Paris, Grandpa's stuffing was definitively Ligurian in origin, as I've learned in recent years from friends who actually have a house on a little street in San Rocco, a *frazione* of the Ligurian town of Ruta. Their street is called *Via Mortola,* a name that persuades me that in some distant ancestral lifetime I too would have been the owner of such a house.

The *Via Mortola* is probably too rough and certainly too narrow for any vehicles except motorcycles to brave its bumps and cracks. It curves around a hillside on the Portofino peninsula that's thicketed with chestnut trees, dotted with olive and lemon groves, and blooming with bay, rosemary, thyme, and other leaves and herbs whose names I don't know. From this road, really a path or track, you can clamber down to the little fishing village of San Fruttuoso or the small resort town of Camogli or up and around the hilly peninsula to elegant Portofino itself, where a dazzle of international yachts bob in the harbor, admired by strolling masses of tourists nibbling at paper cups filled with the wonderfully portable sundae called a *paciugo.* But if you stay on this hillside, from here on the Via Mortola you can see the great plateful of blue that is the Mediterranean and the hilly spine of the Riviera whose *Italianità* once stretched all the way to Nice, until, over the protests of Garibaldi, himself a native of the town some still call Nizza la Bella, the Niçois voted to become part of France.

I guess the farm where Grandpa grew up was reached by another narrow road, not unlike the Via Mortola, high in the hills above Nice, perhaps set among olive and lemon groves, studded with bushes of rosemary and looking toward fields of other herbs—lavender? thyme?—evoking the greenery of Liguria because really primordially part of it.

What did they cultivate on that farm? I've heard they had rabbits. When my aunt Louise visited there as a young girl, her Tante Rosette took her to see those rabbits and asked her which of the tiny, soft, hunched-up quivering creatures she liked best, and when little Louise pointed to the sweetest bunny, beautiful Tante Rosette (for she was beautiful, dark-haired, dark-eyed, and tragically bereft because her fiancé had been killed in the first World War) said, *Bon, we'll have that one for dinner.*

Did they stuff it with some semblance of Grandpa's stuffing? His famous stuffing was green with spinach—which I now realize was a stand-in for the wild herbs that Ligurian cooks pack into ravioli—and dense with sausage and salty with parmesan cheese and creamy with mushrooms and lively with garlic, onion, celery, all bound with a couple of beaten eggs and several cupfuls of good stale bread or bread crumbs, and all seasoned with Grandpa's all-purpose Italian American herb: oregano.

If tarragon was the herb my mother fastened on when she searched the shelves of Bohack's and the A & P in Jackson Heights, oregano was what caught Grandpa's eye. Perhaps there weren't many other herbs available in the forties and fifties. Could anybody in Queens buy basil, rosemary, or thyme at a local supermarket? Surely there weren't any fresh herbs, but there must long have been dried oregano, even then widely used in pizza and pasta sauces, and it kept well. So when Grandpa dictated recipes to me and my young husband as we sat at his kitchen table in the early sixties, bent over our graduate student notebooks, taking down his every word, he always said, "And add a little oregano." Add it to the marinades. Add it to the sauces. Add it, most important of all, to the stuffing.

The indescribably delicious stuffing was of course essential to the turkey, and better, indeed, than the turkey itself, which Grandpa tended to overcook, perhaps out of some fundamental mistrust of American turkeys. After its sojourn in the turkey, however, Grandpa's stuffing had many more uses. On the days after Christmas, Grandma rolled out noodle dough and together she and Grandpa made ravioli that they crammed with the stuffing, thus returning their mix of greens and meat and cheese it to its original Ligurian function as a filling for pasta. And then if there was more stuffing—as, if one was lucky (or provident), there may well have been—it could be used, *can* be used, to stuff mushrooms, or even zucchini, peppers, who knows what other vegetables, in time-worn Ligurian fashion.

I recognize grandpa's stuffing as an Americanized version of a traditional recipe from the Via Mortola because my friends who live on that street have written a book in which a recipe akin to my grandfather's appears, only with exotic wild greens instead of spinach, and local cheeses, mushrooms, and sausages replacing the ingredients Grandpa bought in Queens. Still Liguria survives, though transformed, in Grandpa's stuffing, which my children and I have shared with numerous friends and relatives, many of whom prepare it at least once a year to mark, as Grandpa did, the turnings of the seasons, especially the swivel from fall to winter, when one wants to preserve the spirit of green hillsides for a while, along with the bite of garlic, the zest of oregano.

To be sure, the most famous Ligurian recipe—and one often encountered in Nice as well—is the one for *pesto,* a summery sauce that sanctifies greenery in the marriage of basil with olive oil, pine nuts, garlic, cheese, and sometimes butter. But oddly, my grandfather never produced a single *pesto* that I can remember, nor did any of my other relatives. I learned to make this sauce by reading cookbooks, despite the ancestry in which I take such wistful pride. And this is strange indeed since everyone now knows that *pasta all' pesto* is what one can and *should* eat on the Italian Riviera. My friend, the food and travel writer

David Downie, quotes in *Enchanted Liguria,* his wonderful introduction to the region, a passage that he calls "florid" but that nevertheless exactly summarizes the privileged place of *pesto* among my ancestors:

> "What is that scent of alpine herbs mixing so strangely with the sea spray on the Riviera's cliffs," asked writer Paolo Monelli.... "It is the odor of pesto: that condiment made of basil, Pecorino, garlic, pine nuts, crushed in the mortar and diluted with olive oil.... [It] is purely Ligurian; it speaks Ligurian; the mere smell of it makes your ears ring with a dialect at once sharp and soft, full of sliding sounds, of whispered syllables, of dark vowels."

Yet this is a taste of Liguria I never encountered in my family. Did Grandpa favor oregano as his invariable seasoning *because* it wasn't quintessentially Ligurian? Or did he choose it so often because in the taste of oregano there is a darker hint of basil, as if oregano were basil grown more intense, a little more bitter, a little older? Yet basil must have grown on the farm in the hills above Nice just as it blooms in small, intensely fragrant and flavorful leaves in all the kitchen gardens of Liguria, waiting to be picked and merged with olive oil, garlic, pine nuts, Pecorino.

Maybe Grandpa cooked with oregano because he lost not only the restaurant in the market district but also the farm. In 1960, about a decade after the restaurant failed, my parents went to Europe for a long-deferred second honeymoon. And of course they journeyed not just to the usual tourist places—Rome and Venice and London and whatever—but also to the family places: Paris, Sicily, Liguria, Nice.

Because my father felt so sorry for his father's suffering and bankruptcy, so sad that his father was unmanned by living on Grandma's savings and Auntie's meager earnings, he went to Nice to sell Grandpa's half-share of the family farm in the hills above the old city, and he was pleased that he succeeded in getting about $7,000 for the place. The purchaser was his second cousin, Liline, whose husband had made a good deal of money marketing refrigerators in Tahiti.

A few years later, Liline and her husband—who looked rather like Albert Camus, I thought, even though I knew he was an appliance salesman—built a ten-story condo on the land where the farm had been. Ten years later still, my husband and I visited Nice and went to look at this structure, which then seemed remarkably glamorous. And although we never entered the building, never ascended in what I suspect is rather a fancy elevator, I imagine that from the top story of the condo we would have seen the blue expanse of the Mediterranean and the thorny spine of Liguria, relaxing here and there into gardens dense with rosemary and basil, tables laden with bowls of *pasta all' pesto.*

Basil

When I was a little girl and even when I was a teenager, I don't think I knew what basil was, so I couldn't have known that it had been mysteriously replaced by oregano in my Niçoise-Ligurian grandfather's cooking. Yet I was often surrounded by basil, as I realized when I first began to cook with its distinctively peppery, aromatic leaves. In the tiny yard behind his three-story brownstone in Williamsburg, Brooklyn—then a stronghold of Sicilian culture—my Uncle Frank, the husband of my mother's only sister, Frances, had laid out a miniature formal garden. Just behind the house there was a grape arbor, with a porch swing in its leafy shade, and above the arbor flapped Aunt Frances's clothesline, on which she could pin her wash while standing in her big, second-story kitchen. But for maybe twenty or thirty feet beyond the arbor stretched the sunny *giardino,* with a stone bird bath at its center and little plots of herbs and flowers radiating in all directions.

From these tiny beds of exuberant bloom rose many fragrances, as fascinating as they were mysterious to a child who lived in a fourth-floor, two-bedroom, gray-carpeted apartment in a stolid brick building sur-rounded by prickly, boxy hedges of some dismally indeterminate plant.

One late afternoon in California, when I was tearing the leaves from a bunch of basil in preparation for a *pesto,* I thought, as I often had, how familiar their perfume was, and wondered why I felt that I had long ago—somewhere, but where?—inhaled it. And then I remembered the hot flagstone paths in the miniature Williamsburg garden and the little beds of herbs and flowers. The aroma that rose when the sun leaned hard on them was mostly basil, or basil dominated the others, and I think that when I was very young I came to consider this distinctive perfume coextensive with summer in that garden in that part of New York City.

My Uncle Frank, the garden designer, was swarthy, mustachioed, slightly bald, and very bitter. He almost always wore an unbuttoned suit vest and his sleeves were almost always rolled up, as though he was determined to Get Down to Things, or anyway, do some work in the garden. He was an architect, born on one of the Lipari Islands off the coast of Sicily, I don't know which one, and I believe his family name was *Adami.* But when he arrived on Ellis Island, the immigration offi-cer who greeted him said, "Here we call you *Adams.*" So a genteelly WASP-ish Adams he became, though the name sat strangely on him, given his belligerent, even rather piratical air.

Uncle Frank chain-smoked Camels, a habit that eventually led to his death from emphysema, but in his healthy middle age, the time I re-member best, he neither coughed nor wheezed, but vigorously breathed in and out great hot blossoms of smoke as he pounded on the table, elaborating his rage at America: New Deal, Old Deal, every deal was a bad deal. For he was an impassioned communist (though I doubt that he was what used to be called a "card-carrying" one), who admired Stalin, loathed almost every other politician, and articulated his unswerving beliefs in English, Sicilian, and Italian.

Most likely it was the Depression that drove Uncle Frank to such heights and depths of apoplectic, chain-smoking fury. Things had happened before I was born, I gathered, that had imposed some professional torment on him. He was a brilliant, highly educated architect, and yet the Depression had deprived him of his livelihood. My mother said he "had to work for the WPA," and she made this acronymic fate sound awful to me. Uncle Frank worked for the WPA and as part of his labors he made a beautiful little model of a Mayan Temple, which he kept downstairs in his study. But his family—a wife, two daughters, and a son—had sunk into genteel poverty during his years at the WPA, or so my mother implied when she discussed family history. My mother told me that she and her aged mother had lived with them and she had helped support the whole clan with her wages as a schoolteacher until her mother, a grandmother I never met, had died. Then my mother married my father (once he had passed his trial by sausage), gave birth to me, and moved to Queens.

I have to admit that to this day I don't quite grasp why Uncle Frank constructed a model of a Mayan Temple as part of what was defined as a "demeaning" job for the WPA. But even as a child I understood the reasons for his bitterness, his rage, his intransigent communism. After all, he outlined his grievances in the course of each one of the countless political debates that surged around the long dinner table at which my parents and I frequently joined him, my aunt, and my three cousins for festive meals featuring—yes—hot Italian sausages and platters of *arancini* or great roasting pans laden with Sicilian-style pizza or marvelously layered *pasta infornata* and *cannoli* filled with sweet ricotta.

My three Adams cousins were significantly older than I, and I worshiped them all: dark-eyed, lively Nancy, who spoke perfect Spanish and knew how to tango and rhumba; beautiful Virginia, who looked just like Ava Gardner and dated tall, witty Jules, a Jewish mathematician; and the youngest, Richard, who was so brilliant and dashing, such a great joke-teller and such a devastating debater (especially in arguments with his father) that when I was thirteen I pretended to my schoolmates that he wasn't really my cousin, he was my *boyfriend*!

Theirs was the home I wanted: a tall house, three children, a long

table heavy with pans of pasta, people shouting and laughing in a language incomprehensible to me—Sicilian!—but that seemed somehow
a source of the strange vitality that kept everyone making convivial
noises and pounding the table, and a garden warm with that inexplicable scent I now know to have been the perfume of basil.

In his garden, stooping over his herbs and flowers, perhaps tending
his basil with special care, Uncle Frank did sometimes smile. His sleeves
rolled up, his vest loosened, a Camel fuming in the corner of his mouth,
he was nevertheless more amiable there than he was at the dinner table,
when memories of the Depression and the immigration officer and the
WPA and the Mayan Temple flooded him with bile. The aroma of basil
must have penetrated that cloud of smoke; its sunny flavor must have
left a trace on his tongue.

When, years later, I went with my daughters to Sicily, we spent a day
in the windswept, hilly town of Sambuca-Zabut, where my mother, her
sister, and her seven brothers were born a century ago. Not far from
there, we visited the great ancient ruins of Agrigento, so superb one
doesn't want to call them ruins since they look almost as if someone
had *wanted* them to have the special majesty they have, set against those
vine-covered hills and sun-baked fields. I wondered why Uncle Frank
hadn't made a model of Agrigento for the WPA.

But with his rage, his cigarettes, his bizarrely American name, his
frustrated architectural dreams, my uncle had been forced into strange
compromises. One of the few "real" buildings he designed was my
Grandpa Mortola's restaurant on Franklin Street, in the New York market district. The one that failed in 1950.

Rosemary

Rosemary for remembrance, says Ophelia. But though I studied
Hamlet in high school, I didn't "get" the reference since I didn't actually

know what rosemary *was* and how it can grow wild in fields, or be cultivated in hedges and gardens. And there were songs we sang in the sixties, when we were young and hopeful—"parsley, sage, rosemary and thyme"—but what did those refrains mean? Until I became a serious cook such lines were nearly as opaque to me as Ophelia's ravings, even though I knew they referred to herbs, meaning (to a young New Yorker) dried leaves people used in the kitchen.

But in early September 1970, my husband, Elliot, and I went with our three small children—two daughters and a son, like my dream family in Brooklyn, along with an *au pair*—to vacation for two weeks in a "villa" in Portofino. The six of us had spent the summer in London, where Elliot and I were sometimes really, sometimes just ostensibly doing research at the British Library. Californians that we'd become, we needed a break from city gray, an interval of pure, mindless sun and sea, and somehow, remarkably enough, we'd managed to find a place that was not only available but affordable on our overstretched academic salaries, besides being large enough for what was, as the French put it, a *famille nombreuse.*

Our villa was really a large apartment on the hillside above the town, exactly two hundred steps up from the piazza that was even then basically a parking lot. (Perhaps all those steps up kept the rent down a bit.) But though it was inexpensive, the apartment had cool marble floors, tall shuttered windows, a fine view over rooftops all the way to the glitter of the harbor where the sleek yachts rode at anchor, and a large terrace partly shaded by the vast leaves of a grape arbor like the one in Uncle Frank's garden. Almost every day Elliot and I took the children to the beach in the nearby town of Santa Margherita di Ligure, where they swam and clamored for *tosti*—ordinary melted cheese sandwiches made somehow glamorous by Italian vendors. Later, in the market we would buy *basilico* so I could try my hand at *pesto,* about which I had only then learned, and when we came back to Portofino we sometimes strolled through the piazza, licking versions of that sublime sundae the *paciugo.*

One evening, perhaps after a meal of linguine with *pesto,* the three children—six, eight, and ten—guarded by eighteen-year-old Kathleen, clambered down to the village on their own, to get *paciugi.* Roger, the eldest, was charged with ordering *"Quattro paciugi per favore"* since culture-shocked, California-bred Kathleen absolutely refused even to attempt Italian, and the little girls were too young and shy. But he came back in tears, reporting that in a minute of confusion and self-consciousness he'd blurted out *"Quattro paciugi s'il vous plaît."*

The terrace of that Portofino apartment was lined with flowerpots and with tubs of rosemary, perhaps the first "real" (as opposed to dried) rosemary I'd ever seen. These were trimmed and watered by Elissa, our landlord's daughter, a young blonde woman who also cleaned house for us several days a week. I could barely communicate with her in my broken Italian, so, since, like many Ligurians, she had some French, I usually spoke to her in my not quite so broken French, and perhaps that linguistic mix—one in any case part of my immigrant heritage—was mirrored in what my ten-year-old son feared was an unforgivable solecism.

Often, in the late afternoon, Elissa would appear on the terrace with garden shears, gesturing toward the tubs of rosemary and saying politely in our two languages, *"Rosmarino? Rosmarin?"* Watching her clip the fragrant branches and bear them away for some kitchen project, I too learned to clip branches of *rosmarino* and cook with the bittersweet dark green needles, chopped fine and so strongly perfumed that yes, Ophelia was right, they offer a medicine for memory.

But it's sad that my memories of an Italy I never really knew are so partial, so incomplete, slanting and glinting from the stems of rosemary, the leaves of basil and oregano, then devolving into the tarragon that comforted my mother in her old age.

Before leaving for Europe, we had of course struggled to persuade my mother that she should join us on our trip, and of course, as always, she refused to stir from the apartment in which she had imprisoned herself, though she wrote us regularly, encouraging our travels. She forgot to tell us, however, that the internationally famous resort of Portofino was just across the wooded peninsula from Ruta, the Ligurian town from which her husband's family had emigrated to Nice in the nineteenth century and one of the places she and my father had visited on their European trip in 1960, when they sold the farm in Nice. So the whole time we were in Portofino, eating *pasta all' pesto* and inhaling the enlivening fragrance of *rosmarino,* we didn't know that the Via Mortola, with its herbs and bays, was just on the other side of the hill.

St. Sebastian in Boston

RANDY-MICHAEL TESTA

Prologue: Boston, 2005

The Catholic Church is in Flames. Everybody here knows this. AM talk-radio sportscasters regularly refer to Bernard Cardinal Law, now in exile in Rome, as Bernie the Pimp. Survivors of clergy abuse stand in front of Holy Cross Cathedral each Sunday howling their unrelieved torment to Heaven, while the Archdiocesan newspaper assures churchgoers during flu season they will not become sick at communion by drinking wine from the chalice.

No Boston Catholic I know has a good word to say about the Pope, either the one who just died or the one just elected. Dead or alive, the question for each is the same: What would it take for you to know what you know?

Conversely, the Fire has caused many other men to know what they know and to tell their story: of Italian American upbringings, of Catholic priests and nuns.

Of martyrdom and death without resurrection.

. . . . .

RANDY-MICHAEL TESTA is a teacher, writer, and editor living in Cambridge, Massachusetts. Growing up near Akron, Ohio, Testa was both a choirboy and an altar boy.

Part One: The Answer

St. Sebastian's mortally wounded body is the object of intense scrutiny by a six-year-old Italian American Catholic schoolboy at St. Sebastian's in Akron, Ohio. The boy sneaks into the church when nobody else is around, counting and recounting the bloody arrows, staring at the places where they pierce Sebastian's side, chest, and arms. He follows the maroon trickles down Sebastian's limbs, from the arrow tips that seem to slice right through him all the way down to Sebastian's crotch, the streams of blood converging there, why he is not sure.

At six, the boy is unsure what to make of the maroon feeling that stirs him whenever he follows the streams. He loves Sebastian as much as the nuns tell him he is to love Jesus.

No.

That is a lie.

He loves Sebastian more.

The child sees St. Sebastian's contorted face, pierced more strongly by each newly shot arrow, until this moment, the moment caught by the sculptor.

And when he is a man, he sees St. Sebastian's body as a gnarl of twisted agony and the look on his face of bliss, horror, and unutterable pain, his head cocked back, the arched body high at the small of the back and suspended for just the briefest second in the air.

Like a man about to come.

The child stands at the back of the church, searching St. Sebastian's features, as does the man, each searching for clues to his own eventual martyrdom. A nun is playing the organ in the back choir loft, practicing for Mass. The man and boy remember other music, music in a record store where, under the NOW PLAYING sign is an album cover with St. Sebastian's picture on the front. The boy walks up to the sales clerk at the front counter and asks, "Is that St. Sebastian singing?" and the clerk, smiling, replies, "Well, yes, as a matter of fact, it is. Sebastian's men are afraid to follow the Roman Emperor's orders to kill Sebastian. And if they don't do it, they'll be killed too. So Sebastian is trying to save his men's lives by telling them, 'The one who wounds me the deepest loves me the most.'"

In the orange brick vestibule of St. Sebastian Catholic Church, next to the white marble baptismal font encircled by red velvet cord to keep eighth grade boys from slurping holy water out of it on a dare, the enormous statue of St. Sebastian at the precise moment of his martyrdom halts the chatter of even the noisiest classes upon entrance to the church.

For first graders like me, St. Sebastian's death poses three questions, questions lacking the smug certitude of Baltimore Catechism answers posed during Religion class, or by Italian relatives at pasta dinners served in Pyrex cookware, by aunts with fleshy arms at noon each Sunday after Mass.

Who made us?
God made us.
Why did God make us?
God made us to know Him, love Him, and serve Him.
What is faith?
Faith is the virtue by which—

My own catechism goes like this:

Which of the seven arrows killed Saint Sebastian?
The one that went right through his heart.
Which arrow hurt the most?
The one shot by his best friend.
How will I be martyred for my faith?

The answer to this question will come soon, the words for it, decades later.

Every Friday afternoon during Lent, seven hundred students at St. Sebastian Catholic School enter the enormous church and sit down by age and by grade—in row after row of brown oak pews monitored by ancient nuns—for Mass, Stations of the Cross, and the Adoration of the Blessed Sacrament.

We are the children of the American Dream, in this parish, over-whelmingly Italian American—our parents deciding to speak to us in English not Italian, to straighten our hair, grounding us in Catholicism, to make sure, above all things, that we do not stand out. My mother calls me in from playing outside in a blow-up swimming pool during the summertime, explaining as she dries me off that my olive skin "will get so dark the neighbors will think you're a Spic."

We first graders, from three different classes of some fifty plus kids each, get to sit up front, eighth graders at the back of the church, every-body else in between, flanked by rows and rows of twinkling votive can-dles in red glass cups along the sides of the church, arranged on wrought iron stands painted with cheap paint to look like brass.

The nuns don't really care if you sit with your own class during Mass or not because if you talk out loud, any one of them might smack you on the back of the head, or call out your name in a hoarse whisper.

I am in Sister Gonzaga's class and sit with Donny Sienna from Sister Dominick's first grade class. As legions of schoolgirls in gray plaid skirts and blue wool vests and boys in gray pants and blue oxford shirts troop up to the communion rail, I watch them and whisper to Donny Sienna. "If you could pick how they were going to martyr you," I ask, "what would you pick?"

"Well I dunno—" Donny begins in a whisper. "Sister Dominick said being martyred was the best way to die because if you die for your faith you go straight to heaven." He's stalling. "So how would *you* go?" I press. "If the Romans said, 'Okay, you can either be tortured by having your hands and feet cut off and then being stabbed, or you can be stoned with great big rocks thrown at you by a crowd of mean pagans, or you can have your eyes poked out and then be fed blind to the lions or be tied to a tree and shot with arrows like St. Sebastian,' what would you pick?"

Along the side church walls, near the Stations of the Cross, is a gallery of life-sized saint statues. As first graders we know them all by heart. Ten feet from where Donny Sienna and I now sit whispering stands St. Lucy, holding her eyeballs in a dish. Donny looks over at her. "How would *you* wanna be martyred?" he asks.

Soon we will both find out.

We are copying pictures of the Blessed Mother from holy cards Sister Gonzaga has distributed, redrawing them on paper with colored pencils.

This is art class. Mary wears blue and white robes and she is looking up to God. Her hands are pressed together and she is stepping on the head of a big snake, who manages to coil himself around a globe of the world. I draw the Blessed Mother with green and yellow crayons and I draw her in army boots not barefoot like on the holy card. I don't especially like the Blessed Mother, why I can't really say. Since my favorite television show at the time is *My Favorite Martian* with Ray Walston and Bill Bixby, I draw two antennae coming out of her bowed head.

Sister Gonzaga roams up and down the aisles, her long black robes and wooden rosary beads lapping up against the blond wooden desks like waves against piers. She smells like baby powder and wool. While we are drawing, the kids in my class keep one eye on Sister Gonzaga and one eye on the clock, knowing that as long as she keeps moving, they are fine.

She stops suddenly. Everyone looks up with a jolt from their drawings. The backwash of rosary beads splashes across a kid's desk, whose they can't tell right away.

The crucifix lands in the middle of my picture of Mary. I look at the little crucified Jesus on Sister Gonzaga's long black crucifix. Then I look up.

"And just what do you think you're doing, may I ask?"

I jerk violently, stammering, "I, I was—I thought..." trying to spit out some kind of lie—an explanation, a confession, whatever Sister Gonzaga wants. It's no good.

"Answer me."

"I thought if Mary had—"

"You thought—*what*? That this picture of our Blessed Mother is *funny*? That sacrilege is a *joke*?"

Then comes the ultimate weapon. She takes out her bow.

"Children, what did I ask you to do today? Can someone please tell me what the assignment was?" She points to Rhonda Lawrence. Rhonda Lawrence stands up and says on cue, "You said we should use our colored pencils to copy the picture of Our Blessed Mother exactly the way she appears on our holy cards, Sister Gonzaga." Rhonda Lawrence sits down, smoothing her plaid kilt and giving me a sidelong glance.

"Did the rest of you hear me say this, children?"

"Yes, Sister Gonzaga!" they intone.

"So explain this to me, please." A pause. Silence. "EXPLAIN IT!"

"Yes, Sister—no, I didn't mean to . . . Sister—"

"*No*, Sister? You're going to make your First Communion next year!"

"Yes, Sister—"

Yes, Sister. Anything, Sister. I'm sorry, Sister.

Sister Gonzaga walks to her desk and the desk drawer opens with a scream-like, high-pitched scraping sound. She removes a wooden metal-edged ruler. It's new, and Sister Gonzaga taps it on her palm rapidly several times. There is the flat echoless sound of metal on soft, veiny old lady flesh. She walks over to my desk.

"Stand in the aisle," she says, now possessed. I jump. Beyond terror, thinking if I just do what she asks that maybe this will be over with soon.

"As penance, I want you to offer up three Hail Marys to Our Blessed Mother. Hold out your hands."

I look at her face and say the words but I am not praying. I am too frightened. It flashes into my head how much I hate the Blessed Mother.

"Hail Mary, full of grace, the Lord is with Thee. Blessed art thou among women and blessed is the fruit of thywombjesus—"

"Turn your palms over. I SAID TURN THEM OVER! Put them together. The rest of you: PAY ATTENTION TO THIS!" Sister Gonzaga bellows.

"Holymarymotherofgodprayforussinnersnowandatthehourofourdeathamenhailmaryfullofgracethelordiswiththee—"

She takes aim, then swings as hard as she can. I squeeze my eyes shut. The force of the ruler across my hands knocks me slightly forward, into Sister Gonzaga. The noise of the ruler slams down the main hall of the school. Kids at the drinking fountain stop slurping and look up. This is Italian American Catholic education in the early 1960s.

Terror.

That at any moment, you will suffer, die, and be buried. For nothing at all.

My father's father was gunned down by the Mafia when he stepped outside early one Sunday morning to grab the Sunday paper off the front stoop of his house in Buffalo. A rising Mafia star, a bootlegger during Prohibition, he didn't know what hit him. Years later, when my father and I watch *Godfather II* together he is overwhelmed during the scenes with young Al Pacino and says when the movie's over, "There's more truth in that movie than you'll ever know."

After my grandfather is gunned down, my father is taken to live with his mother under the roof of her parents and large family on the West Side of Cleveland. They are raised for a time as brother and sister. To make sure no one comes after my father.

This of course is never discussed. But it is the story at the heart of the story. My father's greatest terror is that one of his five sons will stick out, be next. Shot through by life before we even get a chance.

So we are in store-bought special shoes with metal braces on their outsides because three of the five of us sons have flat feet, and we are enrolled in Catholic School, my father willing to pay a tuition that will nearly break him, we find out, years and years later.

So here I now stand in front of my entire class. Slow, painful, humiliating death—sticking out for everybody. A crippling spectacle, seamy, unspeakable pleasure for the adults into whose care we are entrusted.

My eyes sting. I squeeze them shut and my hands curl slightly inward at the fingertips when they're struck. Over and over again I am sliced by the piercing gold edge of the ruler—

"—Blessed art thou among women—"

—the piercing gold edge of the ruler—

"and blessed is the fruit of thy womb—"

—the piercing gold edge of the ruler—

"—Jesus?—"

—the piercing gold edge of the ruler—

"—Holy Mary, Mother of God—"

—the piercing gold edge of the ruler—

"—Pray for us sinners—"

—the piercing gold edge of the ruler—

"—Now and at the hour—"

—the piercing gold edge of the ruler—

"—Of our death. Amen?"

She strikes seven times.

I feel a warm trickle between my legs. I have soiled myself. Normally every kid in the class would laugh at this—this, and throwing up in the cafeteria during lunch.

But no one is laughing now. No one.

I suddenly think of the look on St. Sebastian's face in the vestibule and it calms me. I think of the maroon trickle of blood, and the brown stain softening between my legs. I look up, right into Sister Gonzaga's eyes. I am no longer afraid. She looks sad and lost and crazy. Trapped in something, by something. She is surprised by my calm and winded by this spasm of rage that is only the tip of her sadness.

I don't cry. I say softly aloud, as if trying the phrase on for size, "The one who wounds me deepest loves me the most."

Sister Gonzaga stops, her robes heaving up and down. She blinks.

"St. Sebastian said, 'The one who wounds me deepest loves me the most,' " I repeat. "That's you, Sister."

Sister Gonzaga is frozen. Rhonda Lawrence makes the Sign of the Cross.

I know the answer to the third question.

Part Two: The Question

I am happiest in school; the logic of the institution makes perfect sense, and what I least understand I defend with added vehemence. The routine is easy and occasionally interesting, and there are 55 other kids in the room with whom to play at recess. But more than anything else, I can look up at the clock and tell by what time it is exactly what is going to happen next.

When the women from the CYO bowling league come over to play bridge because it's my mom's turn to have the girls over, she calls upstairs, Raaaaaaaaan-Deeeeeeeeeee! and I come downstairs in my pj's and my mom says now tell the girls what you want to be when you grow up and I say shyly I want to be a priest. Then Judy Constanzo says isn't that the cutest goddamn thing you ever heard?

We play this game for decades. This way neither of my parents will have to really own what they know.

The question is: Who—or what—does this serve?

In graduate school, my mentor, Carol Gilligan, used to point out that the hallmarks of loss are idealization and denigration and underneath both, profound sadness. I pretend I will be a cleric one day, so that my celibacy will sanction ideals of goodness and control. Then no one will have to think about what the loss is. Or for whom.

I hear my parents arguing about money then I hear my mom moaning stop it, you're hurting my arm and I remember the picture of my father in the basement as he posed with the Ohio State wrestling team he was pinning another guy twice his size to the mat and then I heard a loud noise so I got up and went into my mom and dad's room they were standing over the bed with their arms up in the air twisted like they were dancing and my dad said you march yourself back into that goddamn bedroom and I looked my dad right in the eye and said in the voice of a penitent you just stop hurting people and my dad blinked his eyes for a minute and took off his belt it slid from the loops of his navy blue salesman's pants with a quick whizzy sound and then a black snake hung in the air above his head and something made me want to fall backward as I watched my glasses go flying off my face and ring the statue of the Holy Family on my mom's dresser just like when we play horseshoes at family reunions in Pepper Pike but nobody yelled that's a ringer and I stared at my dad for a long time and hot red iron and fire burned a line across my face and I stood there in my cowboy and indian pj's with snaps on the front and my mom said go to bed now and the next morning when I came down to breakfast I couldn't open my right eye and my dad put the *Akron Beacon Journal* down.

Jesus, he said.

It was very quiet.

I ate a bowl of Maypo and I looked at my dad. I watched him. He was staring at me. Then he asked, what are you going to tell Sister Gonzaga if she asks what happened to your face. He said it softly.

And I answered I'm gonna tell her my father beats his kids with a strap.

—Dominus vobiscum.

—Et cum spiritu tuo.

I looked at my dad. I heard the high whizzy sound of the snake again. I looked him in the eye.

"Go ahead and hit me," I said. I was seven. "The one who wounds me the deepest loves me the most." I know this by now. Years later a doctor will tell me, "You eroticized the violence in your upbringing in order to make it tolerable."

My father puts the belt down. Then something else happens. Something worse than the belt, worse than the arrows.

He stands with the belt in the air and suddenly he doesn't know where he is anymore.

Then my father breaks in half. Like the communion host, he snaps into two pieces.

Then I become my father and he becomes my son.

—Per omnia secula seculorum.

—Amen.

During Religion class the nuns tell us that on our seventh birthdays we hit The Age of Reason. When we turn seven, our innocence dies. This means we're old enough to know the difference between right and wrong and so God will be watching everything we do from now on and our sins will be burned away in Purgatory like the warts I had on my knuckles and on the back of my head that my dad got rid of by painting on clear medicine that smelled like ether from a dark blue bottle with a thin glass stick attached to the cap.

My Grandma Carmella Randazzo dies when I reach The Age of Reason, she dies just after midnight, right after my birthday and I'm certain she's in Heaven. My grandmother, Carmella—my father's mother—is there because she said the rosary every day on her knees in her living room then attended Mass right before breakfast.

On the morning she becomes a saint, on the morning I reach The Age of Reason, my dad and mom call my brother and me into their bedroom and it was the only time we were ever allowed to get into bed with them and my dad puts his arm around me and says Grandma went to heaven last night boys.

Why? I ask.

What is this question, my father says.

On a corner of their nightstand sits a wool pair of brown pants my Grandma Carmella got me before she went into the hospital because she knew she had something wrong with her blood cells and probably knew she was going to die and my father kept crying she even got you those pants she even got you those pants and I never saw my father cry like that it was high-pitched and scary and he cried right into his hands and my mother cried too and when we got to the funeral my Aunt Rosie walked up to the coffin and she kissed my Grandma and said you were the only good one in this whole goddamn family and then all of us kids are taken downstairs and they give us a piece of dry white cake from a sheetcake that says "Rest in Peace, Carmella" on it but I couldn't eat cake when I could hear my father crying so hard upstairs so that night when we got back home and my parents were watching *The Jack Paar Show* I took the brown wool pants into the backyard where we had a big round metal trash burner way in the back of our house near the woods that began where our yard stopped and I put the pants into the burner with a pronged twig and poked them down under the layer of ashes and the next day when my dad took the trash and the newspapers out to the burner and burned them and I was sitting in my bedroom looking at the *World Book Encyclopedia* under "Blood cells" and I could see black smoke coming from the trash burner and I thought of those pants in the ashes and then I thought of my Grandma Carmella in the ground because we had gone to the cemetery and we watched them lower the casket into a hole that somebody had already dug and then we all threw red carnations into it but I didn't throw mine I hid it in my jacket and when my dad came in from the burner his hands had that smell like ashes with after-shave mixed in and then I knew the pants were burned and I wouldn't have to wear them because then my dad would cry all over again and then I would have to kill myself but suicide is the one sin God never forgives.

Oh, St. Sebastian, how many times I have looked at your slumped body in the vestibule and wondered what it would be like not to die for others, not to find glory in humiliation?

But we are the Flames of Hell.

Epilogue: The Divine Petitions

Slumped, the body hangs in the gold-leafed church vestibule from a brown ceramic tree. In suffering beauty, thick neck and twisted face are up-turned. Like the eyes, the mouth is wide open, frozen in a spasm of pain, the sculpted forearms entwined by delicate purple veins. Tousled, shoulder-length crow-black hair splays across powerful broad, white muscular shoulders, the torso pierced by seven arrows and tied by cords to the tree.

St. Sebastian, patron saint of archers, pray for us.

St. Sebastian, patron saint of athletes, pray for us.

St. Sebastian, patron saint of soldiers, pray for us.

St. Sebastian, whose own men were ordered by the Roman Emperor to kill him on discovery that he was a Christian.

St. Sebastian, the Italian solider whose men refused to carry out the Emperor's orders, putting themselves in danger of being executed until Sebastian made a game of it by saying (says the libretto in Debussy's "The Martyrdom of St. Sebastian"), "He who wounds me deepest loves me the most." Archers. Athletes. Soldiers. Men.

St. Sebastian, Man of the Church.

Patron Saint of Homosexuals, pray for us.

Profound Sadness, pray for us.

Daughters of Mongrassano
· · · · · · · · · · · ·
JEANNA LUCCI CANAPARI

I think it was a few weeks after my first Communion when our neighbor, Priscilla, stormed into the kitchen of our two-family house on Long Island, wringing the hem of her housecoat. I could recognize a worried grandmother from my dishcloth-folding post at the kitchen table, so I folded myself into a safe corner.

"I know that my daughter thinks I'm nuts." Priscilla paced the linoleum in her bedroom slippers. "She thinks Anthony has a cold. I'm telling you, he doesn't." As Priscilla spoke in her heavy Long Island accent, my mother softly translated her rant, selectively, for my grandmother, who was standing at the sink defrosting a chicken under a running tap.

My grandparents, who lived in the second-floor apartment of our house, arrived in Long Island when my mother was a small child, but spoke only the Italian dialect of Mongrassano, the mountaintop town in Calabria where they were born. Though English was our first language, my two younger sisters and I knew all the Calabrese words children would hear from a grandmother (or *Nonna,* which became Nanny

· · · · ·

JEANNA LUCCI CANAPARI is currently at work on a collection of essays on Italian American culture and identity. A graduate of Columbia University and a Long Island native, she lives in Cambridge, Massachusetts.

to us) and a grandfather *(Nonno)*. We knew quiet! *(Chitta!)*, I love you *(ti voglio bene)*, and turn down the television! *(Vascia la televisione!)*

"We saw my sister Mariangela yesterday," Priscilla went on, "the one that lives out in Ronkonkoma? Well, she was all over him. 'Oh what a beautiful child, oh God bless him, oh oh oh.' Yeah, right! I told Mariangela, 'Quit looking at my grandkid and tell your daughter to get busy!' Meanwhile, six hours later, Anthony's throwing up all over the place. He's got a fever. And Marie won't bring him over. What, she thinks St. Joseph's aspirin is gonna cure the evil eye?" she said, extending her pinky and forefinger up toward the ceiling.

I wasn't sure what the evil eye, or *malocchio,* as Nanny would say, was, but it made me shiver whenever anyone mentioned it. When I saw Priscilla make the sign of the curse toward the ceiling I remember thinking, who's upstairs? My sister? Is she going to start throwing up now?

"I'll call Marie and tell her to bring him over," my mother said.

Thirty seconds into the phone call, Priscilla stamped her foot, her slipper muffling the stamp's intended effect.

"Is she coming or not?" she said.

"OK," my mother said into the receiver. "Bye." She hung up the phone and turned to Priscilla, who was looking at her expectantly. "Yes, already! She'll be here in a minute."

It was a mild evening in April, but when Marie showed up with Anthony she had him wrapped in three crocheted blankets to make the trip from her house around the block. All I could see of the two-year-old was one bright red cheek.

"Anthony!" Priscilla hovered over the baby as he started to cry. "Oh! *Menaggia miseria!* He don't look good!"

"Ma!" Marie's pocketbook hit the linoleum with a thunk. "He just has a cold. We were with Daniela the other day and her kid was sick. This evil eye thing is a joke!"

"Oh, what do you know?" Priscilla said, standing closely behind Marie as she settled onto a chair at the kitchen table. "Just let her see! If it's nothing I won't say another word."

As Nanny turned to reach for Anthony, she remembered I was in the corner folding furiously and used her free hand to shoo me out of the room.

"*Vattene!*" she shouted at me. "Go watch TV!"

"Why can't I stay?"

My mother ushered me into the foyer by my shoulders.

"That's not fair!"

"Jeanna, just go upstairs and watch TV with Nonno."

"I'm going already," I said.

I spent a few minutes upstairs trying to listen through the floor while Nonno looked at me over the top of his *Gazzetta dello Sport,* confused. After a few minutes, I gave up and turned on the television. About half an hour later, I heard Priscilla, Anthony, and Marie leave, the jalousie door slamming behind them. I went to the window behind the sofa where Nonno sat and watched them walk away.

"Was that so hard?" Priscilla said to Marie, her piercing voice carrying up to my second-story perch. "He's already better, look!" Marie was aloof. She walked ahead of her mother, ignoring her words and holding the crochet-swaddled Anthony close. When Priscilla didn't bring him back the next day, I knew Nanny had worked her magic.

I was too young then to watch the goings-on, but even as I got older and Priscilla marched in and out of our kitchen with her increasing brood of grandchildren dozens of times, my grandmother never let me watch her perform her craft. The secret prayers and rituals that women

in Calabria were taught on Christmas Eve to remove the *malocchio* remain a mystery to me, even now. I think Nanny thought that I lived in
a new world where the old ways no longer mattered. But my ear was
pressed to the floor every time she did her work.

It occurred to me, only recently, the name for women like my grandmother, who add up the everyday details of a household, the empirical
evidence of spilled olive oil and coffee grains, a flushed cheek of a child,
and see beyond them into the spiritual world.

"Was Nanny a witch?" I asked my mother, as we recalled my grandmother just a while back. It was the fifth anniversary of her death.
Nanny died on a December night, when she was 87 and I was 24.

"No!" my mother said, sitting up in her chair at her kitchen table,
clutching her demitasse cup. Then she slunk back again. "Yes. Well . . ."
she hesitated. "I guess she was a *strega*. But, mind you, she just removed
the evil eye. I don't want you to think she was riding around on a
broomstick and hexing people. She was a good witch."

"You don't have to explain that," I said. "But what I don't understand
is, she was Catholic. Witchcraft isn't in the Bible."

"What Bible? Do you ever remember Nanny reading the Bible, you
know, in her spare time? She didn't even own one. I'm not saying
Nanny wasn't Catholic, because she was . . . but in Mongrassano, I don't
think anyone would have any problem with doing both. I don't know
how to explain it better than that."

Though we lived so close to it, my grandparents rarely went into New
York. But one Christmas, when I was a child, we all went to the city,
Nanny and Nonno, my sisters, my parents, and I. We went to see the
Christmas tree at Rockefeller Center, the shop windows at Saks Fifth

Avenue, and Saint Patrick's Cathedral: the trinity of the American Christmas, pagan, commercial, and spiritual, lined up on Fifth Avenue.

At Saint Pat's, while my grandfather waited outside, Nanny went in to light a candle at the alcove of Saint Anthony of Padua, next to the gift shop. I watched as she put fifty cents in a brass collection box and bowed her head to pray for a moment in front of a statue of the saint.

What she did reminds me of how ancient Romans might have made an offering to a god. In return for her faith, and a bit of her money, she hoped that the saint would provide her with an answer to her prayer. It was the most important code in her religion, more important than any written dogma, and older. This quid pro quo began in the ancient world and became folded into Christianity when it swept across Europe and churches were built on the sites of temples to pagan gods. All over Italy, Minerva overlapped with Mary; in Rome, the Pantheon became home to the legions of saints.

In Calabria, the past is present, preserved in remote mountain towns and riverbeds and the few ancient roads that reach them. There, in the sight of churches, are thickets where you can search for wood nymphs that can improve your love life if you leave food by a certain chestnut tree. There are houses, near overgrown Greek temples, in which palm fronds are tucked behind mirrors and witches make magical potions. There are kitchens where women gather to confront the evil eye. And Saint Anthony, whose figurine rests on dresser tops in the bedrooms of town, replaced a man or beast who took into his charge all fears and desires, things lost and found. When Christianity came to scribble its legacy onto Italy, people still found room for what came before, for all of it: for churches and for the thicket, for witches and abbeys, for Easter and Christmas and potions of love and revenge, for Communion and the Evil Eye.

A thousand years ago, five hundred years ago, and today, in Mongrassano and on Long Island, this is truth: a yawn is a doorway into a baby's soul, an opening allowing evil spirits to enter. And I remember my grandmother, with my sisters on her lap, making a sign of the cross with her thumb over their drooling mouths, locking the evil spirits out.

Shortly after my grandmother died, my mother bought a Strega Nona doll at a children's bookstore, and we started to call the doll Nanny.

The witch of Tomie DePaola's children's book, *Strega Nona,* looked uncannily like Nanny: the two had the same protruding chin and nose that together make a crescent moon, wore aprons that cascaded over round stomachs, and had head kerchiefs that rested above twinkling eyes. And they were both witches, though Nanny never had a magical cauldron, like Strega Nona, that spewed yards of spaghetti; she managed pasta production all on her own.

The doll, embodying Nanny, has been to weddings, to Christmas dinners and afternoon coffee hours, and to the Italian market on Long Island where the local ladies gossiped. When my family went to Italy for vacation and to revisit Mongrassano, Strega Nona came too. We took photographs of her sitting on a crumbling ledge at the Coliseum, peeking out of a backpack on the tracks at the Naples train station, perusing the ruins at Pompeii, and sunning herself on the Amalfi coast. How could we not take her with us? We were going to Calabria to see the people that Nanny used to know, to walk in her steps and remember where we all began before she and Nonno changed their lives completely so we could traipse the clean-swept streets of America, and go to school, and to the city to work, and live in homes with no livestock of any kind in the house.

Strega Nona wasn't in Italy just to sightsee. There was also a piece of unfinished business that we had to take care of for Nanny while we were in Calabria. I had heard my grandmother lament, when she was alive, that she had never gotten the chance to return to Italy. I had thought she had wanted to see her hometown one more time.

"No, are you kidding?" my mother said to me on the train as it left Naples and headed south. "What could she possibly want to see in that dump? You know, Jean, it's interesting for us to go see Mongrassano because we never had to live there, at least not for very long. But for her? Believe me, she was just fine staying on Oak Street."

Instead, my mother told me, Nanny wanted to return because she had long ago promised to make a pilgrimage to the sanctuary of Saint Francis of Paola, to repay the grace of the saint for having fulfilled a wish.

As the train headed toward Paola, on the Tyrrhenian coast, I stared out the window, looking down from cliffside tracks onto unpopulated aqua beaches and half-built homes of stucco and concrete, and wondered what Nanny had done that required her to make a pilgrimage and a bargain with a saint. I had always thought when Nanny prayed at home to her figurine of Saint Anthony, or at Saint Patrick's as she lit a candle, that she sought health or general well-being for her family. But it turns out that what she was after was a more particular quid pro quo.

Maybe she had a secret that she did not want uncovered. A secret love? Did she pray to Saint Francis that her true love never be exposed to the world so she could go to America and leave him behind without anyone the wiser? As I watched the familiar landscapes of her life race by my window, Nanny leapt off her living room couch in my mind, threw down her cane, and tore aside her widow's black to reveal a Technicolor life.

"Nanny, we're going to finish your pilgrimage!" I said to the doll in my mother's lap. My mother made Strega Nona clap her hands.

The sanctuary of Saint Francis is on a hilltop overlooking the city of Paola, which is forty minutes from Mongrassano in the province of Cosenza. Winding up the hill toward the sanctuary, I watched shuttered stucco homes and disused factories give way to black patches of grass, smoldering from the brush fires that plague Calabria throughout summer. I knew that the sanctuary was close when I began to see the Stations of the Cross go by, mounted in the exposed rock. They finished at an enormous parking lot filled with tour buses and overlooking the sea.

I turned away from the sea to the sanctuary, tucked into the side of the hill. The saint's compound is a palimpsest itself. Walking up to the entrance along a broad piazza that marked the homestretch of our pilgrimage, I passed architecture of several centuries that seemed to melt into one rambling structure. A modern glass building found a place within medieval stone walls, and a sixteenth-century cloister attached itself to a church, which was originally early Gothic but rebuilt in the Baroque style. The structures were so ingrained in the land, so organic, that it was difficult to tell where the sanctuary ended and the rocky hillside began.

My mother held Strega Nona carefully, facing out, as we went inside the church, and I dabbed her with holy water. Pilgrims swarming around us, we followed the crowd to the saint's relics, mounted in black and white marble and surrounded with offerings of flowers, real and plastic. My mother propped the doll up on the shrine, and I took her picture. Then she stepped out of the way and left Nanny there by herself.

A nun walked over to where we were standing, and watched us, Nanny's daughter and granddaughter, looking at the doll. Catching the nun's eye, my mother gave her a sheepish look and pulled Nanny down from her perch.

The nun smiled at us, and without speaking, showed my mother a short strand of black yarn ending in tassels, a *conocchia e fusu*. It was a miniature of what the priests and nuns wore around their waists and a souvenir of the sanctuary. The nun tied it around Strega Nona, and walked away as quietly as she came.

I had been a little embarrassed about Strega Nona on our trip, and worried that people who saw my family with the doll might think that what we were doing was strange or disrespectful to the dead. But I cried at the sight of Strega Nona with the *conocchia e fusu* around her waist, her pilgrimage completed. The doll, though a silly thing found in a shop, had kept Nanny close to my family after her death. Something in us, passed on from generations before, understood the sanctity of objects, the comfort of holding something in hand that was a physical symbol of all the things that could never be seen and all the things that we would never want to lose. The impulse we had to carry Strega Nona with us was not unlike lighting a candle, or praying to a figurine, or using the potions and amulets that guarded our family from the evil eye. She was our reinvention of that ancient impulse, and a sign that the old ways were still alive in us and always would be no matter where we lived in the world or how different our lives became from those who came before us.

I sighed. My mother smiled at me, seeming to know what I was thinking. "Let's hit the gift shop," she said.

We loaded up on rosary beads, prayer cards, and ceramic statues of Saint Francis. Wandering the aisles, I passed by thermometers, ashtrays, dishcloths, calendars, all ablaze with brightly colored images of the saint. Behind an overstock of Saint Francis snow globes, I found a tiny wooden figure, green, shaped like two arches and hinged in the middle like a locket, one inch high. On the left side was a picture of Saint Francis, and on the right, in tiny print, on a sticker fastened to the wood, were the words,

"Due cose al mondo non ti abbandono mai: l'occhio di Dio che dovunque ti vede e il cuore della mamma che sempre ti segue."

"There are two things in the world that never abandon you: the eye of God which always sees you and the heart of a mother which always follows you."

I sat close to my mother as we got back in the taxi. With my grandmother, her mother, watching over us, my mother took me to see the place where she was born.

Allium Longicuspis

. . . .

STEPHANIE SUSNJARA

The ancient roots of the garlic bulb and the ever-unfurling roots of
my family tree are so intertwined they're impossible to separate.
Grounded in the past and stretching into the future, these roots are
braided together in solidarity, keeping the branches of identity alive
and intact.

I feel a special kinship with garlic, one that transcends bodily nour-
ishment. However, my relationship with garlic has not always been so
rapturous. At one point I hated garlic and thought I would have to ban-
ish it from my life.

Garlic's ascent from second-class citizenry to comfortable bohemian
chic mirrors my own family's twentieth-century immigrant experience.
Between 1880 and 1920, over four million Italians, including my maternal relatives, migrated to the United States. Language barriers, cultural
differences, and relative poverty placed them toward the bottom eche-
lon of society along with other recent immigrants. To worsen their
plight, the Italians were garlic eaters at a time when garlic was hardly in

. . . . .

STEPHANIE SUSNJARA's essays have appeared in *Brain, Child* and *Women Who Eat:
A New Generation on the Glory of Food.* A graduate of the MFA program in Creative
Nonfiction at Goucher College, she lives in Katonah, New York, and is currently work-
ing on a collection of essays about food.

vogue. In those days, the smell of garlic on one's breath was like the Scarlet Letter pinned to Hester Prynne's chest, the mark of a pariah.

If my Neapolitan great-grandmother were alive today, the main-streaming of garlic would surprise her, considering the prejudices she encountered when she emigrated from her rural village of Calitrie to Washington, D.C. She'd recall how her son and daughter (my grand-mother), the only Italians at their school, were chased home daily with the kids shouting at them "guinea" and "wop."

Despite the cruel taunting of her classmates, my grandmother never betrayed her culinary roots. When I was a young girl in the early '70s, I'd stand on a stepstool beside her stove and watch as she tossed whole garlic cloves into a pot of crushed tomatoes, basil, and olive oil. The sauce would simmer all day until the cloves dissolved, their richness cre-ating a fragrant potion. As I helped my grandmother prepare Sunday family dinner, garlic showed up in every dish. We'd chop garlic coarsely and add it to roasted red peppers that had been doused with extra vir-gin olive oil for the *antipasti*. We'd mince garlic and mix it with bread-crumbs and Parmesan for stuffed artichokes. We'd slice thin garlic slivers and press them into veal roast. As the garlic's papery skins crack-led in my hands and the spicy scent tickled my nostrils, I realized that garlic imparts sensuality to a dish, satisfying a deeper hunger within.

My mother, a second generation, assimilated Italian American, was the first to rebel. In the late '50s she left her hometown of Brooklyn for Rosemont College outside of Philadelphia. The all-girl student body at Rosemont was predominantly White Anglo-Saxon Protestant, a cul-ture far removed from my mother's earthy Italian roots. Whenever she brought friends home from school, she asked my grandmother to omit the garlic. Cook without garlic? My grandmother was stung by this re-quest, which brought back all the painful, taunting memories of her childhood.

But Mom's rebellion was short-lived. Toward the end of college—to the joy of my grandmother—she met a man of Slavic heritage and married him. My father was a serious food lover who was raised on garlic-laden cuisine.

Garlic's association with the lower classes extends beyond my great-grandmother's day. Americans inherited their dislike for garlic from the British, whose disdain can be traced back over 2,000 years to the Roman Empire. Aristocratic Romans abstained from eating garlic, detesting its powerful odor. In Elizabethan times (1558–1603) the word "garlic-eater" signified low social class, and later become a derogatory term used to label foreigners. On December 22, 1818, the poet Percy Shelley wrote from Naples: "There are two Italies... The one is the most sublime and lovely contemplation that can be conceived by the imagination of man; the other is the most degraded, disgusting, and odious. What do you think? Young women of rank actually eat... you will never guess what... garlick!"

Contempt for garlic reverberated into the twentieth century, swooping down upon my mother's WASPy college campus and extending into my teenage life. In the late 1970s I was attending seventh grade at Garden City Junior High School on Long Island. One day I received an anonymous phone call.

"Susnjara, everybody hates you," a voice cackled at the other end of the line. "You're ugly and skinny, you have bushy eyebrows, and you smell." I recognized that high-pitched, whiny voice. It belonged to the female leader of the most popular clique in junior high, a group I had been trying to nudge my way into. I was too stunned to respond before the ringleader hung up.

"Who was that, honey?" asked my mother.

"Wrong number," I said, slipping out of the room. I couldn't possibly tell my mother what had transpired on the phone. I didn't want her to know her daughter was a loser, washed up at thirteen.

That night I curled up on my bed like a frightened snail of a girl, tucked within her shell. Safe and warm, coiled within white sheets, I wondered why God allowed the most powerful clique in junior high to direct their collective hatred toward me. It was true. I was skinny and had thick eyebrows. But smelly, too? What my enemies could be referring to, I had no idea. As a dedicated reader of *Seventeen* magazine, I was well aware of all the beauty products targeted at young girls. Didn't I shampoo every day with Herbal Essence shampoo, sprinkle my body with Shower to Shower bath powder, dab Love's Babysoft behind my ears, and slick my lips with Lipsmacker strawberry-flavored lip gloss? I was dousing myself with so many scents—fruity, floral, spicy, and herbal—there was no way an offensive smell could have been emanating from my pores. I drifted off to sleep, wondering how the hell I would survive seventh grade.

The next day in the cafeteria, I passed by the popular crowd's table and heard someone snicker, "There goes stinky breath."

My cheeks burned. I scurried over to the designated nerd table and hid my head in my lunch box. A strong whiff of garlicky salami, piled on a hard Italian roll, accosted my nostrils.

From then on, I had my mom pack peanut butter and jelly or domestic ham on squishy Wonder Bread—the same stuff the other kids had. Still, I didn't win favor with the popular crowd. On weekends, I slept late and lazed around in my pajamas watching TV. My mother would beg me to call a friend. How could I tell her I didn't have any?

Halfway through the school year, I developed chronic body aches and a low-grade temperature. My mother took me to our family doctor. He believed my illness was psychosomatic, but he wrote a note excusing me from the remaining three months of school. The teachers sent work home, and I earned all A's. They offered little solace. I wanted to be popular, not smart, and at my school the two were mutually exclusive.

The loneliness was unbearable. In the fall of the ninth grade, I reached out to other misfits, those deemed too quirky or brainy or unattractive by the cheerleaders, football players, and other members of the junior high elite. We gathered in each other's basements to smoke pot, read hipster novels by Kurt Vonnegut or Tom Wolfe, and listen to the Grateful Dead. We romanticized our outsider status, and my broken teen spirit began to mend.

In the eleventh grade I fell in love with Larry, an artist who dressed in black, smoked Gitanes, and carried a copy of Albert Camus's *The Stranger* in his back pocket. While our classmates were hanging out at McDonald's and the Roosevelt Field mall, Larry and I would take the Long Island railroad into Manhattan. In the shade of Washington Square Park, we read each other poems by William Blake and listened to musicians strum guitars. At night, we wandered the narrow streets of Greenwich Village chasing down Jack Kerouac's ghost and dined on falafel, humus, and tabouleh at the Middle Eastern cafes that lined MacDougal Street. Sometimes we'd meander down to Chinatown for heaping platters of crabs drowned in black bean sauce.

Eating my way through the cheap joints of Manhattan, I regained respect for garlic, a star ingredient in all those ethnic dishes we were discovering. Like the Indian print blouses that billowed on racks outside the boutiques on Bleecker, garlic now struck me as bold and spirited. Empowered by my new identity as a bohemian refugee, I began walking the high school corridors with my shoulders thrust back, my head held high, puffing garlic's exotic scent over the "in" crowd and their homogenous suburban values. It was a grand moment in my coming of age, with both crises, over garlic and identity, finally resolved.

Throughout my twenties and thirties, I considered myself a genuine garlic lover as well as an enthusiastic connoisseur of its delights. In reality I was a fraud, living in ignorance on generic garlic from my local supermarket. The most common garlic found in supermarkets today, a variety known as Italian, the progenitor of California Early and California Late, was introduced to the United States at the turn of the century. At this time, the influence of Victorian manners on American high society, coupled with the wave of Italian immigration, smashed garlic to an all-time low level of repute. My grandmother's upbringing coincided with this dark period in garlic's history.

One late August morning at the outdoor Greenmarket in New York City's Union Square, I was initiated into the extraordinary gourmet garlic world, populated by a sect beholden to the herb for its many powers over mind, body, and soul. A hazy sun beat down on a throng of early risers who bustled about the stands, gathering the last bounty of summer: succulent corn, spicy-sweet bouquets of basil, and just-picked tomatoes heaving with juice. I pushed through the crowd, past barrels overflowing with eggplant and squash, and past shelves laden with homemade pies, their cross-hatched crusts stretched over mounds of blueberries and other sweet fruit. Soon I found myself standing in front of a table piled high with garlic bulbs still attached to their stiff, ruler-length stems. Unlike the bulbous supermarket variety, these heads were small and uniform, ivory-colored and streaked with pale violet. Scraggly roots hung from their bottoms, coarse and kinky.

"Excuse me," I said. "What kind of garlic is this?" The woman behind the garlic-filled cart wore her silvery hair tied back in a ponytail. She had a clear complexion and a glowing tan.

"Allium longicuspis," she answered, as she picked up a wand of garlic and swirled it in the air like a magician. "It's the most ancient garlic in the world, the only one that hasn't been genetically altered." The woman handed me a tiny sliver of raw garlic. "Taste," she commanded. I examined the wafer of garlic glittering in my palm, then closed my eyes and placed it on my tongue. It was hot and spicy but quickly mellowed, leaving a strong but pleasant aftertaste, not at all bitter. The flavor danced in my mouth. It was as if I were tasting garlic for the first time. At that moment rays of sun zeroed in on the bulbs, igniting them with a supernatural glow.

"I'll take two," I said.

"Wait," said the garlic woman. "Let me get you some better looking ones." She turned on the heels of her Teva sandals and disappeared into the back of her black minivan. A moment later she returned clutching garlic stalks.

I tucked the wands of garlic underneath my arm, toting them the way Parisians carry their beloved baguettes. I practically ran home, eager to get cooking. That night my husband and I dined on *spaghetti con aglio e olio* (spaghetti with garlic and oil). The fresh garlic, with its toothsome bite, transformed this basic dish into a dazzling feast.

I became obsessed, scouring the library bookshelves for garlic history, garlic recipes, and garlic lore. After reading about garlic's origins in Chester Aaron's *The Great Garlic Book,* I began to daydream about the woman at the Greenmarket, with her piercing blue eyes and bright purple flannel shirt flapping in the early morning breeze. I imagined that she was an apparition I'd conjured up out of garlic's very ancient past. Perhaps she was really a 6,000-year-old Kirghiz nomad who, long ago, gathered *allium longicuspis* bulbs as she and her tribe roamed across the mountains of central Asia where food historians pinpoint garlic's origins. Maybe she was a spice trader who transported garlic along the trade routes, spreading it east through China and west through Egypt, eventually bringing it to Europe and then on to North America. Or might she have been among the day laborers who built the Great Pyramid, receiving payment in the form of onions, parsley, and *allium longicuspis*?

I also learned how garlic eventually broke through the class barriers. Thanks must be paid to culinary icons James Beard, who in the 1950s proclaimed that a good cook could not live without garlic, and Julia Child, whose traditional French recipes often featured garlic. By the 1970s, Alice Waters, chef and owner of Chez Panisse in Berkeley, California, began slathering roasted garlic paste on bread as if it were butter and creating unlikely desserts like figs poached in wine and garlic, signaling that the garlic revolution was in full swing. Over the next few decades, the American palate became more and more accustomed to other garlic-laden cuisines as immigrants from Southeast Asia, Mexico, and Latin America settled here. The red-checked tablecloth period of Italian dining, with its southern Italian derivatives such as spaghetti and meatballs and chicken Parmesan, made room for new regional Italian restaurants that featured the foods of Emilia-Romagna and Tuscany. In

2002, Italian chef Mario Batali, of Food Network fame, appeared on the cover of *Gourmet* magazine, his fists bulging with garlic bulbs.

Today garlic is a common staple in the pantries of America's most celebrated chefs. In serious food circles, the growers of high-end specialty garlic become famous. There are garlic magazines such as *Mostly Garlic* and the *Garlic Times,* garlic newsletters such as the *Garlic Press,* garlic restaurants such as San Francisco's *Stinking Rose,* and dozens of nationwide garlic festivals. The story of garlic, its struggles and its successes, echoes the American Dream.

My quest for garlic knowledge culminated with the annual Hudson Valley Garlic Festival. The event is held in Saugerties, New York, in late September—the time to enjoy East Coast garlic at its prime. (Garlic is harvested here in July and August, then cured for two months.) I remember my heart pounding with excitement as I entered the festival gates. Many others had made this same trip, and the unabashed crowd displayed their devotion, with garlic logo T-shirts, 18-carat gold *allium sativum* necklaces, drop-style earrings shaped like delicate white bulbs, and tattoos of fading gray bulbs on forearms. Hobnobbing with garlic growers, garlic chefs, and garlic experts, checking out endless tables groaning with exotic garlic, I quickly grew familiar with names such as Music, Italian Rocambole, Porcelain, Killarney Red, Creole, Red Toch, Georgian, Siberian, and Spanish Roja. I moved from stand to stand sampling raw cloves, filling my backpack with dozens of bulbs.

The heady scent of frying garlic lured me further and further into this Shangri-la. Suddenly, I felt ravenous. The food concession area presented a smorgasbord of garlic delights; I chowed down on corn on the cob slathered with garlic herb butter, tortilla chips blanketed with warm garlic salsa, and string beans blackened in a garlic dry rub.

Licking a shockingly tasty garlic ice-cream cone, I continued my stroll until I came upon a small crowd surrounding a man wearing a black cowboy hat festooned with garlic bulbs, an "I Love Garlic" T-shirt, and boxer shorts with bold garlic-bulb print. With scraggly white hair and skin crinkled by age and sun, he actually resembled a head of garlic. He looked at me and reached out his hand.

"Hello there," he said. "I'm Mr. Garlic."

Suddenly a camera crew from a local news station was on the scene, and Mr. Garlic was on his mission, enthusiastically proclaiming, "I have been growing garlic for over 25 years, and I travel all over, telling people about the health benefits of garlic. Garlic lowers blood pressure and cholesterol, prevents cancer, improves circulation, and can even enhance your sex life."

During my research, I had unearthed a Middle Eastern folk belief that a bridegroom who pins a clove of garlic to his lapel ensures a happy wedding night. I'd also come across a Web site for the Garlic Centre of Sussex, England, which touted garlic as a cure for penile dysfunction. Garlic, it seems, can improve blood circulation and stimulate the enzyme nitric oxide synthase, two essentials for obtaining and maintaining an erection. Why take Viagra when there's garlic, a less expensive, over-the-counter drug?

My thoughts drifted back to Mr. Garlic, who still held the media in rapt attention. I wondered what kind of sacrifices Mr. Garlic had made in order to spend so much time on the road, touring North America as an apostle for garlic. Did he have family? Was there a Mrs. Garlic? My own passion seemed quite pale in comparison. At that moment, I realized that I simply don't have what it takes to renounce all else in the name of garlic. My journey would have a different climax.

In bed that night, I tossed and turned, unable to stop thinking about my new garlic stash. Careful not to wake my husband, I crept out of bed. At the dining room table, I set up my own private taste test, laying out slivers of each bulb, along with water and crackers to cleanse the palate. Like wine experts, garlic growers use a specific vocabulary to describe the taste of garlic, defining it in terms of hotness and aftertaste. Is the garlic hot or mild or bitter at the back of the throat? Does the clove's spiciness mellow, linger, or clear?

Until recently, it was believed that over 200 varieties of garlic existed. However, new studies involving DNA tests confirm just six: rocambole, porcelain, Asiatic, purple stripe, marble purple stripe, and artichoke. The endless taste variations of exotic garlic have more to do with environmental factors such as soil and climate than true genetic differences.

I broke open a bulb of Spanish Roja, chose a plump clove, and peeled back the papery skin to reveal flesh shining with juice. I nibbled on it, savoring its sharp tang. The Killarney Red left a warming aftertaste that lingered on my tongue like a fine Cognac, and the Palermo tasted mellow and smooth, like sweet butter.

I carefully labeled each bag of garlic and jotted down some cooking notes. I constructed a small shrine, lining up the small paper bags of garlic on the middle shelf of my dining room hutch, a cool, dark place that would keep the bulbs fresh for months. I fell asleep dreaming of steak with chimmichurri, shrimp with garlic sauce, bouillabaisse, and chicken stewed with forty cloves of garlic.

The next night I made garlic soup by simmering a whole bulb of spicy German-White in chicken broth. I crushed a handful of *longicuspis* cloves underneath the broad side of a knife—a technique that heightens garlic's potency by breaking down its sulfur-rich cells—and stuffed them into the cavity of a roasting chicken, along with lemon and rosemary, and nestled the bird into a 425 degree oven. Then I sautéed minced Spanish Roja cloves in olive oil, watching to make sure they didn't burn and turn bitter. I folded baby spinach leaves into the garlicky oil, wilting them until they glistened an emerald green.

When my husband walked through the door, a strong, seductive aroma pervaded our apartment. Sulfur compounds in garlic release endorphins, which may have been the reason behind our heightened sense of well-being. Before he could speak, I handed him a thick slab of *bruschetta,* toasted bread rubbed with the Palermo, then dipped in a mixture of olive oil and coarse salt. He took a bite and sighed with pleasure.

We proceeded to the candlelit table, took our seats, and bowed our heads over the bowls of steaming soup. The flavor was rich yet mellow, bewitchingly good for such a simple dish. The chicken had beautiful crisp skin, tangy with garlic, and meat that fell off the bone. The savory whipped potatoes dissolved on the tongue, and the spinach tasted lush in its silky bath of garlic and oil.

After dinner we moved to the living room, both reeling with happiness. We sank into the couch. My husband brought my hand to his lips. "That was one of the best meals I've ever eaten," he said, then slowly nibbled his way up my arm. His lips trailed across my shoulders, sending a sweet rush of desire through my core. We undressed each other, slowly peeling off each layer of clothing. I pushed his naked body down on the couch and climbed on top. We pressed into each other, finding the perfect fit. He buried his face in my neck. "You smell terrific," he whispered.

"You, too," I replied, running my fingers through his hair.

Our bodies rocked back and forth, and we fell to the floor. Both breathing hard, we continued making love, lost in time and enveloped in garlic's celestial perfume.

Lovers' Garlic Feast

Garlic Soup

INGREDIENTS: 1 head of garlic, 1½ quarts chicken broth, four slices toasted Italian bread, salt and freshly ground pepper, Italian parsley, and extra virgin olive oil.

DIRECTIONS: Peel the garlic. Poach the cloves in simmering broth for ten minutes. Add salt and pepper. Ladle the soup into four bowls, top each with a slice of toasted bread. Sprinkle with parsley. Serve hot.

Perfect Roast Chicken

Adapted from a recipe that appeared in the *New York Times,* this is a perfect Sunday supper dish. The secret to roasting chicken is to start roasting the bird at a high temperature—this makes for crispy skin and seals in the juices.

INGREDIENTS: 4-pound roasting chicken, 4 lemons, 1 head garlic, fresh rosemary sprigs, and olive oil.

DIRECTIONS: Heat oven to 425 degrees. Wash chicken thoroughly under cold running water. Pat dry inside and out with paper towels. Cut lemons into quarters. Roll garlic on hard surface to separate cloves. With flat side of a heavy knife, smash garlic cloves (skin need not be removed). Stuff lemons and garlic inside the body cavity. Tie legs together. Tuck rosemary between thighs and breast. Rub chicken lightly with olive oil. Place in roasting pan and bake 30 minutes; reduce heat to 375 degrees and cook about 45 minutes longer or until juices run clear when chicken is pricked with a fork. Serves 6 (or 2, with plenty of leftovers).

Best-Ever Garlic Mashed Potatoes

INGREDIENTS: 4 pounds russet potatoes, peeled and quartered, 5–7 peeled garlic cloves, 3 tablespoons unsalted butter, ¾ cup milk, salt, and freshly ground pepper.

DIRECTIONS: Place potatoes and garlic in a large saucepan and cover them with cold, salted water. Bring to a boil. Lower the heat and cook until potatoes are tender. Drain. Return potatoes to the pot and mash along with the garlic. Stir in milk and butter. Season with salt and pepper to taste.

Jealousy, or The Autobiography of an Italian Woman

GINA BARRECA

I

I was born jealous.

Just as some people know how to sing from the moment they open their mouths, I was able, from the first breath I took, to wonder why somebody else had it better than me. Why was somebody else's layette set more frilly? Why did their mothers get more flowers? Why did the nurse coo more frequently over the bundle in the next crib than over me?

I'm sure I kept track. Somewhere in my infant brain was inscribed a primitive cry at—and for—injustice: "Ignore them; choose me!"

It's still there, that cry, indelible as a tattoo. It was woven into my DNA, right there alongside the love of opera, the distrust of government officials, and sixteen recipes for eggplant.

Maybe I was my mother's favorite, my family's favorite, maybe even my doctor's favorite, but what did they know? Those foolish enough to prefer me did not count—that was automatic. I am certain that what I wanted was to be valued by those who saw no particular difference

GINA BARRECA is a professor of English at the University of Connecticut. She is the author of *Babes in Boyland, They Used to Call Me Snow White but I Drifted,* and *Too Much of a Good Thing Is Wonderful,* as well as the editor of *Don't Tell Mama: The Penguin Book of Italian American Writing.*

between me and other one-day-olds. If only they hadn't been so busy admiring those ridiculous lesser babies, I might have won.

Winning has always been important to me. Even when I don't know what it is that drives me, blind and ruthless. This remains true even though the ferocious presence of jealousy I felt in my youth is no longer quite as palpable.

When I was five and my brother was ten, I tore into confetti the valentines he received from sweet, innocent little girls in his fourth-grade class. They had, I am quite certain, no intention of provoking the fury of a grubby, chubby miniature Medea. They were just being nice.

But "nice" is not what I felt when faced with glittery hearts in pastel colors directed to my one big brother. Once he discovered what I'd done, he ran to my mother and demanded to know why I was so rotten. My poor confused and worried mother didn't know what to say in defense of her daughter's indefensible act. I remember that climactic moment, forty-three years after the fact. I made a decision to suck my thumb and not answer.

What I don't know is whether I was prompted to viciousness by a wish to have my brother all to myself, or by the wish to have the valentines all to myself. No doubt a good shrink would declare it a combination of both. And when my good shrink asks, "Why do you compare yourself to other people? Why aren't you content?" I bite my tongue, as I once thrust my thumb into my mouth, and am silent.

She knows I still struggle with a desire to triumph over my rivals— or my imagined rivals.

Jealousy defies sophistication. "Choose me!" isn't what you'd call a refined request.

We torture ourselves with jealousy, true, but the world makes it easy. A girl hears "Why can't you be as sweet as Ann-Marie? She never cries." And instead of choosing to emulate Ann-Marie, you decide to tie her to railroad tracks. You cry "Not fair! If I always got my way, I'd be sweet too!" You embed this in your fierce six-year-old heart. The emotion sits there, knitting itself into the core of your emerging self, forming a web.

If my father kissed my mother before kissing me after he returned home from work, I would throw myself down a short flight of stairs to manifest my disapproval. This was the story recited to the hilarity and approval of family members on Ocean Avenue in Brooklyn. Nobody suggested that we go to a counselor; it would have been more likely that they'd suggest an exorcist. So there I was, flinging myself down the steps on a regular basis and being regarded as a real Barreca for doing so. It was seen as evidence of an appropriately passionate nature. How my mother—my poor French-Canadian mother—felt about this I don't know. She might not have found it so funny. What could she do? Her voice was drowned out by the much louder, livelier, more persuasive voices of my father's family. And after all, she was the one who had moved in under their roof. No doubt they felt she had very little right to exert any influence. Conspiratorial women, my aunts and grandmother—her other rivals for my father's affections—saw me as one of them. It could not have been easy for her.

We learn to slipcover jealousy with contempt. "You won't catch me brown-nosing" we say when we get a B. Archly we sniff, "I could have done everything she did if I didn't have to work after school, live so far away, deal with inherited self-loathing."

We occasionally attempt to fool ourselves by camouflaging jealousy as compassion: "Poor thing; she tries so hard to look glamorous. I don't care if all the guys look at her all night long. Personally, I feel sorry for her."

. . .

Once in the web, it's tricky to get out. Jealousy is self-sustaining; it feeds on itself, chewing on details and imagination the way you tear at your cuticles and draw blood but somehow find the act satisfying.

Don't wave self-esteem around as if it's a solution, either, however well meant. I have whole closetsful of self-esteem, right behind my winter clothes and my self-respect. Also, don't get me wrong in terms of the Italian American thing, either. I don't think that we're the only ones who get jealous; we don't have a lock on this emotion. But we do it better, like cooking with garlic or writing sonnets. We're not ashamed of it, where non-Italians are embarrassed by the fact that they want to bury their rivals. They giggle when inventing plots of revenge.

"Without jealousy there is no love" declares an old Italian saying. Italian American women love deeply, and we're deeply jealous. It's an emotion that comes from the heart; why hide it?

Since I too come from that passionate, ungovernable, inexplicable part of the world, you couldn't expect me to be any different. All life begins with passion. You wouldn't want to live without it.

Not that it's so easy to live *with* it, either.

Italians inhabit the Lower East Side of emotional life: messy, loud, and confusing to outsiders.

II

Would she and her husband have married under other circumstances, Anna, a paisano, asks me. Or would they have simply split up, leaving each other at an airport, waving good-bye with remorse but also with relief? Would they have dwindled to memories, become increasingly distant as the years passed from where they are now? Is marriage a location, my friend asks me, one that you either head toward—or away from—at any given moment?

She and her husband more or less grew up together. They met when they were twenty-one. What can you learn by twenty-one? You can barely cross the street or cut your own food. Any earlier relationships were strictly amateur. Practice.

It didn't seem so at the time, of course. She cut her sharp, jealous teeth on his former girlfriends, one in particular who was in the same class at medical school. Being his colleague meant this girl was smart and dangerous. Plus she had access to him during the day. They could meet for lunch and tell themselves it counted as work. This girl knitted him a sweater, thereby asserting that she was feminine and domestic— a combination not particularly potent that young except when combined with brains and ambition. Commandeering the sweater within the first month of their dating, Anna's breasts pushed out the subtle pattern knitted into the blue wool. Never saying so out loud, Anna was slit-eyed happy to be shaping it to herself, happy to distort the original version imagined by the medical student, the sweetheart, the knitter. It was like being able to rewrite somebody's love letter, making a parody of the intention behind the original by changing it just a little bit.

Anna positioned herself as the interloper in their relationship, as the "other woman," and relished the part. Uncovering a few details—no, all the details—of the other girl's life, Anna proceeded to make subtle but effective fun of them and thereby undermined the other girl's status as singular object of affection. She disdained knitting and all crafts; she made jokes about female medical students. This scattershot approach to the dismantling of the old girlfriend's fortified hold worked better than she imagined, and soon Anna was the one waiting for the boy to knock on her door, call on her phone, slip into her sheets.

The girl went on to do her residency halfway across the country. Anna is sure that she thinks about the old girlfriend more than her husband does and she wonders why. As if in some kind of fidelity to her younger self, Anna has never wavered from the opinions she held all those years ago, afraid to admit that they were only shallow responses to a young woman who no longer mattered. It's almost as if Anna needs to hold onto the idea of a vanquished rival as a way to prevent the same thing from happening to her. She needs to be the winner, the victor in the struggle. If she doesn't hold onto that position, it might just happen that another woman will fill it.

III

My story is different from Anna's. I am my husband's second wife. He left his first wife. He divorced her and married me. That's the simple chronology.

The story is more complicated.

And so I do what second wives do: I've counted the years until we will have been married longer than they were. It will take some time. I always fear I won't quite catch up. The equation works against me; the numbers are fixed. So if that's how marriages are judged then I lose, but I can't believe that's how marriages are judged. Marriage isn't a marathon, after all. It isn't merely about going the distance, like two fighters who can claim victory because they're still standing, bloodied and incoherent, when the final bell rings. Surely a marriage can't be considered successful simply because it exists over a period of time until one of the combatants, players, partners, dies.

As the second wife, I believe that I'm the real wife, not the required one but the chosen one, the one he picked as a grown-up. I am the woman who married him when his collar had grown a little too tight rather than when his thin neck wobbled inside cheaper shirts, barely touching the sides of the fabric, the version I've seen of him in old photographs.

I claim that young man, too, however. My flag covers old as well as new realms; previously colonized as well as newly acquired territories come under my aegis. That thin-necked boy is mine as surely as a foundation stone is part of the finished building—the original contractor doesn't keep the cornerstone even if he was the one to put it in place. This is about territory, conquest, ownership.

It is about love.

IV

"I bought these pants the other day and they're way too big. They say they're a size ten but they must be a twelve. I think they might fit you. Want to try them on?"

"Thanks. I'll try them on at home."

"Don't you want to try them on here to see if they work?"

"No, I'll do it at home, and I promise I'll return them if they don't fit."

Pause.

"Look, why don't you try to lose the extra weight? A few brisk walks every week, a couple of skipped lunches, and you'd be beautiful."

"I'm fine. I'm happy that everything on my body seems to work. My husband loves me enough to pinch me when I'm in the kitchen making dinner, and besides, I like to eat. I don't want to skip lunch. I do lunch really well."

"But honey, you'd be so much happier with just a few changes. You know that. People think you're ten years older than I am. Tell me that doesn't make you feel bad."

"Meaning that it makes you feel good?"

"This is not about me."

"Everything you've ever said is about you."

V

My ex-husband didn't like my extended family. He said that all anybody talked about was how much money somebody else made, what kind of deal somebody got on a house or a car or a TV, and how many times somebody had been to Italy. He was an Englishman and he simply didn't get it. Why didn't anybody talk about their own money, for example? He didn't see that Italians would never, ever want somebody to know how much they personally had. It was nobody else's business how much you had. What other people had, in contrast, now that was a rich source of conversation. You did not want to call attention to yourself in a way that might make someone envy you. It seemed like bad luck to be the Joneses with whom everyone else wanted to keep up because, after all, everyone hated the Joneses; no one would wish them well. "Rotten bastards, who do they think they are? They think they're so much better than us? Good. Let them think that."

VI

A call before eight from my best friend from junior high school never means happy news. She's another Italian woman, one whose life is different from mine but whom I love as a sister. She leaves a message on my machine while I am in the shower: "Call me."

The edge in her voice is sharp enough to cut bone.

When she picks up the phone, I hear running water and the metallic sound of cutlery being thrown into the sink. "Am I interrupting you?" I ask for form's sake, trying to sound apologetic.

"You're not interrupting anything that shouldn't be interrupted," she mutters. I hear her moving dishes into the sink and I know she is cradling the phone in the hollow of her shoulder, doing other things—stacking the dishwasher, filling the washing machine, drying the silverware.

"I shouldn't be thinking what I'm thinking this morning."

"You want to tell me?" I pull on pantyhose while trying not to miss a word. I put the phone down on the bed so I can use two hands to pull the tights up all the way. I still hear her.

She doesn't want to get to the big subject right away, so instead I ask her about school. She went back to college to finish her degree—this, after raising three kids and being married for twenty-six years to the same man. A man I don't like, have never really liked, have never really trusted. He's like a hyphen between us, her husband, connecting and distancing us from each other at the same time. She usually calls when things are going badly between them. I'm her oldest friend and she doesn't have to give me a history lesson; we're closer when she's furthest away from him. It's not something I encourage, but it is something I acknowledge.

But finally I say, "Look, I really want to hear about all this, but I've got to go to work and the meter's running. Tell me the real stuff."

Silence. And then she starts. "We had his new clerk over for dinner last night and it's just that now I want to murder everybody. I'd wipe everybody out, except the kids. They weren't even home."

"So?"

"Peter asked me to give him the benefit of the doubt, but I don't have those kind of benefits around anymore." She waits, catches her breath. "I know too fucking well that I can make everything harmless by just letting it go but I can't. I hate them all."

I risk interrupting, "Hate who, honey?"

"Him, her, me, everybody." She's banging pots and pans around again, as if providing orchestral accompaniment. "I hate how stupid and useless I feel but mostly I hate that Peter stayed inside the dining room last night after dinner and talked to that woman with big cow eyes while I did every stupid dish, in the manner of all wives everywhere. I was the wife . . . and it wasn't pretty."

"But you've always been the wife, you usually like being the wife. 'I'm the judge's wife' is what you say about yourself when people ask who you are."

"Well, I don't like it anymore." I hear something fall with a crash behind her, but she just keeps going. "I've had two thousand years of being married to this man but just exactly one year of learning to make my own way in the world and you know that I had to carve that path out of my family with a machete. So, from the kitchen, with me out of the room, I hear him making fun of my going back to get my degree— making fun of me to this twenty-eight-year-old lawyer who sat on her ass while I scraped off her plate. Jesus. I thought it was only old women in our neighborhood who felt like I felt last night, at the sink with my hands in hot water, wanting to kill my husband. My hair suddenly felt too short and my feet felt too big and my tits felt too flat and my teeth looked yellow in the downstairs mirror. I kept sneaking looks at myself, can you believe it? I felt like a wife—and like 'wife' was a dirty word, something nobody should be called—because Peter was in there talking to a woman who wasn't a 'wife' and suddenly wifedom seems defined by women who aren't married instead of by the ones who are."

There is silence for a minute. It doesn't matter. I sit at the table and wait. "So?"

"So I'm standing there at the sink and all I kept thinking was my life has been filled with fucking jealousy," she laughs bitterly. "It's all I am. It's what I've become. I'm jealous of the kids who sit next to me in my classes. Their lives will be entirely different from mine because they're actually getting started on making themselves into people before they start having children and need to make *them* into people. I'm jealous of you, of my other friends, of my own daughter, for chrissake. And I am really jealous, seriously jealous, of this ridiculous girl of Peter's."

I stop putting on my earrings, moving the phone from one ear to the other without missing a syllable. I hear what she says about being jealous of me and my heart freezes; I don't want her to think of me that way, it kills me to believe she thinks of me that way. I'm not somebody in that category; I'm not somebody she measures herself against, how can I be, we're from the same place, we're versions of the same person, we're best friends. I want anything but to be a yardstick, a stick she would use to beat herself. What I say is, "Tell me about the girl."

"Let's just say she should be judged by weight, not by volume. I was pissed off when he hired her. I was pissed off when she called at home during dinner for the last month to ask questions about his assignments. Sure, as his clerk she has every right to call, but not during my dinner. She never chews her cuticles. She's younger, sweeter, smarter than I could ever be. Or ever was. I was never that young," she practically yells, and then says, "And neither were you, Gina. Neither of us was ever that young."

My Italian friend, who never cries, starts to cry.

VII

Jealousy makes detectives, clairvoyants, and thieves of us all. We track down private papers; we imagine encounters in gruesome detail and construct passionate conversations; we purloin letters, phone bills, and e-mails; we decode their passwords, the retrieval code for their answering machines, their journal entries. When their phones are busy, we call the other numbers to see if indeed we can make the connection—are they talking to the one we fear? We drive by to see if lights are on, if cars are in driveways; we walk by offices to see if doors are open or shut; we go through trash; we go through credit card statements. We go through hell.

"To be loved is nothing," wrote André Gide. "What I want is to be preferred." Ah, yes: preference. A rival sweetens the captured heart; a vanquished foe flavors the victory. What you really want is to win someone's favor, not to settle for what is offered to all.

Doesn't being first in line depend on the concept of the second, third, and tenth, impatient behind you? To be alone in the queue is comic. Pathetic.

A rival at school, in love, at work, in the family; what would we do without our trusted double?

VIII

Before I went on my first book tour, an Italian friend of mine who grew up in Philadelphia said that I must—no question about it—sew some red thread onto the gold necklace I always wear in order to stave off the evil eye. "People are going to be jealous of you because you did something they haven't done. A lot of people think of success not as something you earn, but something bestowed randomly. Why you and not them, they'll think, and even if they don't mean to, they'll give you the evil eye. Red thread will offer you protection. You don't believe it, do it as a favor to me."

And so, with humble gratitude for the generosity I was offered—generosity being the antidote to jealousy—I find red string around my gold.

IX

Jealousy captures the imagination. It creeps up on us when we least expect it and involves people we love deeply. Of course it does. We long to bite the hand that feeds us, the hand with the ring we are meant to kiss. Jealousy emerges from the most buried part of ourselves; we carry it with us from the oldest of old neighborhoods, the oldest of old countries.

Il Pasto Che Parla
. . . .
VALERIE K. WALDROP

"You're squashing the snake," she says. "Stop. Watch me." Beneath her hands the dough lengthens and smoothes, an obedient potato snake. "Roll it firm but easy," she says. We both watch her square hands, pale with flour, move on the counter. "Go stir the sauce," she says without looking up, and cuddles this snake along the last one she rolled. My mother's kitchen is no laboratory; experiments are not encouraged. If I'm likely to wreck the recipe or make a mess, she will snatch the food away and make it right. She is a small woman, but her way is large, so I, an obedient daughter, step away from the counter and move to the stove.

We are making *gnocchi alla sorrentina,* the Italian dumpling. Sprinkle flour over cold mashed potatoes, add an egg and mix by hand, then knead the dough until it's as soft as an earlobe. The dough is shaped and cut and curled. And once cooked, the potato pasta is piled in a bowl and covered with a simple red sauce and grated *parmigiano* cheese. If made correctly, if the snake is spared the squashing, if the dumpling hollows,

. . . . .

VALERIE K. WALDROP is working toward her MFA in Creative Nonfiction at Western Michigan University. This is her first published story. She lives in Anchorage, Alaska, with her husband and son.

gnocchi is delicious. Each *gnoccho* is a delicate dumpling curl that, once cooked, will slightly resist the tooth and melt on the tongue. "Help me cut the dough," she says, and I do, sure of this part. Holding the snake down on the table with one hand, I slice with the other. I cut off half inch pieces and swipe them to the side. My mother's quick hand keeps the counter dusted with flour, and still her slicing speed is twice mine. Our *pezzetti,* the sweet little dough pieces, slide gracefully to their pile. When all the snakes have been cut, my mother hands me a fork. Here is the art, I think: with my left hand I hold the fork, handle resting between my thumb and first finger, at a forty-five degree angle, concave side facing up with the tips of the tines poised against the counter. With my right hand, I place a lightly floured *pezzo* at the base of the tines. I pet the dough against the tines while rolling it down the fork: too hard and my finger will break through, too soft and the *gnoccho* will not hollow and will remain heavy. The dough wraps perfectly over my finger as it rolls down the fork; the finished *gnoccho* is a ridged curl around my deep finger indentation. My mother and I work quietly, grab a *pezzo,* roll it, slip it aside, and then again. Her occasional closed-lipped *hmmmm* tells me not to press so hard. Together we cover the counter in *gnocchi.*

My mother, Fulvia Maria Rosaria Sanniti, was born in Naples in 1934, to Vicenzo and Rovena Sanniti. Her father was a nobleman; the Sanniti family held the title of "Count" for three centuries, until all titles were stripped after the Second World War. He married Rovena against his family's wishes. My grandmother was a Tuscan farm girl who left the hills to make a living in the city. My mother is a lovely blend of her parents: noble grace and agrarian strength. She has aged easily. Her skin is fair and smooth like the heart of a potato. She draws on her eyebrows each morning, perfect arcs, and matches their angle on her round lips with dark rose lipstick. She has been light blonde all my life, but in photos from her twenties her hair is darker. She likes to show me these photos: "My waist was twenty-three inches," she says, "and that was after two babies." Forty years and two more children later, her perfectly petite Italian frame is fuller, voluptuously sturdy.

I remember how strong she seemed leaning over my father in his hospital bed, fixing the blanket: her hands moved without hesitation. I was twenty years old, standing near the door in the recovery room after his gallbladder surgery. My father was semiconscious, ashen, and skinny. Tears slid down his cheeks, and his lips were caked with dried blood. He would be fine, I knew, but when I saw him on the hospital bed I cried. I felt helpless. The more I tried not to cry, and to be strong, the more I cried, until I was sobbing and gasping. My mother had her arms under my father's torso to adjust him. She straightened up and looked at me and said, "Stop it or leave." I left the room and wondered if I could ever have her strength.

The last of six children in her family, my mother was three years old when her father died of throat cancer. Vicenzo planned for his family to be supported after his death by his wealthy father and stepmother. When his widow, Rovena, asked her in-laws for support, they told her there would never be money for her or the children because Vicenzo had not married nobility. Rovena went to work to support her family. My mother and one of her sisters, Adriana, were not old enough for school and needed watching during the day, so Rovena took them to an orphanage where she intended for them to live until they were old enough for school. "I wouldn't stay there," my mother says. "I wanted to live at home, so I kicked the nun who met us, scratched her arm, and pulled off her habit." My mother tells me the story sixty-five years later with the same feistiness I imagine in that toddler. She grabs high in the air to demonstrate how she reached the nun's habit and pulls down, her fist tossed to the floor. She straightens up and smiles. "Of course I remember what happened; I remember everything," she says. "The nun said I was too young for the orphanage, so I left with my mother. Adriana lived there for several years. I was only a baby, but I knew that I didn't want to live there." Rovena asked her sister-in law to take in my mother. Although the Contessa did not consider her niece, my mother, noble (I'm sure she thought my mother's blood was only half blue), she agreed to care for her at their country estate. "She hardly cared for me," my mother says. "I tried to run away every day for a year, but it was too hard. I was so young. Farmers would pick me up on the side of the road, and I'd go pick potatoes with them, but they always took me back to my aunt's house at the end of the day. The Contessa never looked for me when I was gone. For dinner she would feed her children soup and then give me just bread. I tried to jump out of a window one day, so she returned me to my mother, afraid that I'd kill myself and she'd be blamed." My mother tells the story sitting at the table, leaning over it. Her elbows supporting her, she presses one fist against her heart. "I will never forgive that woman," she says.

My mother was five years old when she left the Contessa's home and finally old enough for school; instead she returned to Naples just in time for war.

Cynthia, my sister, calls our mom a war baby. "It explains everything." The war made Naples poor and hungry and stripped its people of control. Rovena worked even more than before, and so did her four oldest children. While Adriana was in the orphanage, my mother stayed at home alone when she had to, stayed with neighbors when they were home, and went to school when it was available. She tells me a story of sitting up in a tree watching German soldiers walking underneath her, and later rummaging through their dead bodies for money and food. "I would roll them over and reach in their pockets. I was never afraid," she says. During the last two years of the war, Rovena was afraid for her, however. She sent my mother and Adriana to her family's farm in Tuscany, to what she saw as safety.

. . .

Maria, my mother's oldest sister, took care of the family in Naples while Rovena worked. During the first part of the war and for years afterward, my mother was an apprentice to Maria in the kitchen. There wasn't food to waste during the war, and so she learned to make meals from items we might discard these days: potato peels, the stalks of broccoli, leftover pasta. My mother still makes fabulous creations from remnants. I call these meals her "war food," but she doesn't laugh. "You don't know what you're talking about," she says. She's right. I don't know hunger. I mean by the expression only that some of her best dinners are her most modest.

"Make sure the spaghetti is cold before you add the egg." she says. "Otherwise the egg will cook too soon and look like it's been scrambled." We are making *frittata di spaghetti,* my favorite "war food." It is simply a spaghetti omelet. First beat the eggs, and then add grated *parmigiano,* salt and pepper. "Use enough eggs," she says, "but not too many or the meal will be too filling."

"How many eggs?" I ask.

"Enough," she says. Add the egg mix to the cooked and cooled spaghetti and mix well. Use a spaghetti fork to mix it: pull a bunch of spaghetti above the bowl, drop the spaghetti back in, and then fork some more.

"Don't mix it like pancakes," she says, "that's not what I mean, you're splashing, here, give that to me." If a spaghetti fork is not available, then two regular forks will work nicely; use them as if tossing a salad. My mother adds chopped ham and mozzarella to the mix, and I put some olive oil in the frying pan. "Just enough to cover the bottom of the pan," she says, "or it will splash out the sides." Fold the spaghetti mixture into the heated frying pan, cover and cook on medium heat until it's light brown. Then flip the *frittata* over to brown the other side. "Be careful," she says, because she lets me do the flipping. I hold the frying pan in my left hand, place a plate face down, like a lid, over the *frittata,* and I quickly turn the frying pan upside down while pressing on the plate. The cooked side is then up on the plate and I slide the *frittata* back into the pan, keeping the cooked side up. Once again, cook it covered until light brown. Serve the *frittata* hot or cold; it's delicious either way.

Maybe my sister is right and the war can explain everything about our mother. During the war she often went without enough food and for several years she was separated from her family. Now as an adult she seems to require steadiness from both. Or maybe it's simply that food is what she knows best, and therefore it's her favorite gift to those she loves. When I was in grade school, I would walk home from school each day for lunch. My mother refused to pack me a lunch and insisted that I return home for a better meal. She was working then, so she would leave my lunch set out on the table along with a note: "Valerie: don't use the stove, wash your hands, lock the door when you leave. Love Mom." The best lunch was a Thermos of *brodo e pastina,* chicken broth and tiny pasta, and a *Nutella* sandwich. *Nutella,* a chocolate sandwich spread, sounds like junk food, but somehow because it's Italian, my mother tells me, it is not. What I really wanted was a *marshmallow Fluff* sandwich. "It's too American," she'd say. *"Che schifezza!"* She often uses this expression, "what nastiness," to describe over-processed American foods. I didn't mind *schifezza* at eight years old. For me, normal moms fed their kids *Fluff,* and I was desperate for my mom to be normal. I wanted a mom who didn't talk with an accent, a mom who would pack my lunch with those little cheese and cracker snacks, the ones that included a small red plastic spreader, and whose package could double for a matchbox size semitruck.

When I was in middle school my family moved to Colorado for my father's final military assignment. My parents made their home in Denver and slowly, over the following twenty years, all four of us siblings left for college, traveled, worked, and eventually made our homes near them so we could eat our mother's Sunday dinner. She showed us love by cooking for us, and I think eating dinner at her table was our way to return the affection. I was on the Tupperware circuit then. My mother would package leftovers and send each of her children home with a meal for the week. Or if I missed the Sunday dinner, she might leave a container of food hidden on my back porch, and a phone message along with it: "Valerie: I've left some *pasta in bottita* on your porch, hurry, bring it inside, return the Tupperware on Sunday, and don't forget to lock the door. I love you." It comforts me to know that when I visit her, she will say during the hello hug, "Are you hungry?" And perhaps due to some repressed teenage disobedience, I will always respond to her advances with retreat:

"No, not really."

"Oh, just have a little. I've made you something special," she will say. And I will eat because that is what we do. And because my mother does not like to hear "no."

Several years ago, I moved to Michigan. My mother was worried I was losing weight. "Can't you buy good bread there?" she asked. "Have it with butter. Your dinner would be so much better." Really what she was saying, I think, was wouldn't my wedding dress look better if I still had my plump breasts to fill it?

If I live too far for her to feed me, then she mails me food. In college, I received a package every few weeks. In it were my favorite foods: Cinnamon Apple Cheerios, a box of Little School Boy milk chocolate cookies, and a chunk of *parmigiano*. Although I reassured her I could buy these things where I lived, she regularly sent them. In fact, fourteen years later, just last week, I received a package of *parmigiano* from her. "You have to use good cheese," she says.

· · ·

"It's the sauce of the whore," she says, "that's what *puttanesca* means."

"Really," I say, "why haven't you ever told me that before? You've been making this all of my life."

"Don't be ridiculous," she says, "of course I've told you its name. Here," she says, "cut the garlic thin." We prepare the ingredients for this fast sauce, me cutting the garlic thin, and her dicing the tomatoes. "Slice the garlic," she says. "Don't chop the cloves; it's better this way." She puts olive oil into the saucepan, and when it's heated she adds all of the ingredients: garlic, anchovies, capers, olives, fresh tomatoes, salt, and crushed red pepper. "Don't use bad olives," she says, "that American *schifezza*. Make sure they're Greek or Italian, and don't add too much salt. No, the olives are salty enough." She covers the sauce and cooks it on low for fifteen minutes, then adds parsley, and cooks the sauce covered for another five minutes. "The Italian housewife would spend the day with her lover," she says, "while her husband was at work. The wife would rush home in the evening to prepare her husband's dinner and throw these ingredients in a pot. When he ate this sauce, the husband was sure that something this delicious would have taken her all day to prepare, not twenty minutes, and so the sauce was a good cover for her infidelities."

"Oh," I say.

"Hurry," she says, "drain the spaghetti, it's best *al dente.*"

I have been an apprentice to my mother in the kitchen my entire life. I was a reluctant cook as a teenager: "Why doesn't Robert have to cook? Why can't I talk on the phone?" Most of my culinary education has come with the enthusiasm of adulthood, and the realization that I need to cook my own meals now. I have pressed my mother for recipes and direction on some of my favorite foods. She says there are things that are too hard for me to make. A few summers ago I was eating at my aunt's home in Naples. I asked the sisters how to make the *gateau di patate.* They looked at each other, and my *zia* Maria shook her head and laughed. "Ask us in a few years," my mom said. The *gateau* is a dollop of milky potato and *parmigiano* that is delicately bathed in breadcrumbs and then lightly fried. This year my aunt gave me the recipe as a wedding gift.

When I quit my job last fall, my mother was concerned about my finances. To reassure her that my husband and I would be okay, I called her one afternoon to say, "I'm making *risotto,* Mom, with portobello mushrooms."

"Oh," she said, "that takes so long."

"Yes Mom, I have time now," I said.

"Oh good," she said, "you really can't make *risotto* when you have a job." She is pleased that I cook for my new husband. I was raised watching her delight in feeding my brother and father; I'm sure she thinks cooking is my duty after all, and my ability to cook, a reflection on her mothering of me. "What are you cooking for Marc tonight?" she asked last month. "How about *penne alla Bolognese;* do you remember how much he liked mine at Christmas?"

"Yes," I said, "I do remember, Mom." While she wants me to be the primary chef in my home, she will say, occasionally, "Does Marc cook for you?" And she will mean by this, does he take care of you? Is he sweet to you?

"Yes Mom," I will say, "he cooked for me last night."

I can't duplicate some of my mother's recipes in my home. "What's wrong with you?" she says. "Remember it this time." We are making the *Genovese,* my favorite sauce. "It's important," she says, "to use a big enough pot; somehow it doesn't taste the same cooked in a small pot. Here," she says, "cut the celery, onions, and carrots very small. We'll add a few tomatoes, and a little water, and cook these for an hour."

"But Mom," I say, "I thought they were supposed to be cooked in oil first and then water later."

"No," she says and gasps, "oh my God, never. Water first." After an hour of cooking, the vegetables are passed through a hand mill. In Italian this hand mill is called a *passalegumi,* a vegetable passer. "Even Williams Sonoma doesn't carry this," she says. "I've looked, but no luck. So find something like it." My neighbor once lent me an applesauce mill for this task, and although it did pass the vegetables through, the Genovese still failed. Maybe I needed a *passalegumi.* "Put the vegetables back in the pot," she says, "and *now* add the olive oil, not before." Something magical occurs to carrot, celery, and onion when they are cooked together. The three transform into a slightly sweet and tangy paste. I'm of course not the first to notice this. I've read in a cooking magazine that the French have many words to describe these three vegetables together, a word for each way the vegetables may be cut and cooked.

"Mom," I say, "do you know what the French call this mixture?"

"Oh," she says, "French food is so bad." Add salt, pepper, and basil to the pot and cook it on medium. When it dries, add some white wine and cook it until this reduces. "Stir it," she says, "let the sauce almost burn, but not quite, and then stir it. Keep doing that. Drain the pasta," she says. I drain the *rigatoni,* pile it in pasta dishes, and top each with the *Genovese* and grated *parmigiano.*

I'm sure my mother has previously told me to add the oil first. I won't say that now she's lying, just that perhaps, at times, she purposefully omits some recipe details. Often my food comes out good, but not quite right. So I call my mother to find where I went wrong. In this way I need her. I live a thousand miles from her now, too far for the Sunday dinner, but our food conversation keeps our love steady. It is the Italian way: Mom and food are one. A few years ago I overheard my brother speaking with an Italian friend, Davide, at a café in Milan.

"Ciao Robert, how are you?" said Davide.

"Great, and you?"

"I'm well, and how is your mother?"

"Good. And yours?" said Robert.

"She's fine. Did you eat at your aunt's house yesterday?"

"Oh, yes," said Robert.

"What sauce did your mother make?" said Davide.

"She made the *Genovese*."

"Oh, delicious."

I can't think of an American friend who would ask so quickly about my mother, and none that would ever care to know what sauce she had made for dinner. I have come a long way since my *Fluff* fantasies of third grade. I now accept that my mom, although naturalized an American thirty years ago, is still, quite naturally, an Italian.

My mother will call me several times a week to ask what I've eaten for dinner. "I made *pasta zucchini* for first plate," I say, "and then I pan fried trout and had a salad with it." And she will coo, and ask,

"Did you lightly flour the fish like I showed you?"

And of course I will say, "Yes, Mom." What she really wants to know, I think, is how my day went, if I am well, whether I eat healthy. I use this language to learn about her day as well.

"Tonight I made *pasta a'burro* for me and your father," she says. And I know that her day was long, and that she's tired, because all she could manage to cook was spaghetti tossed with butter and *parmigiano*.

Today my husband had a busy day planned at work. I called him and asked what he ate for lunch. He said he ate a Caesar salad with grilled chicken and a side of vanilla yogurt. I told him I was planning to make him *pizza alla Napoletana* for dinner.

"I love you too," he said.

Selling the House

MARIANNA DE MARCO TORGOVNICK

Not a ghost, not a vision, there he was: my father at age sixty-nine (though he had died at eighty), standing in the living room of my house in Durham and looking around as he had the day we moved in. Saying, "This is the kind of house you see in movies, the kind of house rich people live in. Congratulations, Marianna." I was crossing from the foyer to the family room, filled with thoughts of family since I was teaching Philip Roth's *The Plot Against America* the next day—a book about the kind of family I or, perhaps more, my husband, had grown up in. My parents and in-laws were very much on my mind. So there he was: my father, who has been dead since the end of 1992. Not a ghost, not a vision, but simply there. A presence summoned up, I realized, after some thought, not just by the book I was going to teach but also, and more, by my situation, the situation of being ready to sell the house, being at a place in life when it only made sense to sell the house, but being madly and irrationally reluctant to do so.

· · · · ·

MARIANNA DE MARCO TORGOVNICK is Professor of English at Duke University and Director of Duke in New York in the Arts and Media. She is the author of the American Book Award-winning memoir *Crossing Ocean Parkway* as well as acclaimed works of cultural criticism such as *Gone Primitive* and *Primitive Passions.* Her newest book is *The War Complex.*

. . .

How do you sell a house when you have "the *sta' casa* gene"? Furtively, and with considerable angst. I have the *sta' casa* gene, the stay at home gene, I like to call it, which I cannot identify anywhere on a strand of DNA but can recognize in myself and others: the tendency to stay in one house for years and years and decades and decades—and to come from generations that have stayed in one house, so atypical of our America. This is my story.

My parents married on July 4, 1942—a patriotic gesture in a time so far distant that, although I can place it in relation to World War II, I can't really feel and touch it, save through the memory of the apartment they moved into that day, which became, some years later, the place where I was born and grew up. Curtains and bedspreads would change with the season; furniture would come and go; the landlords who owned the house would change at least three or four times. But the apartment remained—a stable place that was the only one my parents ever lived in as a couple.

They stayed married for almost fifty years, until my father's death (longevity in marriage being linked to the *sta' casa* gene). It was a happy marriage but, even if it had not been, anything else would have been, culturally and perhaps genetically, unthinkable for them. After my father's death, my mother continued living at their original place in Bensonhurst. Then, at age 89, amidst events that constitute a separate drama but one related to my own, she moved one flight down and next door into an apartment that looks, feels, and lives almost exactly like the one that she had rented for nearly sixty years.

"The neighborhood," Bensonhurst, was changing, as it had not for decades, and my mother's modest move was a concession to that. The house had been sold to non-Italians, more specifically to "the Chinese"—

a stereotype in this context and not people like you and me—and "the Chinese," as has become folkloric in Brooklyn, want empty houses when they buy. The move triggered a major crisis for my mother, marked by many tearful phone calls and much indecision until she bit the bullet and made the move, albeit into a place next door almost identical to the old one.

My mother's consort, Joe, lived in her building too but lacked the protection long-term tenants like my mother have under New York's rent-control laws. (Rent control is sacred in New York and no one ever gives it up.) Rather than lose Joe's companionship and undergo the trauma of his eviction, my mother chose to move next door into the two bedroom apartment they now share. With sixty years at just two next-door addresses, she may be the origin of my *sta' casa* gene—though I expect that my ancestry is laced through and through by attachments to houses, long-term residences, and anxieties about moving that go beyond the usual uneasiness anyone feels about transitions and change. I envision women in black washing windows and sidewalks in Sicily or clinging to that one room shack in Calabria. Partly out of affection, partly from necessity, my ancestors no doubt stayed in place until the fateful day they were forced to move.

My father's family's day came after my grandfather, a labor union organizer, ran afoul of the Mafia in Sicily. I never knew my mother's family's reasons for immigration but I do know that they, unlike most others, had kept the farm back home in Calabria so that, illogical as it seems, my American-born mother was sent back to Italy as a baby with her mother and the other kids and only returned to the United States when she was sixteen. Economic necessity may have been another name for the *sta' casa* gene or its reluctant subversion in the old country. But I suspect that needy people without the gene can and often must move frequently from place to place (migrants, we call them). And I know that economic necessity does not explain my own tendency to stay in one house—quite the contrary, in fact.

. . .

That house—soon not to be my house—is a beauty. It has gracious, flowing rooms, green trees and plantings all around, including hundreds of azaleas, and—what counts most, I think—an abundance of happy memories. My older daughter was an adorable 14 months when we moved into the house, accompanied by my parents, who drove down with us for the occasion: my daughter all chubby, wobbly legs and dark brown curls, cascading around the place with her favorite bottles in hand; my parents serious about the household details when they were not focused on my daughter's every move. My younger daughter was born while we lived in the house and my parents took the first airplane they had ever flown immediately after her birth to see the baby. Perhaps as a result, my younger daughter has an even worse case of the *sta' casa* gene than I do. The night we told her our house was going on the market—an event we'd been anticipating for years—she tried to be stoic but then broke down on the phone. She wouldn't be able to show the house to her own children, she said; she would never, ever see us all together in a place that she had first seen with a toddler's eyes. No porch would ever seem so special; the wallpaper in the bathroom would never be so dazzling; the cardinals in the trees wouldn't seem, somehow, quite as red. The past would be lost and no amount of searching would ever bring it back. All true. Her sobs made me realize fully why I'd seen my father in the living room; they made me understand why I'd been thinking for days about things associated with my parents in my house.

I might be driving along in my neighborhood and see, almost as if they were really there, my parents, wheeling my older daughter in her stroller, into which they had packed groceries from the store a mile away since, like many New Yorkers, they did not drive. Teasingly unhappy with the load, my Kate would toss things to the ground and my father, with good-humored mock-scolding very typical of him, would say, "that's enough now," and mug a look of pride toward my mother at his granddaughter's feistiness—though I hasten to add that she was usually quite well behaved.

In my kitchen, I saw in my mind's eye my father washing pots and pans with the attention he paid to such things, never having owned a dishwasher of his own and unwilling to use ours. He would scour our pots and pans for hours, his tongue protruding just a jot between his lips, forgotten in his concentration. Afterwards, he'd display the results for me, often with remarks I did not like about my husband's and my lesser standards.

Yes: the past had been a thing of richness and plentitude and I was not eager to shed it. I told myself that my past and my memories did not reside in any meaningful way in the house. That they resided in people, and in me. But was I lying, or at least not yet telling the whole truth about the reasons for selling the house?

For, of course, and perhaps inevitably, the very markers that tie my daughter to the house were the reasons it was time to leave it. My older daughter got her bachelor's degree in 2002; my younger daughter finished college in May 2004. Our beloved cat, Spiral—she of the gentle wisdom and gloriously soft dark tortoiseshell fur—died in my arms on the deck of the house that July. Both my daughters now live in New York—the older one permanently, the younger, perhaps not permanently—it's still possible, though unlikely, she'll return to Durham.

The wallpaper my daughter so admires has been hanging for more than twenty years; like the bathroom it adorns, it could use a renovation and is, quite simply, on the verge of getting shabby. The same can be said for the kitchen and for some of the windows, not to mention the decks we built and love but which, one year within the next five to ten, will surely need replacing.

That sprightly cardinal flitting in and around our one acre plus of land is, truly, one of the glories of the place, a sight that never stops thrilling some part of me. But from time to time, and sometimes dramatically, our land, like any land, needed trees removed, shrubs trimmed, lawns reseeded and so forth, not to mention regular maintenance. Some years the expense can be dramatic: once, Southern pine beetles ravaged forty trees and removing them cost almost ten thousand dollars.

Let's face it, as we try to do: our house is glorious but maintenance-intensive. Is it nice for two people? Yes indeed. Looking way ahead, would it make a great retirement house and take us into old age? Yes indeed once more. Could we keep the house if we wanted to badly enough? Yes, though it would mean some adjustments. But is it necessary for two people? No. Is it sensible for people with our current lifestyle? No, and emphatically no again. For here, life has dealt me a delightful twist, but one I am only now coming to terms with in the form of selling the house.

For the last few years, I have taught for my university for five months each year in New York, doing committee work and the like from afar before returning to North Carolina to teach during spring semesters. It's been a wonderful and fortunate arrangement—one I love—an unexpected mid-career adjustment beyond my wildest dreams. Because finding a new place to live in New York each year is unthinkable for anyone who knows the crazy New York market, let alone for someone with the *sta' casa* gene, I maintain an apartment in New York—and I love that place too, though it is (and will always be) too small and too new to be anything like "home." The problem, not surprisingly, is that it no longer makes sense to maintain a large and elegant place in Durham for only part of the year, especially a place where things often happen in the yard and to the house when we're away. And even if it did make sense, we could not really—read: comfortably—afford to do so. I have the *sta' casa* gene, no doubt about it. But I am also an all-American woman and a briskly professional one at that. It might have taken a feud with the Mafia to motivate my grandparents' generation to pick up stakes and move; it took the threat of dealing with a foreign culture new to Bensonhurst, one she found scary, to move my mother from her Brooklyn apartment of many decades. Me? I stayed put for twenty-four years, no mean feat in these United States. But, finally, I had the luxury and the flexibility (sort of) to sell the house, not out of necessity but for pragmatic reasons.

So where does that leave me? With the need, the real and practical need, to sell the house and downsize in rooms, in maintenance, and in price. But conflicted, torn—far more so, I suspect, than most other downsizing Americans.

My story to this point has been particular to me and to my family, even, perhaps, peculiar to me as the daughter of my parents and a bearer of the *sta' casa* gene. The actual process of selling the house was, well... exciting and boring all at once. In March, when the house went on the market, we learned how to be prepared, at any moment, for a "showing": house clean, desks clear, flowers out, candles lit, and all the rest. In *The God of Small Things,* Arundhati Roy says that *paravans* (untouchables) in the old days were required to sweep away all evidence of their footsteps in the dust as they walked. Getting ready for a "showing" is like that—the art of making yourself disappear in the place where you live, making it as close to a neutral, model house as possible. For Italians, always aware of *la bella figura,* the process is, perhaps, a bit easier than for most. But let's face it, being "shown" is uncomfortable, unsettling—a bit like living in a whorehouse.

As mid-April approached without a sale, my husband and I set a deadline or, in Italian American terms, made what I call a fate-bet: if the house had not sold by April 17th when we returned to Durham from New York following my mother's 90th birthday, we would take it off the market and rent it during my upcoming sabbatical year. We had, we simply had, to be in Venice (oh, the difficulty! It sounds so spoiled to say it!) by May 20th for me to teach a summer school semester. Once in Europe, we would be away for ten weeks—hence the time limit beyond which we felt we could not sell the house.

But April, to my surprise, turned into a frenzy of real estate madness. First, my older daughter, Kate, found a very small but extremely cute and well-located studio in excellent condition. After first losing the apartment, she got it, so we were off on one round of helping her with lawyers, mortgages, deposits, and the rest.

Then, precisely on April 17th, a far-too-low offer on our house turned into one we could consider and within a week the house was sold. Over the next month we endured: a North Carolina ritual called "the inspection," which lists the faults of your house (a *disgrazia*), right down to trivial items such as a two-inch strip of paint on the hidden upper inside of a door that the painters skipped; the removal of an old oil tank we did not know we had (not so trivial—messy and fairly costly); arranging for storage; and, truly horrible, clearing out a 1600 square foot basement that had accumulated stuff for twenty-four robust years.

In the nooks and crannies of time, we looked for a new house, setting a deadline here as well: we had to find one by May 1st or we would wait, perhaps even for the year after my sabbatical. We found the house precisely on May 1st, and almost exactly what we wanted: small enough to be easier to maintain, inexpensive enough to make sense, in a heavily wooded neighborhood we liked, with trees, greenery, cardinals—in fact, a smaller version of our original house, but not so similar that it felt like moving just next door. It's a house that still might strike my father as fit for movie stars but would more likely remind him or anyone else of a solid middle-class house on a sitcom.

By moving day, utter exhaustion ran interference with so many other emotions that it checked any impulse to feel sadness, even though, when I began this essay, the tears came quick and plenty. I'd always thought that our things and perhaps our renovations had made our house so lovely. Now, cleared and cleaned, the house revealed its secret, the secret that my father knew: it always was a beauty, with high and well-proportioned ceilings, great light, good bones, good vibes. Gleaming hardwood floors that we had installed and that I had always, always loved made it shine. I thought of my father, evoked his vision one more time, bid the house farewell, and that was all.

Except, as is only fitting, that wasn't all. Perhaps responding to the house's strong sense of family (we and, before us, the Hollers, had been its only owners since 1963), perhaps even sensing the *sta' casa* gene in the aura of the house, our buyer—who loved the house as we had—offered to let us store some large paintings and our children's many things, so difficult for us to sort while they were in New York, in their rooms downstairs until our return from Europe.

I'd like to end with a vision of my father, bestowing a blessing on my new house. But it's early June of 2005 and we won't move in until August. So that ending just won't be.

I am in Venezia now as I write. The apartment we have rented—small, but comfortable, with windows that get lots of light and participate in the ebb and flow of our Venetian *campiello*—seems, very oddly, like home and is the perfect place to be in between houses. It reminds me of places my parents knew by instinct: lively street life, great vegetable and fish markets nearby, and friendly banter with the people all around. Like the parts of Sicily I've seen, the beauty of Venezia is evident; poverty is not—so that the place seems paradisal, idyllic. As in Sicily, I wonder why anyone born there would leave the place but am aware—as would have been the case in my grandparents' Sicily and Calabria—that economic factors can still prevail. For many modern Venetians as for many Sicilians in the past, work would be elsewhere: on the mainland for the Venetians, across the Atlantic for the generation that emigrated in the 1900s. In Southern Italy, early in the twentieth century, poverty and its grinding needs would have been as evident and perhaps more evident than the splendor of the Sicilian landscape. Contemporary Venetians move to gentler rhythms but rhythms also largely financial. Housing has grown very expensive in the city, largely because of those who purchase vacation houses there, or long-term renters like me and my students; those born in Venice may still want to live there, but roughly 1500 leave each year, a significant number in a population now under 60,000.

Still, right now, as I write, it's the atmosphere and now the statistics about Venice that prevail. It's late morning. The flowers are all out in the stand beneath our kitchen: a riot of oranges, purples, and yellows. The earlier quiet—just neighbors afoot, shopping and talking—has given way to the daily cacophony of tourists making their way to Piazza San Marco. Soon, the tourists and the heat will be at their height. Soon, but not yet.

I look through some photos I have brought along—of my daughters and my parents, of my father at his 80th birthday party, glasses glimmering, smiling into the camera. I tell myself that the people make the home, the feelings, and the memories that travel with them. The very thought makes me feel grounded and certain—but anxious as well. Like my family before me, I knock on wood.

Italian American: The Next Generation

CHRISTINE PALAMIDESSI MOORE

We squeezed past the gray Vespa, parked in the entry, into dizzying sun and another day of a June heat wave. The air smelled muddy. At the end of the *vicolo,* we circled Piazza Trilussa to the Lungotevere. On our left, the pea green Tiber sliced the Centro Storico in half. The shade from the plane trees near the river stretched halfway across the street. We could see the Ponte Sisto and a small curve of St. Peter's Basilica.

I was with my nine-year-old daughter—a very affectionate child— on one of our semi-annual holidays in Rome. Our usual route to the bus stop twisted through the old Trastevere neighborhood, along a cobblestone path, past a bakery, a bookstore, and several cafés. Although the Lungotevere, the busy road that paralleled the curving Tiber River, was the shorter route, I usually avoided taking it because of the soldiers.

But that morning we were in a hurry—nearly late—to meet a friend. I opted for the busy road along the Tiber. Three olive drab armored tanks were parked on the sidewalk like ugly intrusive shouts in this city of beauty. A dozen steel-helmeted special force *carabinieri* in thick black boots surrounded the tanks.

. . . . .

CHRISTINE PALAMIDESSI MOORE writes reviews, articles, and stories. Her novel, *The Virgin Knows,* was published by St. Martin's Press. She teaches writing at Boston University.

Ruby balked, half-embarrassed to be approaching tanks and soldiers, and both scornful and confused that tanks were in her way.

We heard a school bell and then a flood of children's voices. We'd have to circle the tanks, since there was no sidewalk on the other side of the busy street.

"They're guarding the school." Heavy ammunition harnesses were slung across the soldiers' green uniforms. The men held matte-surfaced, desert-colored machine guns twice as large around as my daughter's skinny legs.

"Why?" We headed into a military zone. I'd been around soldiers and guns, in Nicaragua in the early 1980s. My daughter had never seen a gun, and we'd not yet suffered through the monstrousness of 9-11. Striking a balance between honesty and not scaring her stiff, I said, "There are some people in Israel—Jews and Palestinians—who have continued to fight over the same land for thousands of years. They both want to control it. They even fight in places outside of their country." In October 1982, in a call for revolution within the Arab world, the Abu Nidal Organization (ANO) attacked a synagogue in Rome.

"The soldiers are here because before you were born a Palestinian terrorist group tossed grenades and fired guns into a synagogue and killed a two-year-old boy."

We walked a few steps. "It doesn't seem right, does it?"

She shook her head in agreement.

"The Italians were horrified. They wanted the Jewish people in Rome to feel safe and to know that the Italian government understood their concerns. So the military made a pledge to the Jewish community to guard this school day and night."

"Why did they kill the boy?" Her eyes darted from side to side.

"For a lot of reasons, but mostly because the terrorists didn't like Jews."

"Daddy's Jewish."

We slowed down between tanks to peer into the schoolyard where the children played quite happily. "They're your age."

Immediately, a soldier brandishing his machine gun pointed the barrel at my face. "*Avanti. Subito.* Keep moving." His helmet shadowed his forehead. He was shorter than I am. Nonetheless, my feet froze to the sidewalk. My mouth went dry. The paralyzing fright was like what I had felt when neighborhood kids used to jump out from behind hedges on summer nights just to scare the bejesus out of passersby. Worse, I couldn't turn my head to see Ruby. I couldn't speak; yet, in that short moment, an entire horrid scene from the De Sica movie *Two Women* reeled through my mind: a World War II widow, played by Sophia Loren, and her daughter, Rosetta, are attacked and raped in a church outside Rome by a band of Moroccan soldiers.

A second *carabiniere,* out of kindness or duty, nudged my shoulder, breaking the trance. His touch should have been more terrifying than the threat of being shot, but it ended the surreal moment, bringing blood back to my limbs. I scooped up my daughter. She seemed to weigh no more than a sack of semolina flour.

I put her down ten yards beyond the third tank.

"You okay?" Her brow puckered. Her irises shrank and with savage grace she smoothed the front of her pink dress. I patted the top of her head.

"We won't stop there again," I said.

Ruby, a child of few words, put on her straight face—I knew the look from when she competed in gymnastics—a firm resolve to proceed despite challenge.

We began walking. "Would they have shot us?"

"No. Like good Italians, they take care of children. The soldiers aren't allowed to let anyone stop. That's their job."

I could smell the river and the acrid exhaust of automobiles. The encounter had shaken my sense of safety, and I didn't want to communicate that to Ruby. Still, I knew how much more sophisticated Italian children's awareness of politics had to be compared to my daughter's. Yes, taking her to Europe, exposing her to more than American ways and people, was a deliberate educational move on my part, but standing in front of a loaded gun wasn't part of the plan. We walked under an archway. I elaborated on the ongoing tension between the Jews and Palestinians, intellectually lessening our encounter with the soldiers. As usual, Ruby wasn't saying much. "Have you studied Israel in school?"

She shook her head no.

"Hitler?"

"Yes." She answered in a quick clip to let me know not to tell her more, but I did.

"Well, he had a friend Mussolini, an Italian. Italy was on the same side as Hitler during the War. Did you know that?"

"No."

Mussolini's damaging 1938 racist laws barred Jews from public schools and universities, barred Jews from marrying non-Jews, and prohibited Jews from taking vacations.

A handful of scooters ripped by on the left.

"I really don't want to be Jewish." She stared down the street, as though, if she really wanted, she could run after the scooters and catch them.

Ahead, a traffic jam incited drivers to sound their horns. While we waited on an island on viale Trastevere for the #116 bus, Ruby leaned against me and wrapped her arms around my waist. "I want to be Italian, like you."

One way I had embedded my Italianness into her being was through her mouth: feeding her white beans, crusty bread sprinkled with salt and olive oil, anisette biscotti, prosciutto, and Christmas Eve *baccalà*. Food and an unthwartable sense of loyalty, which could at times be as much a prison as an asset, penetrated my core, occupying the eternal spiral of my being, which was Italian.

I looked down at my daughter and then straight ahead into the traffic. Totally enjoying himself, a middle-aged man dressed in an expensive suit drove by on his scooter. In one hand he held a cell phone and was carrying on a conversation, and in the other hand a cigarette. Beagles balanced on the scooter's sideboards, tucking their spotted shoulders under the driver's calves. So, she'd rather be like the man on the scooter than the kids in the Hebrew School, like her mother rather than her father.

Though I was pleased by her choice, I could not dismiss the fact that she was half-Jewish, and, as the poet Adrienne Rich pointed out, "from the beginning split at the root." I had not connected the two cultures because I didn't know how to be Jewish. My husband, who does not practice Judaism, does consider himself to be a cultural Jew. Though he is often mistaken for being Italian, he asserts, "If they came looking again to round up the Jews, they'd take me."

Prior to World War II, immigrants to the United States, such as my grandparents and my husband's grandparents, lived in Italian, Irish, Polish, and Jewish enclaves. In our case, near Pittsburgh and in the Bronx. Children of the immigrants rarely intermarried; their children, however, who include my husband and me, grew up in suburban settings and then went to college where we were thrown together with people who came from families with similar economic lifestyles.

In 1986, when my husband and I married, the Jewish side felt more concern. Our marriage threatened to contribute to the shrinking Jewish population in the United States. In 1970, a National Jewish Population Survey discovered that in the previous five years, 30 percent of new Jewish marriages were to non-Jews. By 1990, that figure was more than 50 percent. Moreover, according to a later study, 28 percent of children of intermarriage were raised as Jews, and only 15 percent of that group ultimately married Jews themselves. In other words, the Jewish grandparents felt the children were already lost to them—as ethnic replacements—before they were born. At the time, embracing my sweet husband and new family, I was oblivious to the dynamic our offspring would let loose into the larger community.

The Italian side celebrated the marriage. My father thanked Matthew, my husband, for taking me off his hands. "Someone else can worry about her." My mother prayed my husband would convert, and probably still does. As a Christian, my mother thinks Matthew only has to take one more step: "He already knows the Old Testament: he just needs to add on the New Testament."

When my daughter was born, my Italian aunt had said to me, "Oh, how lucky, she'll have the best of two worlds." The best of two worlds never happened: my husband did not bring Judaism into the home. In Jewish households the women pass on the traditions. I was hardly prepared to take on a culture I knew little about while I was struggling to pass on my own ethnic identity, which had no generational guidelines.

I don't blame my husband for not teaching her more about his culture. Perhaps my daughter is less confused, perhaps her root is less split. By saying she wants to be Italian, she is choosing what is more familiar and safe. Would I want my daughter to walk around Boston, New York, London, or Rome wearing an ITALIA T-shirt or an ISRAEL T-shirt?

Choosing an identity is always a verbal act, whether it's a T-shirt that identifies its wearer or a statement, such as Ruby's "I want to be Italian." For my daughter and other children three times removed from their immigrant ancestors, ethnicity is voluntary and satisfies the American urges for both community and individuality. Ruby can be different from her friends because, for example, she puts an Italian twist on her holiday celebration. At the same time, just by saying she's Italian, she's become a member of a larger community that shares the same ancestry.

In the first week of a new semester, the students in my Ethnic Literature class at Boston University name their ethnic identities. Of twenty students at least 60 percent of them identify with one ethnic group in their multiethnic backgrounds. A student with the last name Camp says he is Italian; a tiny blonde says she is Korean, because she has one Korean grandmother; a fellow with the surname Pisaturo identifies himself as Polish.

In mixed marriages, Italian is often chosen by parents to simplify ancestry on questionnaires and surveys. In the 2000 census, the number of Americans claiming Italian ancestry increased over previous years. A

1990 survey by Harvard sociologist Mary Waters asked participants: "If you could be a member of any ethnic group you wanted, which one would you choose?" Italian was the most common answer. The reason might be more than good food, sensuality, and appreciation for beauty. Additionally, we can consider that Italy is a fiction: a country of provinces, dialects, and regions, and historically, because of its location, an incorporator of invaders, empires, and bloodlines.

Interesting, too, is the increase in Italian language studies. From 1998 to 2002, enrollment in Italian language courses in both high schools and universities grew in America by 30 percent, faster than the enrollment rates for Spanish. French and German language studies actually decreased.

Memory and similarity create a group identity. Because memory is strongly tied to childhood, whatever ethnic culture dominates the family when the child is young is the culture that the child is most likely to identify with as an adult. So families like mine, who develop food preferences for pasta and risotto over macaroni and cheese and Uncle Ben's, and who are members of Italian American organizations, and who teach or encourage their children to speak Italian, raise children who choose to identify themselves as Italian Americans. For Ruby the origins of her Italianness come from what I have passed on to her, her travels in Italy, her Italian family, and media images—some good, some not so good. Here's an irony: for members of her generation, the genuineness of the ethnicity they choose becomes more obscure and questionable because of its mixed origins; however, because it is voluntary, the act of choosing sustains the identity. The eighteenth-century philosopher David Hume said it this way: "That which ceases to exist cannot be the same as that which afterwards begins to exist." If my daughter's grandson chooses to be Jewish, his ethnic identity will not embody the Jewish memories of my mother-in-law and her ancestors.

We're chameleons, able to change our way of being in order to survive or to fit in. There are optional add-ons to subjective ethnic identity. During Chanukah, my daughter is happy to be Jewish. Because of how it sounds, when teachers, friends, or gymnastic trainers hear her Russian Jewish last name—Bagedonow: (BAG-a-dawn-oh)—they think it's Italian. Similarly, for the third-generation Americans in my Literature class who have multiple identity pools to draw from, how they choose to characterize their ancestry depends on time, place, and whether they've been influenced by me, their instructor, or the cute girl sitting next to them.

I admit I've influenced my child: I would rather her Italian ancestry stand guard, as the Italian *carabinieri* stand guard over the Hebrew School. Her Jewishness is her vulnerability, both personally and internationally.

When she was an infant, just about every day after I finished my workday, I turned on Verdi's *La Traviata* or Puccini's *Tosca,* lowered the lights, and massaged her strong, tiny body with warm olive oil, defining each soft toe, smoothing not only my energy but also Italy's nectar into her skin, priming her muscles for pleasure. Her father returned home before seven. While I washed her in the kitchen sink, he played the guitar and sang. He didn't sing Jewish songs but folk tunes, rock 'n' roll, and the theme from *Pippi Longstocking.* In an obvious way Matthew has been less concerned about Ruby's being Jewish than I am about her being Italian.

So why didn't I marry an Italian man? I think, in the end, DNA makes the choice. The human race wants to survive and multiethnic children like Ruby have an array of biological resources.

Later that day in Rome, after Ruby and I had gone about the business of being guests and tourists in Rome's Centro Storico, we returned to Trastevere, but not directly to our flat, nor did we pass the tanks in front of the Hebrew School. We got off the #116 bus farther down the road, at via Glorioso, and slowly walked up a steep hill, stopping to rest under blocks of shade, until we reached via Dandolo. That June the grass, browned early because of lack of rain, clung close to the earth. We followed a gravel path to a playground near the Villa Sciarra, a spot we often visited when in Rome. Statues and fountains surrounded the swing set, slide, and sandboxes. Water spewed from frogs' mouths into a tiny low water fountain, from the nipples of a row of bare-breasted women into a small pool, and from a small to a larger tier into a large basin flanked by a circle of creatures half-female, half-crouching-animal. A ten-foot tall statue of a naked man chasing a naked woman stood guard over the sliding board. No American playground could hold a candle to the sensuality of Italian ones.

Ruby amused herself on the edge of a sandbox, sifting and rearranging piles, while I sat watching, taking out a sketchbook and colored pencils. Where I grew up, in Western Pennsylvania, the park along the Allegheny where my sister and I often played proudly displayed a row of heavy cannons, dating from the Civil War to World War II. The cannons pointed over the water to the hill on the other side of the river. After we tired of the swings, we'd climb to the end of the cannon barrels to watch the river.

I collected a cup of water from a fountain to wet my paper before drawing. Two cute, chubby Italian girls, both younger than Ruby, followed me back to the bench to watch me draw. After a few minutes, when she saw potential playmates, Ruby joined us.

Using my best Italian, I asked the girls their names and ages. They looked at each other.

"*Sono straniere.* They're foreigners," one said to the other, lifting her shoulders in a perfect Italian gesture. *Non italiane.* Not Italians.

"They say we're not Italian," I translated for my daughter.

The girls laughed. "You speak really funny." The blonde one put her arm on my lap and leaned close to my drawing of the naked woman.

"*Ma, dove ha imparato l'italiano?* Where did you learn Italian?" she asked, and then, "Where are you from?"

"Boston," I said.

"Americane," she shouted.
A bevy of mothers and nannies looked our way.
That afternoon, neither Ruby nor I was Italian.

My daughter, who is now seventeen, continues to say she is Italian whenever anyone asks about her ethnicity. She studies Italian language and culture in school. Speaking the language is the only real way to maintain a connection to an ethnic identity. She has grown to look Italian, in a Botticelli sort of way, and dresses well—which means coordinating everything on her body as carefully as Italian words are coordinated in a sentence. On random Italian American days, she wears gold jewelry or sports a red ITALIAN GIRL T-shirt. Her boyfriend, who is half-Anglo, says he is Palestinian. Together they are quite an exotic pair, even in their multiethnic and racially diverse Cambridge high school where "white" people are a minority,

I often think about the Italian soldier pushing me away from the Hebrew School in Rome. During the War, Jews fared less badly under the Italians than anywhere else in German-occupied Europe. Although not every Italian helped the Jews, and though deportations and shootings did happen, no ingrained anti-Semitism existed or continues to exist, as unfortunately it does in France and Germany. Perhaps the origins of Italian-Jewish compatibility began in the Middle Ages when both Jews and Italians in Italian city-states provided banking services to the rest of Western Europe. For these reasons, Jewish Italian marriages seem less charged than, for example, Jewish German marriages. I also wonder what ethnic identities the children of Rome's Hebrew School chose: simply Italian, or Jewish, or Russian Jew, Polish Jew, Iraqi Jew, or Italian Jew? In the United States, as recently as 20 years ago, Jews considered marriage between distinct subgroups an out-marriage, a crossing of ethnic lines.

Along with the foodways that my grandmother passed on to me, the language, and travel to Rome and Italy to understand more about the intricacies of the culture, I want to pass on the age-old tradition of hospitality to my daughter. In Italian, the word *ospite* means both the host and the guest, which is a clear indication of the selflessness of caring for one another, no matter what side of the door he is on.

What I don't want her to catch wind of is the idea that sons are much more valuable than daughters and the consequent mindless privileges that go along with being a boy. I don't intend to diminish the sensuality of the feminine element. The loyalty, which I have called both an asset and a prison, stems from the son–daughter complex and has clouded clear calls for me, too often in my life, on issues of work and love. At the same time, the loyalty has kept me in a marriage that keeps getting better.

The Anglo American writer Iris Origo, Marchesa of Val d'Orcia, who lived most of her life in Italy, noted, "The Italians live in the continuous present." Maybe this is why people choose to be Italian. What better way to start a day than as a new day, while at the same time claiming membership in an ancient culture that, rather than controlling and organizing, perseveres and adapts to the chaos of life?

Mama, Che Cosa Vuoi Che Faccio?
· · · · · · · ·
JAMES VESCOVI

"Che cosa vuoi che faccio?!" my father hollered at his mother. "What do you want me to do?!"

He knew what she wanted. I knew what she wanted. Even a man visiting his ailing wife seated near us knew what Desolina wanted, and he didn't speak a word of Italian.

Desolina Vescovi, my ninety-four-year-old grandmother, had broken her hip. She had passed through surgery with flying colors, but now came the hard part: physical therapy.

"Che cosa vuoi che faccio?!" my father repeated. "Huh, Mama?!"

My grandmother detested the nursing home, where she'd been sent two weeks earlier from the hospital. She'd expected to return to her pleasant room at Director's Hall, an assisted living community whose residents had to be fully ambulatory. Until she could walk, however, she was stuck at the nursing home, where patients lined up along the halls in wheelchairs babbled all day.

"You've abandoned me here," she whimpered.

"Mama, I've told you a hundred times. It's not me who made you

· · · · ·

JAMES VESCOVI's unpublished collection of stories, from which this essay is excerpted, is called *Eat Now; Talk Later*. He lives in New York with his wife and three children.

come here. It's your doctor. When you're walking again, you can go back to the other place."

Desolina waved that notion away. "Why do I have to learn to walk again? I'm an old woman!"

My father bit his lower lip so hard I was afraid he'd draw blood. He turned to me for help. I was the grandson, whom Desolina and Antonio, my grandfather, had spoiled as a boy. My youth brought sunshine into their lives. Most importantly, my grandmother and I didn't share an entangled history.

"Nonna, what he says is right," I said. "All you have to do is listen to the nurses."

Desolina had no interest in my opinions; she was fighting for her life. She gave me a glare that produced goose bumps on the back of my neck.

The head nurse had told us that Desolina's therapy was not going well. She refused to cooperate. Though she wouldn't come out and say it, she wanted to give up, toss in the towel, and move in with my father.

She did not want to accept that in American society this was no longer the norm. Most adult children didn't give their parents twenty-four-hour care; they sent them to assisted living communities and nursing homes.

What made the home arrangement truly impossible was their complex relationship. My father was an only child and, since his youth, Desolina had inserted herself into his life. She doted on him as a boy, tried to rein him in as a teenager, chastised him for moving away from her as an adult. He was her world. In my father's eyes, what she passed off as love and affection were suffocating. Her moving in was out of the question. Mother and son hadn't lived under the same roof since he was twenty-two, and he wasn't going to allow it four decades later.

"Mama, che cosa vuoi che faccio?" My father wiped his brow with a handkerchief.

It was 10 A.M. We were sitting in a sunny atrium, Desolina in a wheelchair staring at her shoes.

"What do you do all day?!" she asked. "You're retired!"

"Semi-retired," my father shot back.

Born in 1900 in a peasant hamlet in northern Italy called Casalasagna, Desolina had no conception of "semi" retirement. Either you worked or you didn't.

"Why do you still have to work? Don't you have enough money in the bank?" she asked sarcastically.

My father looked away and shook his head in disgust.

"There was money when Papa died!" she continued.

"He left it to you," my father countered.

The man near us was shifting uncomfortably. Even his wife, who seemed to have Alzheimer's, looked alarmed at the scene.

Feeling helpless, my grandmother attacked.

"As soon as Papa died, you deserted me!" she cried. "You put me in this zoo!"

My father's face reddened; veins on his neck appeared. His eyes looked as if they would pop out of their sockets. I was afraid he was going to have a stroke and that my grandmother would get her wish: to spend her last days with him, though the two of them would be living side by side in a nursing home instead of his condominium. I grabbed his arm and pulled him outside to the parking lot.

Throughout his adult life, my father was engaged in paying off a debt to his parents. He was thwarted at every turn. Tony and Desolina were from another time. They had grown up as impoverished peasants in the Province of Parma and immigrated to New York City in 1930. They'd fed my father, loved him, and kept him out of trouble. He'd gone on to college and become an executive in a Fortune 500 company. Some of his success, he believed, was the result of sacrifices they'd made. He wanted to pay them back, but he didn't have a currency that they understood and accepted.

After working for several years in New York, he and my mother moved away. Desolina was crestfallen. She didn't understand that in 1962, an American businessman went where his company told him to go—in this case, to Kalamazoo, Michigan.

Several years later, my grandfather retired from his job in the terrazzo trade. My father felt increasing pressure—some of it he himself created—to make their later years enjoyable and productive. Wasn't this the American dream, after all? To work until you were sixty-five and then settle down to enjoy the fruits of your labor: travel, golf, cooking, tennis.

My father encouraged Tony to spend afternoons with friends playing bocci or Briscola, but Tony wasn't interested. His discomfort with using the telephone kept him from calling to get bus times to Asbury Park, New Jersey, where he and Desolina could have enjoyed a few days with friends at the beach. An evening at the cinema? Their English was too poor. And Fellini? Or Pasolini? For Italians who'd grown up in a culture that had hardly changed since medieval times? My father bought his parents subscriptions to Italian newspapers but, with only a third grade education, reading did not come easily to them.

It pained my father to envision Tony and Desolina sitting around their kitchen watching the clock till the next meal. He took their obsolescence personally.

Had my grandparents lived back on the farm in Italy, they would have been busy. *Their* grandparents had been sent to look for mushrooms. Or they fed chickens and darned socks. Or they looked after the babies and toddlers. There was a strange irony to the lives of Tony and Desolina. As youths in Italy, they had tended sheep in the mountains; as retirees in Queens, New York, they were like lost sheep.

What made the situation worse was that their lives remained at a standstill until we came from Michigan for our yearly visit. Only then could they be persuaded to come into Manhattan for a dinner or spend $6 on a cab to visit cousins in Flushing. As soon as we left, we knew they returned to their tedious days.

Guilt pounded away at my father. If he lived closer, he could enrich their lives. What was he doing all the way out in Kalamazoo? He called them every week. Occasionally, Desolina fired a broadside: *"Noi hanno abbandonato!* You've abandoned us!" After hanging up, he went off to mope for an hour.

It was a strange juxtaposition of power. My father had four thousand people reporting to him at work. He paid his country club dues on time. He kept his sons in line. He'd once even knocked out a hippie harassing him in a Sears parking lot. But he could not make Tony and Desolina budge from their frozen world.

From an early age I had a special affection for my grandparents. Our annual visits to New York were one of the high points of my year. We drove seven hundred miles overnight and arrived at their three-story apartment house in Astoria, Queens, just before lunch. Even before my father had thrown the Ford station wagon into park, I burst out of the car and, with my brother and sister at my heels, raced up the stoop and into the vestibule. We fought to press the bell. There was a wait that lasted only a few seconds but seemed interminable. The door buzzed loudly, like an obnoxious alarm clock, but to me it was music. It meant the lock was disengaged, and we shoved open the door and raced down the hallway, its walls sculpted in fleur-de-lis.

We ran up the stairs, two steps at a time. Soon, we could smell the scent of mothballs emanating from Desolina's closet. My grandparents waited for us on the third floor landing, next to the dumbwaiter. When they saw us, they clapped their hands. Tears sparkled in their eyes.

"Tesoro della Nonna!" my grandmother cried. "Grandmother's treasure!"

After hugs and kisses, we raced around the apartment like dogs that needed to sniff at familiar places. First stop: the aluminum breadbox in the kitchen. Yes! Stocked with marshmallow cookies we could not get in Michigan.

"Tesoro della Nonna!" Desolina said.

My brother put on Tony's fedora and strutted around the apartment, while I slipped into the bathroom. The toilet had an old fashioned pull chain, the only one I had ever seen, and in a green plastic cup on the sink sat Tony and Desolina's toothbrushes, the bristles yellowed like old newspaper.

"Tesoro della Nonna!" Desolina yelled, to no one in particular.

After suitcases were lugged upstairs we all sat down to eat. There was prosciutto, salami, capponata, and cheese. The crust of the fresh-baked bread from the pizzeria crackled when we broke it into sandwich lengths. My brother dug out the fluffy white, shaped it into a communion wafer, and slipped it on his tongue. After the antipasti, Desolina served up bowls of tortellini in brodo.

None of my friends in Kalamazoo had grandparents like these. Theirs simply looked like older versions of their parents. Tony and Desolina were exotic. They spoke a strange dialect of Italian. They didn't know how to drive a car and would never learn. Desolina, a short heavy woman with the smooth skin of a child, wore a dress and kerchief and, underneath, a girdle with a million snaps. Tony mixed his own shave cream, used a straight razor, and never shaved without a lit cigar in his mouth. It looked like a black licorice stick.

My grandparents had grown up in villages within sight of each other. At the age of nine, they were pulled from school and made to work on the farm, which most years barely supported their families. Tony worked with the animals and, when older, in the fields. Desolina shepherded the cows up into the mountains. After arriving in America, my grandfather, a compact, muscular man with a square jaw, laid terrazzo in office towers and churches, while Desolina sewed pom-poms for a hat manufacturer and looked after my father.

During our visits, while my parents spent their days shopping or visiting old friends, we shopped daily at small markets, threw a "Spaldeen" around on the stoop, and watched TV shows that we couldn't get in Michigan. What was most peculiar about spending time with my grandparents was the lack of conversation. We hardly said a word to each other. Their philosophy was that if things were going well, there was no need to talk about it; if we needed help, they knew we would ask. We soaked up their aura and they soaked up our youth.

The week went quickly and departing was painful—for all of us. Even brave Tony, who, when prodded, told my brother and me his World War I stories of combat, capture, and flight, wept.

My father took extra time tying the suitcases onto the roof rack, then announced it was time to go. We said our final good-byes and drove off. My grandparents did not stop waving until we'd rounded the corner and headed for the Major Deegan Expressway. As my sister curled up with an Etch-a-Sketch and my brother pulled out a Hardy Boys book, my heart felt hollow. That emptiness was not assuaged until long after we crossed the George Washington Bridge.

I am sure that my father felt relief. Like a good son, he'd done his duty, though the fact that they'd spend a year waiting for our next visit continued to eat at him.

When I moved to New York in 1983 to attend graduate school, it must have been like a dream come true for my father: finally, someone he trusted to look in on his aging parents and add variety to their lives. He saw it not as a chance to abdicate his responsibility. He simply accepted my relocation as a gift, much the same as when, on a cleaning crew, one person says, "Windows? I don't mind doing windows."

By my own choice, I visited my grandparents every Saturday. We had a ritual. I rang their bell; received sloppy kisses from Desolina, who still called me *Tesoro della Nonna*; the bowl with artificial fruit was moved from the center of the table; we ate antipasti followed by tortellini, ravioli, or spaghetti, with red wine served in small glasses; we sat on the stoop; there was a little talk; we went back in for dessert, usually vanilla ice cream and Entenmann's apple pie. While my grandfather washed the dishes, Desolina returned to its place the fruit bowl, which had been sitting on top of the television next to an assemblage of family photographs. On these days, I felt like the happy, big-toothed seven-year-old I was in one of those photos.

While my friends were eating eggs Benedict at Manhattan's latest brunch spot and talking about sports or getting laid, I was eating mortadella wrapped around Stella D'oro bread sticks and listening to my grandfather recount stories from his youth, this time with details he'd left out in previous tellings. Each one was like finding a bit of gold. I played cards with my grandmother, who cheated when she could get away with it.

I arrived home in the late afternoon and called my father. He liked to have a report after every visit. He listened carefully. He knew his parents well and could recognize any signs of trouble. That was his burden. It couldn't be transferred to me. My role was simply to be the sun that rose in their lives once a week. He saw himself as the oxygen responsible for keeping them alive.

Tony and Desolina were mostly self sufficient until their early 90s, and then things began to deteriorate quickly. Their diet fell apart. Their medical conditions needed frequent supervision. They grew forgetful. My father and I talked the situation over, and he decided the best option was to move them to Kalamazoo, where he could keep a close eye on them.

Convincing them was not going to be easy. My grandfather was especially independent and stubborn. He hated nursing homes. He'd seen his friends enter them only to die.

My father flew in from Michigan and sat them both down at the kitchen table. After a long prologue—I'm sure Tony knew what was coming—he explained in great detail how an assisted living facility was different from a nursing home. He produced brochures with photos of an elegant dining room, lounges, and an outdoor garden. He swore to them on a stack of bibles that he had seen the place, and it was clean and well operated.

They shook their heads.

"*E che bel post!* And it's such a beautiful place," he told them. "Look at the dining room and the garden. And I live five minutes away!"

"*No,*" Desolina said flatly.

He now tried to work on their stomachs. There was little more important in their lives than eating.

"There are four meals a day! Breakfast, lunch, dinner, and *un spuntino prima che dormire*! A snack before bedtime!" he pleaded. "*Hanno il 'ros bif' tutte le Domeniche.* They serve prime rib every Sunday."

"No, Selvi, it's time for you to come back here to take care of us," my grandmother said.

My father turned to his father, but Tony, wagging his index finger back and forth—which meant not in a million years—said he wouldn't live under anyone else's thumb and, besides, these places were expensive.

My father now deployed all his firepower. He pointed out to Tony that, yes, he didn't so much need help himself, but Desolina did. She was forgetful, a little unstable on her feet, and now needed help getting in and out of the bathtub. Tony knew it was true and also knew he was not equipped by age or temperament to assist her.

Tears came to his eyes. He had lived in New York for more than six decades. Maybe it was time to go.

My father now had to tip the scale and get Tony to say "yes." He accomplished this by doing the one thing he rarely did—as a child or an adult. He lied to his father.

"And Pa, you're not going to believe it, but the place is free."

Tony wiped his eyes and looked up.

"*È* free?"

"*Sì.*"

"*Ma, no!*" Tony said.

"*Sì.*"

"*Ma, chi paga?* Who pays for this?"

"My company. One of the benefits I get is to move into this beautiful place, but I don't need it now. But, my parents can stay there—for free."

"*È vero?*" he asked. "Is this true?"

My father nodded. "*Tutto* free. Everything is free."

Tony couldn't stop shaking his head.

Desolina, who was growing more and more deaf in her old age, leaned forward and asked: "What are you people talking about? *E al Papa, perche al pianga?* And why is Papa crying?"

"*Porco cane,* free!" said Tony. "*Che compagnia!* God bless America!"

"Then you'll go? It really is a nice place, Papa," my father said.

Tony sighed. "*Sì,*" he said, and tears came again.

"*Selvi, perché piange il Babbo?* Why is Papa crying?" Desolina repeated.

"He said he'll come to Kalamazoo," my father replied.

"*No,*" she said. "*È vero?*"

My father nodded.

"Tony," she said to him across the table. "*At ve a Kalamazoo?*"

He nodded.

Desolina looked at her son. "*Se va il Babbo, vengo anch'io.* Well, if he's going, I'm going."

And so on a hot August day they flew first class to Kalamazoo. My mother met them at the airport and chauffeured them to Director's Hall, which had two hundred residents. At ninety-four and ninety-three, Tony and Desolina were not even the oldest couple in the place.

Tony especially grew fond of his new home. The staff was deferential, the residents were kind, and everything was spic and span. He liked to sit in an inner courtyard, where he'd made friends with the resident cat, a tabby who wrapped her tail around his legs while he stroked her head. He would sit in the dining room, his plate heaped with food, and aides serving all the iced tea he wanted. The chairs were soft, the carpet plush.

After a few months, I flew in from New York and went to lunch with them. He looked at me with wonder and said, "Jimmy, *chi paga per questa roba?* Who pays for all this stuff around here?"

"*È* free," I said.

Unfortunately, my grandfather did not live to enjoy it long. He died just before Christmas. We had done a few tests that suggested lung cancer and called everything to a halt. It wasn't worth putting him through the pain and anxiety of a biopsy. It was his time to go.

The day of his wake was brutally cold. The daytime highs hovered around nine degrees. We bundled up Desolina and brought her to the funeral home. The moment she saw her husband laid out, she broke away from my father and rushed up to the casket. She gripped the sides and began wailing.

Tony and Desolina had outlived all their friends and hadn't made any new ones in Kalamazoo. To fill the void, my father had invited some of his friends and former business colleagues, but they hadn't arrived yet. Desolina wailed and wailed, drowning out saccharine music being piped in on ceiling speakers.

My father tried to escort her away, but Desolina wouldn't budge. She jammed her palm in her mouth and bit it. She looked up at the heavens and wailed.

A funeral director haltingly approached me to make sure everything was to our satisfaction.

Yes, I told him, everything was fine. Tony looked good in his favorite Barney's suit, bought long before the store became chic, in an era when suits came with two pair of pants.

We finally coaxed my grandmother to a couch, where she made an occasional dash for the casket. I could see my father praying that she wouldn't explode in the presence of his guests. When they began arriving, her face lit up. She grew calm and was quite charming.

After they left, she returned to her husband. In the end, we had to wrench her away.

In the months afterward, she continued to mourn her husband but, at heart, Desolina was a survivor. One afternoon while my brother was visiting, she cried, "My poor husband. He was such a good man. And now he's gone...*povereto.*"

My brother put his arm around her and let her spill her grief. Finally, she looked up at a military photograph of Tony in his Bersagliare uniform in 1917 and sighed, "Ah, well, better him than me."

Tony's passing set my father and grandmother up for a showdown. In his quiet but forceful way, Tony had run interference between the two of them, keeping them on their best behavior. Now he was gone, and feelings long suppressed could crack through their relations like lava through rock.

At first my father was encouraged by Desolina's widowed status. Without her husband around, she might be more willing to try new things. Maybe now he could pay off some of that debt. He spent a lot of time with her, taking her around Director's Hall to show her art classes, the card room, and an outdoor patio.

At an exercise class, she watched residents raise and lower their arms, try to touch their toes, clap—anything to get the blood moving. After two minutes, Desolina turned to my father and remarked, "What the hell are these people doing? They look like idiots."

One afternoon he took her to a church service. Desolina believed in God but like many peasants had little time for organized religion. As they left the service, my father said he thought it was a good way to pass some time, to which Desolina, folding her hands together to imitate the minister in prayer, responded, "Blah, blah, blah, blah...."

His final hope was to help her make friends with some of the other widows. My mother even hunted down one woman who spoke decent Italian, but Desolina had no interest in a new acquaintance.

"*Tutti nasone qui,*" she muttered to my mother. "They're all nosy busybodies here."

My father stewed over her intransigence. It seemed like Desolina was shutting everything out so as to make her only option moving in with him. On my occasional trips to Kalamazoo, when my father and I went for a visit, I could tell he was near a breaking point. Resentment had built up. He deflected everything she said, whether she was trying to hook him in or not.

Then she broke her hip. I believe my father could smell an imminent showdown. As he and I went to visit her that day in the solarium, he seemed to have the vulnerability of a boy. He drove nervously, silently. He walked quickly into the nursing home. He wanted to get whatever was going to be said or done over with. Would the power she had had over him as a child—roiling for forty years—now rear its head and overwhelm him?

He was torn in half. The voice from the Old Country told him that good sons knuckled under to their mother's demands; the voice of the New World insisted that she was responsible for her own life.

After we wheeled her into the solarium, she began complaining: the food was awful, the people were pathetic, and she didn't want to have to walk again.

"*Che cosa vuoi che faccio?!*" my father cried. He was daring her to ask him to let her move in.

Desolina knew that if she asked outright she was likely to be turned down. She hated the thought of being alone. Would her son actually slash the apron strings?

"*Che cosa vuoi che faccio?!*" he repeated.

She didn't want to risk the question, so she worked him from other angles.

"I have no friends here!"

"I'm a tired old woman!"

And finally, "If your father was alive he'd be ashamed of you," she said, "leaving me in a place like this. Maybe you just want his money!"

It was her last broadside—an attempt to deflate his honor, not to mention his masculinity which, poor woman, was how her overbearing love also affected him. He stood up from his chair with the clearest of eyes.

"You don't wanna walk again, Mama? You don't have to walk again. As far as I'm concerned, you can stay here for the rest of your life!" he yelled, gesturing toward the slumping souls in their wheelchairs. "It's not my fault that you're here. You broke your hip. You can get up and go back to Director's Hall or I'll visit you here for the rest of your life— while you stare at the walls!"

She looked up at the two of us with hate-filled eyes and then, in a kind of Old Testament gesture of futility, stuck a hand in her mouth and bit it.

We turned around and left. Wiping tears from our eyes, we got into my father's Cadillac. He jumped on the gas and screeched out of the parking lot. As we turned onto the main road, we passed the solarium. In a picture forever frozen in my mind, Desolina was sitting in her wheelchair with her face buried in her hands.

Desolina walked again and returned to Director's Hall. She refused to attend jazzercise or the new ecumenical Passover service for Jews and Christians. She made no new friends, but she didn't have to. Her short-term memory, already on shaky ground, slowly failed, and she retreated into the distant past. She forgot about Astoria and Hell's Kitchen. Her mind increasingly filled with images of her youth. She spoke of her brothers and sisters and noted the dates of their births and deaths. She began singing love songs in Italian, one of which was bawdy.

Had she even tasted the satisfaction and freedom of forcing herself to get up and walk? Who can say?

My father's outburst in the solarium, combined with her retreat into the Old World, had broken her gravitational pull on him. He was more relaxed with her; she was less manipulative with him. He cut down the number of his visits, which made them more enjoyable. Most surprising and beautiful to me was his response to her death: it was one not so much of relief as of sorrow.

Two months before her ninety-seventh birthday, Desolina broke her other hip. She survived the surgery, but not her recovery.

Her funeral was attended by immediate family, my father's cousin, and my mother's cleaning lady. Desolina was the last of nine siblings. We called a niece back in Italy and told her to spread the word.

She was laid out in a favorite dress. Strung around her fingers—by the funeral director, who knew nothing about her indifference to the Catholic Church—was a rosary. We invented our own service: a string of reminiscences and a few readings from—of all things—*The Book of Common Prayer.* We brought her to the cemetery and laid her next to my grandfather in a location she would have loved: on top of a hill, backed by a forest, and within sight of a tranquil pond.

It is strange to see their plot among the descendants of Dutch colonists, whose tombstones have interlocking hearts and greeting-card poetry. Desolina's and Tony's is as they lived, square and simple:

VESCOVI

ANTONIO   DESOLINA

1899–1993   1900–1997

After her funeral, my father took me aside to thank me for caring for his parents.

Had *I* paid back a debt? If so, it was not difficult to discharge. I played a role as the grandson who could do no wrong. Moreover, I was fortunate that a gulf, with modern America on one side and medieval Italy on the other, did not separate my father and me. Consequently I held a currency that, in his eyes, was more valuable than gold.

My father, while mostly at peace, still has days when—no matter how you try to convince him—he wonders whether his parents knew what he gave and tried so hard to give them.

Italian Bride

. . . .

MARY BETH CASCHETTA

When I am 12 years old, my mother starts dragging me off to the back pews of dark churches to watch perfect strangers get married.

"Someday that'll be you," she whispers, pinching me.

I'm supposed to want to be the bride but picture myself more the priest, holy and disinterested. I like his crisp white collar, asexual demeanor, and his purported closeness with God, but have learned to keep my mouth shut. I have a typical Italian American mother who is obsessed with marrying me off, a mother for whom weddings are the ultimate sport. There's no room in her agenda for fantasies of priests. She trains me hard: double sessions, field trips to St. Anthony's, St. Michael's, St. John's.

Each time a new bride stands at the ready, my mother cries into a wadded Kleenex. "So beautiful," she says.

It isn't true: some brides are scrawny, with beaky noses. Some are heavy, with wire-like curls sprayed into a nest. Other brides are just plain homely.

Still, my mother can detect the beauty in any girl about to be given

. . . . .

MARY BETH CASCHETTA is the author of the short story collection *Lucy on the West Coast.* The recipient of the 2004 Sherwood Anderson Fiction Award, she lives in Massachusetts.

away to a man. And we both know that it's me she sees in that long white dress with matching veil and shoes. Not a stranger, but her daughter. Me, flanked by a line-up of broad-shouldered attendants clad in taffeta and men in rented shoes.

In Italy, as in my corner of Rochester, New York, wedding receptions are a birthright: soggy macaroni and chicken thighs. D.J.'d music and an open bar.

My mother can't wait to show me off to the crowd of whiskery *gumbas,* my great aunts, who magically appear at every reception. *"That's* who knows about marriage," my mother says, when the old women from Calabria stand en masse to dance the tarantella. This is their blessing on every bride, their warning for every groom, the promise of what awaits him. Watching from a distance, I can feel the weight of their swollen stomping feet, their arthritic clapping hands.

Long ago, they let me in on the secret of matrimony: that a man (my father, say, or one of my brothers) could be so *stoonad* as to believe he is king, when everyone knows that women rule. Italian women.

The youngest of four, the only girl in our family, I nod and smile, as if I'm interested.

Aunt Peppie points a gnarled finger. "You too."

I believe her. I have seen her perform magic: she and her sisters, my grandmother included, can make headaches go away by dripping oil into water and saying *mal'occhio,* the evil eye. (Mumbo-jumbo, my father calls it.) Any one of them can snap a rabbit's neck in half, skin it, and fry it with greens, conjuring up the most delicious dinner imaginable. Probably they are witches—Italian witches, of course, the good kind. Any prediction they make is likely to come true.

Unable to shake off Aunt Peppie's words as I walk the halls of junior high, I find myself agreeing to go out with a boy who's been pursuing me since seventh grade. Not Italian. It might not actually matter, I decide, since for years I've resigned myself to an eerie certainty that nuptials (like train wrecks and cancer) are what await other people—

my cousins, my brothers—not me. At the time, anyway, my secret emergency back-up plan is to join the nuns, but somehow I end up a lesbian.

Imagine my surprise, twenty-five years later, when Massachusetts, a state in which by utter chance I am living, makes it legal for people like me to marry.

"Are you sure?" I ask my partner, Meryl. We watch the news on New England Cable. "Do you think it's really going to happen?"

I never figured on becoming a modern bride.

Something Old

I come of age in the early '80s, an era of acquiescence and yuppies. Mornings, my mother curls my hair with a hot iron, picks out pastel clothing, and talks *at* me until I have no desire that isn't hers originally. This includes becoming a cheerleader. Forced into lacy anklets and patent leather shoes long after other kids are wearing jeans, I lurch haltingly out the door each morning, the first of many surrenders toward my long, illustrious career as a heterosexual.

My mother is happy at first, elaborately dressing me up for Friday night dinners with my pimply boyfriend, his doughy parents, and a sister who's as blonde as he is. They are Episcopalians from Maine, practiced at eating fish dinners without ever once breaking out into a quarrel, unlike the nightly brawls at my house. Their whispery voices alone are like miracles.

Studying my boyfriend's Teutonic family, I learn to speak low and order salad with buttermilk dressing. It feels like a science experiment, gaining access to this strange planet where no one belches at the table. In time my mother will grow to fear them, these un-Italians, and yet I love them. They talk *to* me, never once mentioning marriage, my hair, my odds for landing the title of homecoming queen. They are teachers, who know things; they discuss nuclear weapons, the economy, saving the environment, our entering high school. Their sole agenda is their son's happiness.

For adults, they seem remarkably unafraid.

"He's not good enough for you," my mother says, when it finally dawns on her that I've been adopted by this kindly Anglo tribe. In her mind, I am Jacqueline Kennedy with princes and presidents en route for my hand. But she is wrong about Chris.

Nerdy and sweet, he is endlessly patient with my hesitancy about romance. "You don't have to," he tells me, "it doesn't matter." Whenever I'm near him, I listen for the blood pumping through his body, striving to open the clenched fist of my own heart, to feel what other people feel. I spend the summer doing research, lying on the front porch reading *Anna Karenina,* wondering if love has to be that hard. Every night I get on my knees and pray to Jesus: "Please let it happen tomorrow. Amen."

At last Jesus answers. I fall in love.

From the age of 13 until I am about to turn 22, Chris is my one-and-only, my heartthrob, sidekick, my entire world. He and I grow up together, navigating our stormy adolescent emotions and dreams, exploring the electric thrill of our bodies together. We take a trip to California to visit his grandmother. We are easy socializing with adults and our friends, but steal away to be alone whenever possible. We laugh. To my mother's great pride, we are actually voted Homecoming King and Queen. He is the only boy I can ever imagine loving—and, as we move toward adulthood at Cornell and Vassar, the only man.

Freshman year, Valentine's Day, I take a humiliating bus ride from Poughkeepsie to Ithaca, with a freshly minted diaphragm in my overnight bag. Going to a Cornell hockey game, we walk around the campus, drinking a bottle of pink champagne. For the first time I get drunk, and we have sex on a single cot in his dorm room. Afterwards I cry, because he's dating other girls but pretending not to, because I'm no longer a virgin. When I throw up in a toilet in the girl's bathroom, Chris waits for me in the hall. He walks me back to his dorm room, apologizing miserably.

Years later, it occurs to me that his parents might have been the ones who wanted him to date other girls. Likely, he was only trying to please them; possibly, they were even right. But because we've made no arrangements to include other people into our twosome, I am stung and bitter, and he is unprepared for my unhappiness.

In time Chris becomes more careful about hiding his infidelity, or maybe he decides to lie to his parents instead of me and stops it altogether. There's no discussion on the matter; he simply becomes more attentive. Eventually we master the art of intercourse, and I begin to trust him again, determined to maintain my devotion. Even later, when I find a letter from a girl he is sleeping with, I try to break it off, but somehow I only fall in love with him more deeply. It's as if Jesus has answered my prayers in one direction: forward. I imagine Him looking down on me with a patient face. *Be careful what you pray for.*

"Date someone," my friends back at school advise. I do. I go to dinner with a couple of nice guys. I even have lackluster sex with one of them, while shoring up my plans for the nunnery. Then, on a lark, I go with my bisexual roommate to see a couple of movies offered by the American Culture Department.

"You only come to the lesbian films," mentions my writing professor and mentor, Paul Russell, who teaches Queer Studies. "People are going to talk."

I am the straightest, squarest person on campus, but I have a versatile mind and a bold imagination. As I am standing there, laughing at his joke, it hits me who I might really be.

Within weeks, I stop caring if Chris dates other girls; I've fallen in love with a girl of my own. A woman actually, my Major advisor, someone who is not technically even gay.

It happens so fast, there isn't time to pray.

Here is a memory, a terrible one: I am standing with Chris in my childhood bedroom. It is December 1987, the first few minutes of Christmas break, our senior year. We have just driven home from school, and I am telling him that I can no longer be his girlfriend.

"See this other thing through," I am saying.

I've been telling Chris all about my theoretical sexuality since Thanksgiving. He wants to marry me anyway.

There is a look in his eye, alternating between fierce and defeated. He listens hard, as if I am speaking a new language.

Then suddenly, like a shade snapping, he understands. He knows not only what I'm saying, but what I mean.

I am no longer his.

It's surprising to watch his knees buckle, the way he falls silently to the pink shag rug of my youth, like a grown man taken down by a gun. He is 22, 6′4″, nearly 200 pounds. He lands just a few inches from the canopy bed where we sometimes secretly make love. He doesn't utter a sound, just looks out the window for a moment, as if there might be a message etched there in the dark pane.

I try to decipher it myself.

I am so young, so optimistic. How can I know that he will never speak to me again? That who I am inside will somehow destroy the people I love?

Like a Muslim deep in prayer, my boyfriend rests his forehead against the carpet, surrendering. Then he stands up and leaves.

Something New

The next time true love makes an appearance in my life, it's late one night in 1999, while I'm watching a rerun of Oprah. I'm visiting friends in Berkeley after a harrowing year-long break-up with a woman who has broken my heart and stolen my money. My adult life has been characterized by a series of bad romantic choices. Perhaps I've just been unlucky, though I sometimes wonder if I am subconsciously punishing myself.

This particular night, I lie sprawled out across a strange futon in a spare apartment reserved for married graduate students. It is a few days before Christmas, the last Noel before the year 2000, and I am 33 years old, depressed, and jet-lagged. In an overcrowded world of 5.8 billion people, I feel utterly, hopelessly alone.

Flipping the channels, I happen upon one TV talk show after another. The topic on Oprah is etiquette, but I stay tuned anyway, because her theme song cheers me up. "O" is for openness. Optimism! All I really have to do, I realize, is get through the holidays: another hour, this evening, the rest of my life. How hard could it be with Oprah always there to rely upon at 3 A.M., ready with her pragmatic advice? I watch commercials for mascara, feminine pads, rejuvenating shampoo.

When the show returns, I find myself suddenly staring into my future. I sit up, pointing. "Hey!" I tell the scraggly house plants that are my only company. "There she is!" *She* is Meryl Cohn, a writer I've met on several occasions.

I've sat across from her—Thanksgiving, Fourth of July, New Year's—at tables of fellow writers. Still, I've never actually *looked* at her before. Now, on TV, she exudes sex appeal and confidence. Even Oprah seems won over by her charm: green eyes, auburn hair, the cheekbones of a 1940s movie star.

During a brief Q&A, edited to one Q *(Should straight people ever ask gay people if they are gay?)* Meryl chats easily, explaining to the studio audience how to know when something is offensive. She offers a quick rundown on the dos and don'ts of queer etiquette. Joking about the age-old question, "What do women like in bed?" Meryl says wryly, "Other women, of course."

Oprah, lovely and velvety, responds with a deep-throated laugh.

Then, in a flash, the moment (and magic) passes: she is just someone I've met, friend of a friend, on Lifetime Television for Women: only Meryl Cohn, writer of the tongue-in-cheek advice column known widely in the gay and lesbian community as "Ms. Behavior." It's just as well. I'm not looking for thunderbolts and romance. I can barely manage a change of clothes.

Closing my eyes, I sink back into my familiar funk. My life is a troubled narrative, but at least I know what to expect: bad choices, difficult women, anxiety, despair. I fall asleep to the sound of the TV, cozy in my misery, unaware that somewhere not far away, a perfect stranger is taking my life into her hands.

Messages are being received—and some of them, it turns out, are about me.

Back in New York in February, I seek out Meryl's advice about a woman I'm casually dating. (Meryl *is* an advice columnist, after all, and it's obvious I could use some help.) It turns out she is in town for a few weeks, so we arrange to meet at a gay bookstore in lower Manhattan, which is now sadly defunct. I launch into my problem without prelude.

"Dump her," Meryl says.

She brings up a little story of her own, how her good friend Linda Brown has been receiving messages about her from someone in California. "My friend Psychic Mary wants me to tell you that you've already met your new girlfriend," Linda tells her. "Psychic Mary sees books."

Meryl doesn't know the woman making these predictions about her future. "I *have* a girlfriend, thank you very much." Her relationship is troubled, but she's loyal nonetheless.

Linda claims she is only passing messages. "Psychic Mary hears voices. Are you going to argue with voices?"

We laugh off the prediction over tea.

Linda has said something else that Meryl won't tell me until months later: a prediction about Meryl getting married and Linda making the wedding cake.

It's the turn of the new century, but, even so, a prediction of marriage seems absurdly far from reality. The world is hardly our oyster. Even if it were, Meryl is not exactly the blushing bride type, which is part of her allure.

That day in February, Meryl strikes me as definitely attractive, but I fancy myself too short for her. I am 5'3", a good 7" shy of matching her height. Even so, after that meeting, I invite her to lunch, the movies, dinner. Each time I share my latest adventure: a blind date who is actually blind, a woman who wants to take me camping after one cup of coffee, a trainer who asks me out for kick-boxing. I'm trying to renew my childhood faith in love; also, I'm lonely. My stories make Meryl laugh.

Between us we have two Seven Sisters degrees, two Masters' degrees, a couple of literary grants, one very successful advice column, two published books, and four books-in-progress. We're not exactly dumb. It's just we're unaccustomed to living out someone else's narrative, a psychic's no less. Who believes in voices, anyway—coming from where, the great beyond?

In my life so far, all predictions have turned out wrong; love has been a disaster. My only good relationship happened in puberty.

With tickets I can't get rid of, I take Meryl to Puccini's *Butterfly*—by chance, on Valentine's Day. And despite the fact that there is nothing like Italian opera to spur on romance, we manage to maintain our ignorance.

To reciprocate, she invites me to Eve Ensler's *Vagina Monologues*.
"Are you kidding?" I say, the guise of friendship beginning to wear.
We spend the entire following Sunday together. After the *Monologues,* we walk downtown in the rain, eat Mexican, cruise a bookstore.
Sitting in the self-help aisle, we diagram each other's personalities, confess our biggest flaws. At a coffee shop around the corner, I grill her about her talk show tour. Flashing back to that lonely California night on a borrowed futon, I can't bring myself to mention Oprah.

Walking down the street, I am suddenly aware of how tall Meryl is; how wide the world, how mysterious. For the first time since junior high, I am truly afraid. But here it is: late and chilly on a dark street corner in Chelsea, my future unraveling before me.

Wary, I look into Meryl's eyes, and suddenly understand how Anna Karenina ended up under that train.

Something Borrowed

I go for long stretches without hearing from Meryl. It turns out Ms. Behavior practices what she preaches: no hint of a new relationship will be permitted until her current one comes to its natural conclusion.

Not to worry, my shrink reassures me: "There's no cure for love." *House with a swing,* Psychic Mary continues her predictions. *Little girl in the swing. A life together, growing old.*

May 17, 2004, 8:30 A.M., a raw morning in Cape Cod, Massachusetts. Meryl and I stand waiting to fill out some paperwork. It is the first day gays can legally be married, and we have the first appointment. A line is already forming, couples standing shoulder to shoulder on the steps of town hall.

By 9, the streets are filled. Hundreds of onlookers watch and wait, cheering. People throw confetti, take photographs. Some carry signs; others hand out roses to every bride, male or female. Volunteers from the Human Rights Campaign cut wedding cake for any two waving a license to marry. The festive atmosphere harkens back to earlier days: the first Gay Pride parades in New York City, the Marches on Washington, the 1980s, the 1990s. Though now we are decades from our youth. Our friends are no longer dying in droves.

"This one's pretty," my mother has said about Meryl. She liked her on first sight, because Meryl is good looking and my mother is vain. Still, she has come a long way since the days of hysterical crying, breast-beating, throwing herself at me; my mother hasn't cornered me in a kitchen or attacked my short haircut in years. We are in easy daily contact, thanks to the computer we gave her for her seventieth birthday, and while she may say a secret novena now and then, petitioning the Virgin on my behalf, she seems okay with my current situation.

Handing over our paperwork, we race up the Cape to Orleans District Court, where we pay for our waiver of the three-day waiting period, an arcane holdover from the days of syphilis and shotgun weddings, when a few days of clarity might have made a difference. (Formerly $65, this waiver now costs $195, the special homosexual rate.) Greeting us in chambers is Judge Welch, a small, worn New Englander in formal robes, whose father, like his father before him, was the sitting judge.

His office is dark and smells of cherry tobacco. "I'm pleased to take part in this special day." His eyes twinkle. He presses our hands into his small but binding grip. "You love each other a lot."

We hold our breaths. Here we are: among the first gay people to marry in the United States of America, in the first state to go legal, on the fiftieth anniversary of Brown v. the Board of Education.

"A fine day for civil rights!" the judge says, breaking into a smile.

Returning to Provincetown for our final license, we are greeted by an army of television cameras. Over the past few weeks we've turned down media requests from *Newsday* to TV Japan, politely declining reporters who want to follow us around to document our wedding day. We are camera shy. Still, the local news catches our happy moment. (The reel later runs in a continuous loop on the *New York Times* website.) We head for home.

At four o'clock, we are married in our living room by someone we have only just met. After angry Republican Governor Mitt Romney has made sure that friends of gay people are not swiftly deputized and pressed into service, we hire a lovely, elderly, gay African-American minister who walks with a cane. She speaks solemnly of candles and circles and unions. It feels suddenly meaningful to participate in an institution designed for our exclusion, more meaningful than expected. It's funny how one can be unaware of one's oppression until the instant it is lifted.

We read our vows.

Flown in from New York, Meryl's brother is our witness, ring bearer, flower boy. Her sister calls a few moments after we've taken our vows; my father-in-law and his wife phone that evening. Meryl's mother sends flowers.

From my family, there is only eerie silence. On May 17th, well through the following Sunday, when our marriage is announced in the *New York Times,* I hear nothing.

I can feel my mother's grief, but I fight it.

All my life, I've struggled against absorbing her quiet devastation over who I am. Surrounded by my dearest and queerest friends, I feel happy, lucky, proud. I wish I could somehow show my mother that I am not so different from who I used to be.

If there were queerleaders, I'd still be captain. My life is a testament to this fact. At Vassar, for instance, I helped start a lesbian and gay alumni group; in New York, I was in the vanguard, working at Gay Men's Health Crisis, marching with ACT UP and The Lesbian Avengers. I helped some friends to die and others to live. I was quoted about things homosexual in the *Wall Street Journal* and *Newsweek*. I even published a collection of short stories, changed from the original title of *Nuclear Family and Other Fictions* to *Lucy on the West Coast and Other Lesbian Short Fiction* by a publisher keen to expand the market.

Yet I feel bad about my family. I imagine them opening the paper to our smiling newsprint faces, cringing each time the word *lesbian* appears in the inky text.

Later, a college professor and former colleague will express her disapproval over our little miraculous publication. "I expected to find your name in the Book Review section," she says, "not in Styles." My parents make their embarrassment at being outed known. When I probe for details, they offer terseness: "Yeah, we saw it." Everyone else seems puzzled and wants to know how we pulled it off, as if Meryl and I have somehow managed to fool the press. "How'd *you* get in the *Times*?" people want to know.

When the moment arrives, of course, none of it matters. Not even my mother.

"Do you take this woman?" the minister asks.

And I do. Completely and happily, I do.

Something Blue

Italians may not be big fans of the lesbian, but they love a good party. Hence my mother's dilemma: I can practically feel her blanch at the thought of her relatives crossing state lines to dance the tarantella at my queer wedding.

Since Meryl and I don't want (and can't afford) a traditional wedding reception, we decide to have two small parties: one in New York in June and one on Cape Cod in September.

My mother comes to both.

In New York, the party is at our best friends Kenny and David's apartment on Central Park South, overlooking the park. Meryl's friend Linda makes an amazing wedding cake from scratch, towering layers with four fillings and a cascade of purple orchids. (Somewhere in California a psychic is smiling.)

Accompanying my mother are my two least homophobic brothers, one with his girlfriend, the other with his wife. My father neither comes to the wedding nor acknowledges it. I try to prepare my mother as much as I can, telling her that Meryl's family is happy for us, that she should be happy too.

With lingering trepidation, I prepare myself as well.

My family arrives late. My brothers stand around in the corner drinking beer, one of them in a baseball cap and sneakers. ("Kind of hot!" Kenny says of him, trying to put a good spin on the situation.)

My brothers can't seem to stop gawking at our forty dearest friends, though they manage to refrain from making ugly jokes. As I catch them passing shocked glances twice during the toast, I realize that they have never been in a room with so many gay people. To them, this party— my life—is a spectacle.

My mother is more at ease; she receives daily e-mails about my queer life. She circulates, chatting with everyone, recognizing names and details.

Only when Debbie, my college roommate, arrives with her husband do my brothers and my mother truly come to life. They pump her husband's hand, questioning her about her kids, the suburbs. For a happy moment, they locate me in Debbie, the me with Chris, with the future they could understand.

Later, in a corner while talking to Meryl's father, my mother cries. She tells him how disappointed she is at my father's lack of interest, at the fact that her only daughter, her baby, is gay. Several friends overhear her admit that her own 92-year-old mother is more accepting of my lesbianism than she is.

I know it's true; from the haze of her nursing home decline, my Nonnie has repeatedly told my mother she should be happy I've found someone to love.

Even so, at the end of the evening, my mother looks around at my friends and says, "I didn't know you had so many *people*." For Italians this is a high compliment, meaning people who love you. It's almost as good as praising the food at a wedding. Which she also does.

Despite her public tears, I am proud of my mother for her struggle. I take it as a sign that our relationship is alive and well.

Our second wedding party is also magical, despite a September hurricane on the Cape: Ivan the Terrible. My mother attends, this time with my sister-in-law Helen and her alcoholic best friend. (My brothers have apparently had enough of my gay friends to last a lifetime.) During the speeches and readings, my mother sits across the room like an outsider; she seems smaller than before, vulnerable. Several of my chivalrous lesbian friends from Brooklyn attend to her every need, refilling her drink, chatting with her about the weather.

We take photographs.

After the party, my sister-in-law's best friend, completely hammered, hits on me. My sister-in-law, herself a little tipsy, gets behind the wheel to drive my mother back to their hotel. It brings back memories of my drunken father driving us home late at night after weddings, my mother quiet in the passenger's seat.

The next morning at brunch, my mother and my sister-in-law stay only a few minutes, eager to get started on the ten-hour drive ahead. My mother gives Meryl and me a gift: her mother's china. "Nonnie always wanted you to have it," she says, not looking at me.

I try to imagine how it would have felt to have those old women, my grandmother and her sisters, dancing at my wedding.

As I walk my mother down to the car, a terrible thing happens. The hem of her denim skirt gets caught on her rubber sandal and she takes a nasty spill down a long, narrow set of wooden stairs off the back deck.

My mouth goes dry. I'm standing on the top step, looking down at her sprawled across the landing, and my heart lurches. This is my 72-year-old Italian mother, a woman I have loved and disappointed all my life. Irrationally, I feel I am to blame for this fall.

Up on her feet in a flash, she brushes herself off, blaming her skirt and shoes.

I rush down the steps, choking back tears, and hug her for as long as she'll let me.

"I'm sorry," I tell her. Sorry about everything. And I am.

And I'm not.

About Creative Nonfiction

Our Roots Are Deep with Passion is Issue 30 of the literary journal *Creative Nonfiction*. Founded in 1993, *Creative Nonfiction* was the first and continues to be the largest literary journal devoted exclusively to the creative nonfiction genre. As the premiere publisher of compelling true stories told through excellent writing, *Creative Nonfiction* sets the standard for the literary world by publishing the finest work of today's greatest emerging and established writers.

For more information, or to subscribe, please contact:

Creative Nonfiction Foundation
5501 Walnut St., Suite 202
Pittsburgh, PA 15232

www.creativenonfiction.org